D1558815

Isaac T. Hopper

ISAAC T. HOPPER:

A TRUE LIFE.

BY

L. MARIA CHILD.

Thine was a soul with sympathy imbued,
  Broad as the earth, and as the heavens sublime;
Thy godlike object, steadfastly pursued,
  To save thy race from misery and crime.

Garrison.

TWELFTH THOUSAND.

NEGRO UNIVERSITIES PRESS
NEW YORK

Originally published in 1854
by John P. Jewett & Co., Boston

Reprinted 1969 by
Negro Universities Press
A DIVISION OF GREENWOOD PUBLISHING CORP.
NEW YORK

SBN 8371-1737-2

TO

HANNAH ATTMORE HOPPER,

WIDOW OF THE LATE

ISAAC T. HOPPER.

THIS VOLUME IS RESPECTFULLY AND AFFECTIONATELY INSCRIBED,

BY HER GRATEFUL AND ATTACHED FRIEND.

L. MARIA CHILD.

PREFACE.

THIS biography differs from most works of the kind, in embracing fragments of so many lives. Friend Hopper lived almost entirely for others; and it is a striking illustration of the fact, that I have found it impossible to write his biography without having it consist largely of the adventures of other people.

I have not recounted his many good deeds for the mere purpose of eulogizing an honored friend. I have taken pleasure in preserving them in this form, because I cherish a hope that they may fall like good seed into many hearts, and bring forth future harvests in the great field of humanity.

Most of the strictly personal anecdotes fell from his lips in familiar and playful conversation with his sister, or his grandchildren, or his intimate friends, and I noted them down at the time, without his knowledge. In this way I caught them in a much more fresh and natural form, than I could have done if he had been conscious of the process.

The narratives and anecdotes of fugitive slaves, which form such a prominent portion of the book, were originally written

v

by Friend Hopper himself, and published in newspapers, under the title of "Tales of Oppression." I have re-modelled them all; partly because I wished to present them in a more concise form, and partly because the principal actor could be spoken of more freely by a third person, than he could speak of himself. Moreover, he had a more dramatic way of *telling* a story than he had of *writing* it; and I have tried to embody his unwritten style as nearly as I could remember it. Where-ever incidents or expressions have been added to the publish-ed narratives, I have done it from recollection.

The facts, which were continually occurring within Friend Hopper's personal knowledge, corroborate the pic-tures of slavery drawn by Mrs. Stowe. Her descriptions are no more fictitious, than the narratives written by Friend Hopper. She has taken living characters and facts of every-day occurrence, and combined them in a connect-ed story, radiant with the light of genius, and warm with the glow of feeling. But is a landscape any the less real, be-cause there is sunshine on it, to bring out every tint, and make every dew-drop sparkle?

Who that reads the account here given of Daniel Benson, and William Anderson, can doubt that slaves are capable of as high moral excellence, as has ever been ascribed to them in any work of fiction? Who that reads Zeke, and the Quick Witted Slave, can pronounce them a stupid race, unfit for freedom? Who that reads the adventures of the Slave Mother, and of poor Manuel, a perpetual mourner for his en-slaved children, can say that the bonds of nature are less strong with them, than with their more fortunate white brethren? Who can question the horrible tyranny under which they suffer, after reading The Tender Mercies of a Slaveholder, and the suicide of Romaine?

Friend Hopper labored zealously for many, many years; and thousands have applied their best energies of head and heart to the same great work; yet the slave-power in this country is as strong as ever—nay, stronger. Its car rolls on in triumph, and priests and politicians outdo each other in zeal to draw it along, over its prostrate victims. But, lo! from under its crushing wheels, up rises the bleeding spectre of Uncle Tom, and all the world turns to look at him! Verily, the slave-power is strong; but God and truth are stronger.

CONTENTS.

GENERAL INDEX.

PARTICULAR INDEX.

I was a father to the poor : and the cause which I knew not I searched out.

When the ear heard me, then it blessed me: and when the eye saw me, it gave witness to me :

Because I delivered the poor that cried, and the fatherless, and him that had none to help him.

The blessing of him that was ready to perish came upon me: and I caused the widow's heart to sing for joy. Job xxix. *16, 11, 12, 13*.

LIFE OF ISAAC T. HOPPER.

Isaac Tatem Hopper was born in Deptford
Township, near Woodbury, West New-Jersey, in
the year 1771, on the third day of December, which
Quakers call the Twelth Month. His grandfather
belonged to that denomination of Christians, but forfeited membership in the Society by choosing a wife
from another sect. His son Levi, the father of Isaac,
always attended their meetings, but never became a
member.

A family of rigid Presbyterians, by the name of
Tatem, resided in the neighborhood. While their
house was being built, they took shelter for a few
days, in a meeting-house that was little used, and
dug a pit for a temporary cellar, according to the
custom of new settlers in the forest. The country
at that time was much infested with marauders ; but
Mrs. Tatem was an Amazon in physical strength and
courage. One night, when her husband was absent,
and she was alone in the depths of the woods with

three small children, she heard a noise, and looking
out saw a band of thieves stealing provisions from
the cellar. They entered the meeting-house soon after, and she had the presence of mind to call out,
"Hallo, Jack! Call Joe, and Harry, and Jim!
Here's somebody coming." The robbers, supposing
she had a number of stout defenders at hand, thought
it prudent to escape as quickly as possible. The
next day, her husband being still absent, she resolved
to move into the unfinished house, for greater security. The door had neither lock nor latch, but she
contrived to fasten it in some fashion. At midnight,
three men came and tried to force it open; but every
time they partially succeeded, she struck at them
with a broad axe. This mode of defence was kept
up so vigorously, that at last they were compelled to
retreat.

She had a daughter, who was often at play with
neighbor Hopper's children; and when Levi was
quite a small boy, it used to be said playfully that
little Rachel Tatem would be his wife, and they
would live together up by the great white oak; a
remarkable tree at some distance from the homestead.
The children grew up much attached to each other,
and when Levi was twenty-two years old, the prophecy was fulfilled.

The young man had only his own strong hands
and five or six hundred acres of wild woodland.

He grubbed up the trees and underbrush near the big white oak, removed his father's hen-house to the cleared spot, fitted it up comfortably for a temporary dwelling, and dug a cellar in the declivity of a hill near by. To this humble abode he conducted his young bride, and there his two first children were born. The second was named Isaac Tatem Hopper. and is the subject of this memoir.

Rachel inherited her mother's energy and courage, and having married a diligent and prudent man, their worldly circumstances gradually improved, though their family rapidly increased, and they had nothing but land and labor to rely upon. When Isaac was one year and a half old, the family removed to a new log-house with three rooms on a floor, neatly white-washed. To these the bridal hen-house was append-ed for a kitchen.

Isaac was early remarked as a very precocious child. He was always peeping into everything, and inquiring about everything. He was only eighteen months old, when the new log-house was built; but when he saw them laying the foundation, his busy little mind began to query whether the grass would grow under it; and straightway he ran to see whether grass grew under the floor of the hen-house wher‹ he was born.

He was put to work on the farm as soon as he could handle a hoe; but though he labored hard, he had plenty of time and strength left for all manner of roguery. While he was a small fellow in petticoats, he ran into a duck-pond to explore its depth. His mother pulled him out, and said, "Isaac, if you ever go there again, I will make you come out faster than you went in." He thought to himself, "Now I will prove mother to be in the wrong; for I will go in as fast as I can; and surely I can't come out any faster." So into the pond he went, as soon as the words were out of her mouth.

A girl by the name of Polly assisted about the housework. She was considered one of the family, and always ate at the same table, according to the kindly custom of those primitive times. She always called her mistress " Mammy," and served her until the day of her death; a period of forty years. The children were much attached to this faithful domestic; but nevertheless, Isaac could not forbear playing tricks upon her whenever he had opportunity.— When he was five or six years old, he went out one night to see her milk the cow. He had observed that the animal kicked upon slight provocation; and when the pail was nearly full, he broke a switch from a tree near by, slipped round to the other side of the cow, and tickled her bag. She instantly raised her heels, and over went Polly, milk-pail, stool, and all. Isaac ran into the house, laughing with all his might, to tell how the cow had kicked over Polly and the

pail of milk. His mother went out immediately to
ascertain whether the girl was seriously injured.—
" Oh, mammy, that little rogue tickled the cow, and
made her do it," exclaimed Polly. Whereupon, Isaac
had a spanking, and was sent to bed without his supper. But so great was his love of fun, that as he lay
there, wakeful and hungry, he shouted with laughter
all alone by himself, to think how droll Polly looked
when she rolled over with the pail of milk after her.

When he was seven or eight years old, his uncle's
wife came one day to the house on horseback. She
was a fat, clumsy woman, and got on and off her
horse with difficulty. Isaac knew that all the family
were absent; but when he saw her come ambling
along the road, he took a freak not to tell her of it.
He let down the bars for her; she rode up to the
horse-block with which every farm-house was then
furnished, rolled off her horse, and went into the
house. She then discovered, for the first time, that
there was no one at home. After resting awhile,
she mounted to depart. But Isaac, as full of mischief as Puck, put the bars up, so that she could not
ride out. In vain she coaxed, scolded, and threatened. Finding it was all to no purpose, she rode up
to the block and rolled off from her horse again.—
Isaac, having the fear of her whip before his eyes,
ran and hid himself. She let down the bars for herself, but before she could remount, the mischievous

urchin had put the bars up again and run away.—
This was repeated several times; and the exasperated visitor could never succeed in catching her tor-
mentor. His parents came home in the midst of the
frolic, and he had a sound whipping. He had calculated upon this result all the time, and the uneasy
feeling had done much to mar his sport; but on the
whole, he concluded such rare fun was well worth a
flogging.

The boys at school were apt to neglect their les-
sons while they were munching apples. In order to
break up this disorderly habit, the master made it a
rule to take away every apple found upon them.—
He placed such forfeited articles upon his desk, with
the agreement that any boy might have them, who
could succeed in abstracting them without being observed by him. One day, when a large rosy-cheeked
apple stood temptingly on the desk, Isaac stepped
up to have his pen mended. He stood very demure-
ly at first, but soon began to gaze earnestly out of
the window, behind the desk. The master inquired
what he was looking at. He replied, "I am watching a flock of ducks trying to swim on the ice. How
queerly they waddle and slide about!" "Ducks
swim on ice!" exclaimed the schoolmaster; and he
turned to observe such an unusual spectacle. It was
only for an instant; but the apple meanwhile was
transferred to the pocket of his cunning pupil. He

smiled as he gave him his pen, and said, "Ah, you rogue, you are always full of mischief!"

The teacher was accustomed to cheer the monotony of his labors by a race with the boys during play hours. There was a fine sloping lawn in front of the school-house, terminating in a brook fringed with willows. The declivity gave an impetus to the runners, and as they came among the trees, their heads swiftly parted the long branches. Isaac tied a brick-bat to one of the pendant boughs, and then invited the master to run with him. He accepted the invitation, and got the start in the race. As he darted through the trees, the brick merely grazed his hair. If it had hit him, it might have cost him his life; though his mischievous pupil had not reflected upon the possibility of such a result.

There was a bridge across the brook consisting of a single rail. One day, Isaac sawed this nearly in two; and while the master was at play with the boys, he took the opportunity to say something very impertinent, for which he knew he should be chased. He ran toward the brook, crossed the rail in safety, and instantly turned it over, so that his pursuer would step upon it when the cut side was downward. It immediately snapped under his pressure, and precipitated him into the stream, while the young rogue stood by almost killing himself with laughter. But this joke also came very near having a melancholy termination; for the master was floated down several rods into deep water, and with difficulty saved himself from drowning.

There was a creek not far from his father's house, where it was customary to load sloops with wood. Upon one of these occasions, he persuaded a party of boys to pry up a pile of wood and tip it into a sloop, in a confused heap. Of course, it must all be taken out and reloaded. When he saw how much labor this foolish trick had caused, he felt some compunction; but the next temptation found the spirit of mischief too strong to be resisted.

Coming home from his uncle's one evening, he stopped to amuse himself with taking a gate off its hinges. When an old Quaker came out to see who was meddling with his gate, Isaac fired a gun over his head, and made him run into the house, as if an evil spirit were after him.

It was his' delight to tie the boughs of trees together in narrow paths, that people travelling in the dark, might hit their heads against them; and to lay stones in the ruts of the road, when he knew that farmers were going to market with eggs, in the darkness of morning twilight. If any mischief was done for miles round, it was sure to be attributed to Isaac Hopper. There was no malice in his fun; but he had such superabounding life within him, that it *would* overflow, even when he knew that he must suffer for it. His boyish activity, strength, and agility were proverbial. Long after he left his native village, the neighbors used to tell with what astonishing rapidity he would descend high trees, head foremost, clinging to the trunk with his feet.

The fearlessness and firmness of character, which he inherited from both father and mother, manifested itself in many ways. He had a lamb, whose horns were crooked, and had a tendency to turn in. His father had given it to him for his own, on condition that he should keep the horns carefully filed, so that they should not hurt the animal. He had a small file on purpose, and took such excellent care of his pet, that it soon became very much attached to him, and trotted about after him like a dog. When he was about five or six years old, British soldiers came into the neighborhood to seize provisions for the army, according to their custom during our revolutionary war. They tied the feet of the tame lamb, and threw it into the cart with other sheep and lambs. Isaac came up to them in season to witness this operation, and his heart swelled with indignation. He sprang into the cart, exclaiming, "That's *my* lamb, and you shan't have it!" The men tried to push *h*im aside; but he pulled out a rusty jack-knife, which he had bought of a pedlar for two-pence, and cut the rope that bound the poor lamb. A British officer rode up, and seeing a little boy struggling so resolutely with the soldiers, he inquired what was the matter. "They've stolen my lamb!" exclaimed Isaac; "and they shan't have it. It's *my* lamb!"

"*Is* it your lamb, my brave little fellow?" said the officer. "Well, they shan't have it. You'll make a fine soldier one of these days."

So Isaac lifted his lamb from the cart, and trudged off victorious. He had always been a whig; and after this adventure, he became more decided than ever in his politics. He often used to boast that he would rather have a paper continental dollar, than a golden English guinea. The family amused themselves by exciting his zeal, and Polly made him believe he was such a famous whig, that the British would certainly carry him off to prison. He generally thought he was fully capable of defending himself; but when he saw four soldiers approaching the house one day, he concluded the force was rather too strong for him, and hastened to hide himself in the woods.

His temper partook of the general strength and vehemence of his character. Having put a small quantity of gunpowder on the stove of the schoolhouse, it exploded, and did some injury to the master. One of the boys, who was afraid of being suspected of the mischief, in order to screen himself, cried out, "Isaac Hopper did it!"—and Isaac was punished accordingly. Going home from school, he

seized the informer as they were passing through a
wood, tied him up to a tree, and gave him a tremendous thrashing. The boy threatened to tell of it;
but he assured him that he would certainly kill him
if he did; so he never ventured to disclose it.

In general, his conscience reproved him as soon as
he had done anything wrong, and he hastened to
make atonement. A poor boy, who attended the
same school, usually brought a very scanty dinner.
One day, the spirit of mischief led Isaac to spoil the
poor child's provisions by filling his little pail with
sand. When the boy opened it, all eagerness to eat
his dinner, the tears came into his eyes; for he was
very hungry. This touched Isaac's heart instantly.
"Oh, never mind, Billy," said he. "I did it for fun;
but I'm sorry I did it. Come, you shall have half of
my dinner." It proved a lucky joke for Billy; for
from that day henceforth, Isaac always helped him
plentifully from his own stock of provisions.

Isaac and his elder brother were accustomed to set
traps in the woods to catch partridges. One day,
when he was about six years old, he went to look
at the traps early in the morning, and finding his
empty, he took a plump partridge from his brother's
trap, put it in his own, and carried it home as his.
When his brother examined the traps, he said he
was sure *he* caught the bird, because there were
feathers sticking to his trap; but Isaac maintained

that there were feathers sticking to his also. After
he went to bed, his conscience scorched him for
what he had done. As soon as he rose in the
morning, he went to his mother and said, "What
shall I do? I have told a lie, and I feel dreadfully
about it. That *was* Sam's partridge. I said I took
it from my trap; and so I did; but I put it in there
first."

"My son, it is a wicked thing to tell a lie,"
replied his mother. "You must go to Sam and
confess, and give him the bird."

Accordingly, he went to his brother, and said,
"Sam, here's your partridge. I did take it out of
my trap; but I put it in there first." His brother
gave him a talking, and then forgave him.

Being a very bright, manly boy, he was intrusted
to carry grain several miles to mill, when he was
only eight years old. On one of these occasions,
he arrived just as another boy, who preceded him,
had alighted to open the gate. "Just let me drive
in before you shut it," said Isaac, "and then I shall
have no need to get down from my wagon." The
boy patiently held the gate for him to pass through;
but, Isaac, without stopping to thank him, whipped
up his horse, arrived at the mill post haste, and
claimed the right to be first served, because he was
the first comer. When the other boy found he was
compelled to wait, he looked very much dissatisfied,

but said nothing. Isaac chuckled over his victory at first, but his natural sense of justice soon suggested better thoughts. He asked himself whether he had done right thus to take advantage of that obliging boy? The longer he reflected upon it, the more uncomfortable he felt. At last, he went up to the stranger and said frankly, "I did wrong to drive up to the mill so fast, and get my corn ground, when you were the one who arrived first; especially as you were so obliging as to hold the gate open for me to pass through. I was thinking of nothing but fun when I did it. Here's sixpence to make up for it." The boy was well pleased with the amend thus honorably offered, and they parted right good friends.

At nine years old, he began to drive a wagon to Philadelphia, to sell vegetables and other articles from his father's farm; which he did very satisfactorily, with the assistance of a neighbor, who occupied the next stall in the market. According to the fashion of the times, he wore a broad-brimmed hat, and small-clothes with long stockings. Being something of a dandy, he prided himself upon having his shoes very clean, and his white dimity small clothes without spot or blemish. He caught rabbits, and sold them, till he obtained money enough to purchase brass buckles for his knees, and for the straps of his shoes. The first time he made his appearance in the city with this new finery, he felt his ambition concerning personal decoration completely satisfied. The neatness of his dress, and his manly way of proceeding, attracted attention, and induced his customers to call him "THE LITTLE GOVERNOR." For several years, he was universally known in the market by that title. Fortunately, his father had no wish to obtain undue advantage in the sale of his produce; for had it been otherwise, his straight-forward little son would have proved a poor agent in transacting his affairs. One day, when a citizen inquired the price of a pair of chickens, he answered, with the utmost simplicity, "My father told me to sell them for fifty cents if I could; and if not, to take forty."

"Well done, my honest little fellow!" said the gentleman, smiling, "I will give you whatever is the current price. I shall look out for you in the market; and whenever I see you, I shall always try to trade with you." And he kept his word.

When quite a small boy, he was sent some distance of an errand, and arrived just as the family were about to sit down to supper. There were several pies on the table, and they invited him to partake. The long walk had whetted his appetite, and the pies looked exceedingly tempting; but the shyness of childhood led him to say, "No, I thank you." When he had delivered his message, he lingered, and lingered, hoping they would ask him again. But the family were Quakers, and they understood yea to mean yea, and nay to mean nay. They would have considered it a mere worldly compliment to repeat the invitation; so they were silent. Isaac started for home, much repenting of his bashfulness, and went nearly half of the way revolving the subject in his mind. He then walked back to the house, marched boldly into the supper-room, and said, "I told a lie when I was here. I did want a piece of pie; but I thought to be sure you would ask me again." This explicit avowal made them all smile, and he was served with as much pie as he wished to eat.

The steadfastness of his whig principles led him to take a lively interest in anecdotes concerning revolutionary heroes. His mother had a brother in Philadelphia, who lived in a house formerly occupied by William Penn, at the corner of Second Street and Norris Alley. This uncle frequently cut and made garments for General Washington, Benjamin Franklin, and other distinguished men. Nothing pleased Isaac better than a visit to this city relative; and when there, his boyish mind was much occupied with watching for the famous men, of whom he had heard so much talk. Once, when General Washington came there to order some garments, he followed him a long distance from the shop. The

General had observed his wonder and veneration, and was amused by it. Coming to a corner of the street, he turned round suddenly, touched his hat, and made a very low bow. This playful condescension so completely confused his juvenile admirer, that he stood blushing and bewildered for an instant, then walked hastily away, without remembering to return the salutation.

The tenderness of spirit often manifested by him, was very remarkable in such a resolute and mischievous boy. There was an old unoccupied barn in the neighborhood, a favorite resort of swallows in the Spring-time. When he was about ten years old, he invited a number of boys to meet him the next Sunday morning, to go and pelt the swallows. They set off on this expedition with anticipations of a fine frolic; but before they had gone far, Isaac began to feel a strong conviction that he was doing wrong. He told his companions he thought it was very cruel sport to torment and kill poor little innocent birds; especially as they might destroy mothers, and then the little ones would be left to starve. There was a Quaker meeting-house about a mile and a half distant, and he proposed that they should all go there, and leave the swallows in peace. But the boys only laughed at him, and ran off shouting, "Come on! Come on!" He looked after them sorrowfully for some minutes, reproaching himself for the suffering he had caused the poor birds. He

then walked off to meeting alone ; and his faithfulness to the light within him was followed by a sweet
peacefulness and serenity of soul. The impression
made by this incident, and the state of mind he enjoyed while in meeting, was one of the earliest influences that drew him into the Society of Friends.—
When he returned home, he heard that one of the
boys had broken his arm while stoning the swallows,
and had been writhing with pain, while he had been
enjoying the consolations of an approving conscience.

At an early age, he was noted for being a sure
shot, with bow and arrow, or with gun. A pair of
king-birds built in his father's orchard, and it was desirable to get rid of them, because they destroy ho-
ney-bees. Isaac watched for an opportunity, and one
day when the birds flew away in quest of food for
their young, he transfixed them both at once with his
arrow. At first, he was much delighted with this exploit ; but his compassionate heart soon became troubled about the orphan little ones, whom he pictured
to himself as anxiously expecting the parents that
would never return to feed them again. This feeling
gained such strength within him, that he early relinquished the practice of shooting, though he found
keen excitement in the pursuit, and was not a little
proud of his skill.

Once, when he had entrapped a pair of partridges,
he put them in a box, intending to keep them there.

But he soon began to query with himself whether creatures accustomed to fly must not necessarily be very miserable shut up in such a limited space. He accordingly opened the door. One of the partridges immediately walked out, but soon returned to prison to invite his less ventursome mate. The box was removed a few days after, but the birds remained about the garden for months, often coming to the door-step to pick up crumbs that were thrown to them. When the mating-season returned the next year, they retired to the woods.

From earliest childhood he evinced great fondness for animals, and watched with lively interest all the little creatures of the woods and fields. He was familiar with all their haunts, and they gave names to the localities of his neighborhood. There was Turkey Causeway, where wild turkies abounded; and Rabbit Swamp, where troops of timid little rabbits had their hiding places; and Squirrel Grove, where many squirrels laid in their harvest of acorns for the winter; and Panther Bridge, where his grandfather had killed a panther.

Once, when his father and the workmen had been cutting down a quantity of timber, Isaac discovered a squirrel's nest in a hole of one of the trees that had fallen. It contained four new-born little ones, their eyes not yet opened. He was greatly tempted to carry them home, but they were so young that they

needed their mother's milk. So after examining
them, he put them back in the nest, and with his
usual busy helpfulness went to assist in stripping
bark from the trees. When he went home from his
work, toward evening, he felt curious to see how the
mother squirrel would behave when she returned and
found her home was gone. He accordingly hid
himself in a bush to watch her proceedings. About
dusk, she came running along the stone wall with a
nut in her mouth, and went with all speed to the old
familiar tree. Finding nothing but a stump remaining there, she dropped the nut and looked around in
evident dismay. She went smelling all about the
ground, then mounted the stump to take a survey of
the country. She raised herself on her hind legs and
snuffed the air, with an appearance of great perplexity and distress. She ran round the stump several
times, occasionally raising herself on her hind legs,
and peering about in every direction, to discover
what had become of her young family. At last, she
jumped on the prostrate trunk of the tree, and ran
along till she came to the hole where her babies
were concealed. What the manner of their meeting
was nobody can tell; but doubtless the mother's
heart beat violently when she discovered her lost
treasures all safe on the warm little bed of moss she
had so carefully prepared for them. After staying a
few minutes to give them their supper, she came out,

and scampered off through the bushes. In about fifteen minutes, she returned and took one of the
young ones in her mouth, and carried it quickly to a
hole in another tree, three or four hundred yards off,
and then came back and took the others, one by one,
till she had conveyed them all to their new home.
The intelligent instinct manifested by this little quad-
ruped excited great interest in Isaac's observing mind.
When he drove the cows to pasture, he always went
by that tree, to see how the young family were getting along. In a short time, they were running all
over the tree with their careful mother, eating acorns
under the shady boughs, entirely unconscious of the
perils through which they had passed in infancy.

Some time after, Isaac traded with another boy
for a squirrel taken from the nest before its eyes
were open. He made a bed of moss for it, and fed it
very tenderly. At first, he was afraid it would not
live; but it seemed healthy, though it never grew
so large as other squirrels. He did not put it in a
cage; for he said to himself that a creature made to
frisk about in the green woods could not be happy
shut up in a box. This pretty little animal became
so much attached to her kind-hearted protector, that
she would run about after him, and come like a kit
ten whenever he called her. While he was gone to
school, she frequently ran off to the woods and play-

ed with wild squirrels on a tree that grew near his path homeward. Sometimes she took a nap in a large knot-hole, or, if the weather was very warm, made a cool bed of leaves across a crotch of the boughs, and slept there. When Isaac passed under the tree, on his way from school, he used to call "Bun! Bun! Bun!" If she was there, she would come to him immediately, run up on his shoulder and so ride home to get her supper.

It seemed as if animals were in some way aware of his kindly feelings, and disposed to return his confidence; for on several occasions they formed singular intimacies with him. When he was six or seven years old, he spied a crow's nest in a high tree, and, according to his usual custom, he climbed up to make discoveries. He found that it contained two eggs, and he watched the crow's movements until her young ones were hatched and ready to fly. Then he took them home. One was accidentally killed a few days after, but he reared the other, and named it Cupid. The bird became so very tame, that it would feed from his hand, perch on his shoulder, or his hat, and go everywhere with him. It frequently followed him for miles, when he went to mill or market. He was never put into a cage, but flew in and out of the house, just as he pleased. If Isaac called "Cu! Cu!" he would hear him, even if he were up in the highest tree, would croak a friendly answer and come down directly. If Isaac winked one eye, the crow would do the same. If he winked his other eye, the crow also winked with his other eye. Once when Cupid was on his shoulder, he pointed to a snake lying in the road, and said "Cu! Cu!"— The sagacious bird pounced on the head of the snake and killed him instantly; then flew back to his friend's shoulder, cawing with all his might, as if delighted with his exploit. If a stranger tried to take him, he would fly away, screaming with terror. Sometimes Isaac covered him with a handkerchief and placed him on a stranger's shoulder; but as soon as he discovered where he was, he seemed frightened almost to death. He usually chose to sleep on the roof of a shed, directly under Isaac's bed-room window. One night he heard him cawing very loud, and the next morning he said to his father, "I heard Cupid talking in his sleep last night." His father inquired whether he had seen him since; and when Isaac answered, "No," he said, "Then I am afraid the owls have taken him." The poor bird did not make his appearance again; and a few days after, his bones and feathers were found on a stump, not far from the house. This was a great sorrow for Isaac. It tried his young heart almost like the los of a brother.

His intimacy with animals was of a very pleasant nature, except on one occasion, when he thrust his arm into a hollow tree, in search of squirrels, and pulled out a large black snake. He was so terrified, that he tumbled headlong from the tree, and it was difficult to tell which ran away fastest, he or the snake. This incident inspired the bold boy with fear, which he vainly tried to overcome during the remainder of his life. There was a thicket of underbrush between his father's farm and the village of Woodbury. Once, when he was sent of an errand to the village, he was seized with such a dread of snakes, that before entering among the bushes, he placed his basket on an old rail, knelt down and prayed earnestly that he might pass through without encountering a snake. When he rose up and attempted to take his basket, he perceived a large black snake lying close beside the rail. It may well be believed that he went through the thicket too fast to allow any grass to grow under his feet.

When he drove the cows to and from pasture, he often met an old colored man named Mingo. His sympathizing heart was attracted toward him, because he had heard the neighbors say he was stolen from Africa when he was a little boy. One day, he asked Mingo what part of the world he came from; and the poor old man told how he was playing with other children among the bushes, on the coast of Africa, when white men pounced upon them suddenly and dragged them off to a ship. He held fast hold of the thorny bushes, which tore his hands dreadfully in the struggle. The old man wept like a child, when he told how he was frightened and distressed at being thus hurried away from father, mother, brothers and sisters, and sold into slavery, in a distant land, where he could never see or hear from them again. This painful story made a very deep impression upon Isaac's mind; and, though he was then only nine years old, he made a solemn vow to himself that he would be the friend of oppressed Africans during his whole life.

He was as precocious in love, as in other matters. Not far from his home, lived a prosperous and highly respectable Quaker family, named Tatum. There were several sons, but only one daughter; a handsome child, with clear, fair complexion, blue eyes, and a profusion of brown curly hair. She was Isaac's cousin, twice removed; for their great-grandfathers were half-brothers. When he was only eight years old, and she was not yet five, he made up his mind that little Sarah Tatum was his wife. He used to walk a mile and a half every day, on purpose to escort her to school. When they rambled through the woods, in search of berries, it was his delight to sit beside her on some old stump, and twist her glossy brown ringlets over his fingers. A lovely picture they must have made in the green, leafy frame-work of the woods—that fair, blue-eyed girl, and the handsome,

vigorous boy! When he was fourteen years old, he
wrote to her his first love-letter. The village schoolmaster taught for very low wages, and was not remarkably well-qualified for his task; as was generally the case at that early period. Isaac's labor
was needed on the farm all the summer; consequently, he was able to attend school only three
months during the winter. He was, therefore, so
little acquainted with the forms of letter-writing,
that he put Sarah's name inside the letter, and his
own on the outside. She, being an only daughter,
and a great pet in her family, had better opportunities for education. She told her young lover that
was not the correct way to write a letter, and instructed him how to proceed in future. From that
time, they corresponded constantly.

Isaac likewise formed a very strong friendship
with his cousin Joseph Whitall, who was his school-
mate, and about his own age. They shared together
all their joys and troubles, and were companions in
all boyish enterprises. Thus was a happy though
laborious childhood passed in the seclusion of the
woods, in the midst of home influences and rustic
occupations. His parents had no leisure to bestow
n intellectual culture; for they had a numerous
family of children, and it required about all their
time to feed and clothe them respectably. But they
were worthy, kind-hearted people, whose moral pre-

cepts were sustained by their upright example. His father was a quiet man, but exceedingly firm and energetic. When he had made up his mind to do a thing, no earthly power could turn him from his purpose; especially if any question of conscience were involved therein. During the revolutionary war, he faithfully maintained his testimony against the shedding of blood, and suffered considerably for refusing to pay military taxes. Isaac's mother was noted for her fearless character, and blunt directness of speech. She was educated in the Presbyterian faith, and this was a source of some discordant feeling between her and her husband. The preaching of her favorite ministers seemed to him harsh and rigid, while she regarded Quaker exhortations as insipid and formal. But as time passed on, her religious views assimilated more and more with his; and about twenty-four years after their marriage, she joined the Society of Friends, and frequently spoke at their meetings. She was a spiritual minded woman, always ready to sympathise with the afflicted, and peculiarly kind to animals. They were both extremely hospitable and benevolent to the poor. On Sunday evenings, they convened all the family to listen to the Scriptures and other religious books.— In his journal Isaac alludes to this custom, and says: "My mind was often solemnized by these opportunities, and I resolved to live more consistently with the principles of christian sobriety."

When he was sixteen years old, it became a question to what business he should devote himself.— There was a prospect of obtaining a situation for him in a store at Philadelphia; and for that purpose it was deemed expedient that he should take up his abode for a while with his maternal uncle, whose house he had been so fond of visiting in early boyhood. He did not succeed in obtaining the situation he expected, but remained in the city on the look-out for some suitable employment. Meanwhile, he was very helpful to his uncle, who, finding him diligent and skillful, tried to induce him to learn his trade.— It was an occupation ill-adapted to his vigorous body and active mind; but he was not of a temperament to fold his hands and wait till something "turned up;" and as his uncle was doing a prosperous business, he concluded to accept his proposition. About the same time, his beloved cousin, Joseph Whitall, was sent to Trenton to study law. This was rather a severe trial to Isaac's feelings. Not that he envied his superior advantages; but he had sad forebodings that separation would interrupt their friendship, and that such a different career would be very likely to prevent its renewal. They parted with mutual regret, and did not meet again for several years.

When Isaac bade adieu to the paternal roof, his

mother looked after him thoughtfully, and remarked
to one of his sisters, "Isaac is no common boy.—
He will do something great, either for good or evil."
She called him back and said, "My son, you are
now going forth to make your own way in the world.
Always remember that you are as good as any other
person; but remember also that you are no better.'
With this farewell injunction, he departed for Philadelphia, where he soon acquired the character of a
faithful and industrious apprentice.

But his boyish love of fun was still strong within
him, and he was the torment of all his fellow apprentices. One of them, named William Roberts,
proposed that they should go together into the cellar
to steal a pitcher of cider. Isaac pulled the spile,
and while William was drawing the liquor, he took
an unobserved opportunity to hide it. When the
pitcher was full, he pretended to look all around for
it, without being able to find it. At last, he told his
unsuspecting comrade that he must thrust his finger
into the hole and keep it there, while he went to get
another spile. William waited and waited for him
to return, but when an hour or more had elapsed, his
patience was exhausted, and he began to Halloo!—
The noise, instead of bringing Isaac to his assistance, brought the mistress of the house, who caught
the culprit at the cider-barrel, and gave him a severe

scolding, to the infinite gratification of his mischievous companion.

Once, when the family were all going away, his uncle left the house in charge of him and another apprentice, telling them to defend themselves if any robbers came. Having a mind to try the courage of the lads, he returned soon after, and attempted to force a window in the back part of the house, which opened upon a narrow alley inclosed by a high fence. As soon as Isaac heard the noise, he seized an old harpoon that was about the premises, and told his companion to open the window the instant he gave the signal. His orders were obeyed, and he flung the harpoon with such force, that it passed through his uncle's vest and coat, and nailed him tight to the fence. When he told the story, he used to say he never afterward deemed it necessary to advise Isaac to defend himself.

Among the apprentices was one much older and stouter than the others. He was very proud of his physical strength, and delighted to play the tyrant over those who were younger and weaker than himself. When Isaac saw him knocking them about, he felt an almost irresistible temptation to fight; but his uncle was a severe man, likely to be much incensed by quarrels among his apprentices. He knew, moreover, that a battle between him and Samson would be very unequal; so he restrained his indignation as well as he could. But one day, when the big bully knocked him down, without the slightest provocation, he exclaimed, in great wrath, "If you ever do that again, I'll kill you. Mind what I say. I tell you I'll kill you."

Samson snapped his fingers and laughed, and the next day he knocked him down again. Isaac armed himself with a heavy window-bar, and when the apprentices were summoned to breakfast, he laid wait behind a door, and levelled a blow at the tyrant, as he passed through. He fell, without uttering a single cry. When the family sat down to breakfast, Mr. Tatem said, "Where is Samson?"

His nephew coolly replied, "I've killed him."

"Killed him!" exclaimed the uncle. "What do you mean?"

"I told him I would kill him if he ever knocked me down again," rejoined Isaac; "and I *have* killed him."

They rushed out in the utmost consternation, and found the young man entirely senseless. A physician was summoned, and for some time they feared he was really dead. The means employed to restore him were at last successful; but it was long before he recovered from the effects of the blow. When Isaac saw him so pale and helpless, a terrible remorse filled his soul. He shuddered to think how nearly he had committed murder, in one rash moment ot unbridled rage. This awful incident made such a solemn and deep impression on him, that from that time he began to make strong and earnest efforts to control the natural impetuosity of his temper; and he finally attained to a remarkable degree of self-control. Weary hours of debility brought wiser thoughts to Samson also; and when he recovered his strength, he never again misused it by abusing his companions.

In those days, Isaac did not profess to be a Quaker. He used the customary language of the world, and liked to display his well-proportioned figure in neat and fashionable clothing. The young women of his acquaintance, it is said, looked upon him with rather favorable eyes; but his thoughts never wandered from Sarah Tatum for a single day. Once, when he had a new suit of clothes, and stylish boots, the tops turned down with red, a young man of his acquaintance invited him to go home with him on Saturday evening and spend Sunday. He accepted the invitation, and set out well pleased with the expedition. The young man had a sister, who took it into her head that the visit was intended as an especial compliment to herself. The brother was called out somewhere in the neighborhood, and as soon as she found herself alone with their guest, she began to specify, in rather significant terms, what she should require of a man who wished to marry her.—

Her remarks made Isaac rather fidgetty; but he replied, in general terms, that he thought her ideas on the subject were very correct. "I suppose you think my father will give me considerable money," said she; "but that is a mistake. Whoever takes me must take me for myself alone."

The young man tried to stammer out that he did not come on any such errand; but his wits were bewildered by this unexpected siege, and he could not frame a suitable reply. She mistook his confusion for the natural timidity of love, and went on to express the high opinion she entertained of him. Isaac looked wistfully at the door, in hopes her brother would come to his rescue. But no relief came from that quarter, and fearing he should find himself engaged to be married without his own consent, he caught up his hat and rushed out. It was raining fast, but he splashed through mud and water, without stopping to choose his steps. Crossing the yard in this desperate haste, he encountered the brother, who called out, "Where are you going?"

"I'm going home," he replied.

"Going home!" exclaimed his astonished friend, "Why it is raining hard; and you came to stay all night. What does possess you, Isaac? Come back! Come back, I say!"

"I won't come back!" shouted Isaac, from the distance. "I'm going home." And home he went.—

His new clothes were well spattered, and his red-top boots loaded with mud; but though he prided himself on keeping his apparel in neat condition, he thought he had got off cheaply on this occasion.

Soon after he went to reside in Philadelphia, a sea captain by the name of Cox came to his uncle's on a visit. As the captain was one day passing through Norris Alley, he met a young colored man, named Joe, whose master he had known in Bermuda. He at once accused him of being a runaway slave, and ordered him to go to the house with him. Joe called him his old friend, and seemed much pleased at the meeting. He said he had been sent from Bermuda to New-York in a vessel, which he named; he had obtained permission to go a few miles into the country, to see his sister, and while he was gone, the vessel unfortunately sailed; he called upon the consignee and asked what he had better do under the circumstances, and he told him that his captain had left directions for him to go to Philadelphia and take passage home by the first vessel. Captain Cox was entirely satisfied with this account. He said there was a vessel then in port, which would sail for Bermuda in a few days, and told Joe he had better go and stay with him at Mr. Tatem's house, while he made inquiries about it.

When Isaac entered the kitchen that evening, he found Joe sitting there, in a very disconsolate atti-

tude; and watching him closely he observed tears
now and then trickling down his dark cheeks. He
thought of poor old Mingo, whose pitiful story had
so much interested him in boyhood, and caused him
to form a resolution to be the friend of Africans.—
The more he pondered on the subject, the more he
doubted whether Joe was so much pleased to meet
his "old friend," as he had pretended to be. He took
him aside and said, "Tell me truly how the case
stands with you. I will be your friend; and come
what will, you may feel certain that I will never betray you." Joe gave him an earnest look of distress
and scrutiny, which his young benefactor never forgot. Again he assured him, most solemnly, that he
might trust him. Then Joe ventured to acknowledge that he was a fugitive slave, and had great
dread of being returned into bondage. He said his
master let him out to work on board a ship going to
New-York. He had a great desire for freedom, and
when the vessel arrived at its destined port, he made
his escape, and travelled to Philadelphia, in hopes of
finding some one willing to protect him. Unluckily,
the very day he entered the City of Brotherly Love
he met his old acquaintance Captain Cox; and on
the spur of the moment he had invented the best story he could.

Isaac was then a mere lad, and he had been in
Philadelphia too short a time to form many acquain-

tances; but he imagined what his own feelings would be if he were in poor Joe's situation, and he determined to contrive some way or other to assist him. He consulted with a prudent and benevolent neighbor, who told him that a Quaker by the name of John Stapler, in Buck's County, was a good friend to colored people, and the fugitive had better be sent to him. Accordingly, a letter was written to Friend Stapler, and given to Joe, with instructions how to proceed. Meanwhile, Captain Cox brought tidings that he had secured a passage to Bermuda. Joe thanked him, and went on board the vessel, as he was ordered. But a day or two after, he obtained permission to go to Mr. Tatem's house to procure some clothes he had left there. It was nearly sunset when he left the ship and started on the route, which Isaac had very distinctly explained to him. When the sun disappeared, the bright moon came forth.— By her friendly light, he travelled on with a hopeful heart until the dawn of day, when he arrived at Friend Stapler's house and delivered the letter. He was received with great kindness, and a situation was procured for him in the neighborhood, where he spent the remainder of his life comfortably, with "none to molest or make him afraid."

This was the first opportunity Isaac had of carrying into effect his early resolution to befriend the oppressed Africans.

While the experiences of life were thus deepening and strengthening his character, the fair child, Sarah Tatum, was emerging into womanhood. She was a great belle in her neighborhood, admired by the young men for her comely person, and by the old for her good sense and discreet manners. He had many competitors for her favor. Once, when he went to invite her to ride to Quarterly Meeting, he found three Quaker beaux already there, with horses and sleighs for the same purpose. But though some of her admirers abounded in worldly goods, her mind never swerved from the love of her childhood. The bright affectionate school-boy, who delighted to sit with her under the shady trees, and twist her shining curls over his fingers, retained his hold upon her heart as long as its pulses throbbed.

Her father at first felt some uneasiness, lest his daughter should marry out of the Society of Friends. But Isaac had been for some time seriously impressed with the principles they professed, and when he assured the good old gentleman that he would never take Sarah out of the Society, of which she was born a member, he was perfectly satisfied to receive him as a son-in-law.

At that period, there were several remarkable individuals among Quaker preachers in that part of the country, and their meetings were unusually lively and spirit-stirring. One of them, named Nicholas

Waln, was educated in the Society of Friends, but in early life seems to have cared little about their principles. He was then an ambitious, money-loving man, remarkably successful in worldly affairs. But the principles inculcated in childhood probably remained latent within him; for when he was rapidly acquiring wealth and distinction by the practice of law, he suddenly relinquished it, from conscientious motives. This change of feeling is said to have been owing to the following incident. He had charge of an important case, where a large amount of property was at stake. In the progress of the cause, he became more and more aware that right was not on the side of his client; but to desert him in the midst was incompatible with his ideas of honor as a lawyer. This produced a conflict within him, which he could not immediately settle to his own satisfaction. A friend, who met him after the case was decided, inquired what was the result. He replied, "I did the best I could for my client. I have gained the cause for him, and have thereby defrauded an honest man of his just dues." He seemed sad and thoughtful, and would never after plead a cause at the bar. He dismissed his students, and returned to his clients all the money he had received for unfinished cases. For some time afterward, he appeared to take no interest in anything but his own religious state of feeling. He eventually became a preacher, very popu-

lar among Friends, and much admired by others.—
His sermons were usually short, and very impressive.
A cotemporary thus describes the effect of his preaching : "The whole assembly seemed to be baptized
together, and so covered with solemnity, that when
the meeting broke up, no one wished to enter into
conversation with another." He was particularly
zealous against a paid ministry, and not unfrequently
quoted the text, "Put me in the priest's office, I
pray thee, that I may eat a piece of bread." One of
his most memorable discourses began with these
words : "The lawyers, the priests, and the doctors,
these are the deceivers of men." He was so highly
esteemed, that when he entered the court-house, as
he occasionally did, to aid the poor or the oppressed
in some way, it was not uncommon for judges and
lawyers to rise spontaneously in token of respect.—
Isaac had great veneration for his character, and was
much edified by his ministry.

Mary Ridgeway, a small, plain, uneducated woman, was likewise remarkably persuasive and pene-
trating in her style of preaching, which appeared to
Isaac like pure inspiration. Her exhortations took
deep hold of his youthful feelings, and strongly
influenced him to a religious life.

But more powerful than all other agencies was the
preaching of William Savery. He was a tanner by
trade ; remarked by all who knew him as a man who

"walked humbly with his God." One night, a quantity of hides were stolen from his tannery, and he had reason to believe that the thief was a quarrelsome, drunken neighbor, whom I will call John Smith. The next week, the following advertisement appeared in the County newspaper : "Whoever stole lot of hides on the fifth of the present month, is nereby informed that the owner has a sincere wish to be his friend. If poverty tempted him to this false step, the owner will keep the whole transaction secret, and will gladly put him in the way of obtaining money by means more likely to bring him peace of mind." This singular advertisement attracted considerable attention ; but the culprit alone knew whence the benevolent offer came. When he read it, his heart melted within him, and he was filled with contrition for what he had done. A few nights afterward, as the tanner's family were about retiring to rest, they heard a timid knock, and when the door was opened, there stood John Smith with a load of hides on his shoulder. Without looking up, he said, "I have brought these back, Mr. Savery. Where shall I put them ?" "Wait till I can light a lantern, and I will go to the barn with thee," he replied.— "Then perhaps thou wilt come in and tell me how this happened. We will see what can be done for thee." As soon as they were gone out, his wife prepared some hot coffee, and placed pies and meat on the table. When they returned from the barn, she said "Neighbor Smith, I thought some hot supper would be good for thee." He turned his back toward her and did not speak. After leaning against the fire-place in silence for a moment, he said, in a choked voice, "It is the first time I ever stole anything, and I have felt very bad about it. I don't know how it is. I am sure I didn't think once that I should ever come to be what I am. But I took to drinking, and then to quarrelling. Since I began to go down hill, everybody gives me a kick. You are the first man who has ever offered me a helping hand. My wife is sickly, and my children are starving. You have sent them many a meal, God bless you! and yet I stole the hides from you, meaning to sell them the first chance I could get. But I tell you the truth when I say it is the first time I was ever a thief."

"Let it be the last, my friend," replied William Savery. "The secret shall remain between ourselves. Thou art still young, and it is in thy power to make up for lost time. Promise me that thou wilt not drink any intoxicating liquor for a year, and I will employ thee to-morrow at good wages. Perhaps we may find some employment for thy family also. The little boy can at least pick up stones.— But eat a bit now, and drink some hot coffee. Perhaps it will keep thee from craving anything stronger

to-night. Doubtless, thou wilt find it hard to abstain
at first; but keep up a brave heart, for the sake of
thy wife and children, and it will soon become easy.
When thou hast need of coffee, tell Mary, and she
will always give it to thee."

The poor fellow tried to eat and drink, but the
food seemed to choke him. After an ineffectual effort to compose his excited feelings, he bowed his
head on the table, and wept like a child. After a
while, he ate and drank with good appetite; and his
host parted with him for the night with this kindly
exhortation; "Try to do well, John; and thou wilt
always find a friend in me."

He entered into his employ the next day, and remained with him many years, a sober, honest, and
faithful man. The secret of the theft was kept between them; but after John's death, William Savery
sometimes told the story, to prove that evil might be
overcome with good.

This practical preacher of righteousness was likewise a great preacher orally; if greatness is to be
measured by the effect produced on the souls of
others. Through his ministry, the celebrated Mrs.
Fry was first excited to a lively interest in religion.
When he visited England in 1798, she was Elizabeth
Gurney, a lively girl of eighteen, rather fond of dress
and company. Her sister, alluding to the first sermon they heard from William Savery, writes thus:

"His voice and manner were arresting, and we all liked the sound. Elizabeth became a good deal agitated, and I saw her begin to weep. The next morning, when she took breakfast with him at her uncle's, he preached to her after breakfast, and prophesied of the high and important calling she wôuld be led into." Elizabeth herself made the following record of it in her journal; "In hearing William Sa very preach, he seemed to me to overflow with true religion; to be humble, and yet a man of great abilities. Having been gay and disbelieving, only a few years ago, makes him better acquainted with the heart of one in the same condition. We had much serious conversation. What he said, and what I felt was like a refreshing shower falling upon earth that had been dried up for ages."

This good and gifted man often preached in Philadelphia; not only at stated seasons, on the first and fifth day of the week, but at evening meetings also, where the Spirit is said to have descended upon him and his hearers in such copious measure that they were reminded of the gathering of the apostles on the day of Pentecost. Isaac was at an impressible age, and on those occasions his thirsty soul drank eagerly from the fountain of living water. He never forgot those refreshing meetings. To the end of his days, whenever anything reminded him of William Savery, he would utter a warm eulogium on his deep

spirituality, his tender benevolence, his cheerful, ge-
nial temper, and the simple dignity of his deportment.

Isaac was about twenty-two years old, when he
was received as a member of the Society of Friends.
It was probably the pleasantest period of his existence.   Love and religion, the two deepest and
brightest experiences of human life, met together,
and flowed into his earnest soul in one full stream.
He felt perfectly satisfied that he had found the one
true religion.   The plain mode of worship suited the
simplicity of his character, while the principles incul
cated were peculiarly well calculated to curb the violence of his temper, and to place his strong will under the restraint of conscience.   Duties toward God
and his fellow men stood forth plainly revealed to
him in the light that shone so clearly in his awaken-
ed soul.   Late in life, he often used to refer to this
early religious experience as a sweet season of peace
and joy.   He said it seemed as if the very air were
fragrant, and the sunlight more glorious than it had
ever been before.   The plain Quaker meeting-house
in the quiet fields of Woodbury was to him indeed a
house of prayer, though its silent worship was often
undisturbed by a single uttered word.   Blended with
those spiritual experiences was the fair vision of his
beloved Sarah, who always attended meeting, serene
in her maiden beauty.   The joy of renovated friend-

ship also awaited him there, in that quaint old gathering place of simple worshippers. When he parted from his dear cousin, Joseph Whitall, they were both young men of good moral characters, but not seriously thoughtful concerning religion. Years elapsed, and each knew not whither the other was travelling in spiritual experiences. But one day, when Isaac went to meeting as usual, and was tying his horse in the shed, a young man in the plain costume of the Friends came to tie his horse also. A glance showed that it was Joseph Whitall, the companion of his boyhood and youth. For an instant, they stood surprised and silent, looking at each other's dress; for until then neither of them was aware that the other had become a Quaker. Tears started to their eyes, and they embraced each other. They had long and precious interviews afterward, in which they talked over the circumstances that had inclined them to reflect on serious subjects, and the reasons which induced them to consider the Society of Friends as the best existing representative of Christianity.

The gravity of their characters at this period, may be inferred from the following letter, written in 1794:

"Dear Isaac,—

While I sat in retirement this evening, thou wert brought fresh into my remembrance, with a warm desire for thy welfare and preservation.

Wherefore, be encouraged to press forward and
persevere in the high and holy way wherein thou
hast measurably, through mercy, begun to tread.
From our childhood I have had an affectionate regard for thee, which hath been abundantly increased;
and, in the covenant of life I have felt thee near.
May we, my beloved friend, now in the spring time
of life, in the morning of our days, with full purpose
of heart cleave unto the Lord. May we seek Him
for our portion and our inheritance; that He may
be pleased, in his wonderful loving kindness, to be
our counsellor and director; that, in times of trouble
and commotion, we may have a safe hiding-place,
an unfailing refuge. I often feel the want of a
greater dependance, a more steadfast leaning, upon
that Divine Arm of power, which ever hath been, and
still is, the true support of the righteous. Yet, I am
sometimes favored to hope that in the Lord's time
an advancement will be known, and a more full
establishment in the most holy faith. "For then
shall we know, if we follow on to know the Lord,
that His going forth is prepared as the morning, and
He will come unto us as the rain, as the latter and
the former rain upon the earth." May we, from
time to time, be favored to feel his animating presence, to comfort and strengthen our enfeebled minds,
that so we may patiently abide in our allotments,
and look forward with a cheering hope, that, what-

ever trials and besetments may await us, they may tend to our further refinement, and more close union in the heavenly covenant. And when the end comes, may we be found among those who through many tribulations have washed their garments white in the blood of the Lamb, and be found worthy to stand with him upon Mount Zion.

So wisheth and prayeth thy affectionate friend,

JOSEPH WHITALL."

The letters which passed between him and his betrothed partake of the same sedate character; but through the unimpassioned Quaker style gleams the steady warmth of sincere affection. There is something pleasant in the simplicity with which he usually closed his epistles to her: "I am, dear Sally, thy real friend, Isaac."

They were married on the eighteenth of the Ninth Month, [September,] 1795; he being nearly twenty-four years of age, and she about three years younger. The worldly comforts which a kind Providence bestowed on Isaac and his bride, were freely imparted to others. The resolution formed after listening to the history of old Mingo's wrongs was pretty severely tested by a residence in Philadelphia. There were numerous kidnappers prowling about the city, and many outrages were committed, which would not have been tolerated for a moment toward any but a despised race. Pennsylvania being on the frontier of the slave states, runaways were often passing through; and the laws on that subject were little understood, and less attended to. If a colored man was arrested as a fugitive slave, and discharged for want of proof, the magistrate received no fee; but if he was adjudged a slave, and surrendered to his claimant, the magistrate received from five to twenty dollars for his trouble ; of course, there was a natural tendency to make the most of evidence in favor of slavery.

Under these circumstances, the Pennsylvania Abolition Society was frequently called upon to protect the rights of colored people. Isaac T. Hopper became an active and leading member of this association. He was likewise one of the overseers of a school for colored children, established by Anthony Benezet ; and it was his constant practice, for several years, to teach two or three nights every week, in a school for colored adults, established by a society of young men. In process of time, he became known to everybody in Philadelphia as the friend and legal adviser of colored people upon all emergencies. The shrewdness, courage, and zeal, with which he fulfilled this mission will be seen in the course of the following narratives, which I have selected from a vast number of similar character, in which he was the principal agent.

CHARLES WEBSTER.

In 1797, a wealthy gentleman from Virginia went
to spend the winter in Philadelphia, accompanied
by his wife and daughter. He had a slave named
Charles Webster, whom he took with him as coachman and waiter. When they had been in the city a
few weeks, Charles called upon Isaac T. Hopper,
and inquired whether he had become free in consequence of his master's bringing him into Pennsylvania. It was explained to him, that if he remained
there six months, with his master's knowledge and
consent, he would then be a free man, according to
the laws of Pennsylvania. The slave was quite
disheartened by this information; for he supposed
his owner was well acquainted with the law, and
would therefore be careful to take him home before
that term expired.

"I am resolved never to return to Virginia," said
he. "Where can I go to be safe?"

Friend Hopper told him his master might be ignorant of the law, or forgetful of it. He advised him
to remain with the family until he saw them making
preparations to return. If the prescribed six months
expired meanwhile, he would be a free man. If not,
there would be time enough to consult what had better be done. "It is desirable to obtain thy liberty
in a legal way, if possible," said he; "for otherwise

thou wilt be constantly liable to be arrested, and may never again have such a good opportunity to escape from bondage."

Charles hesitated, but finally concluded to accept this prudent advice. The time seemed very long to the poor fellow; for he was in a continual panic lest his master should take him back to Virginia; but he did his appointed tasks faithfully, and none of the family suspected what was passing in his mind.

The long-counted six months expired at last; and that very day, his master said, "Charles, grease the carriage-wheels, and have all things in readiness; for I intend to start for home to-morrow."

The servant appeared to be well pleased with this prospect, and put the carriage and harness in good order. As soon as that job was completed, he went to Friend Hopper and told him the news. When assured that he was now a free man, according to law, he could hardly be made to believe it. He was all of a tremor with anxiety, and it seemed almost impossible to convince him that he was out of danger. He was instructed to return to his master till next morning, and to send word by one of the hotel servants in case he should be arrested meanwhile.

The next morning, he again called upon Friend Hopper, who accompanied him to the office of William Lewis, a highly respectable lawyer, who would never take any fee for his services on such occa-

sions.   When Mr. Lewis heard the particulars of the
case, he wrote a polite note to the Virginian, informing him that his former slave was now free, according to the laws of Pennsylvania; and cautioning him
against any attempt to take him away, contrary to
his own inclination.

The lawyer advised Friend Hopper to call upon
the master and have some preparatory conversation
with him, before Charles was sent to deliver the
note. He was then only twenty-six years of age,
and he felt somewhat embarrassed at the idea of calling upon a wealthy and distinguished stranger, who
was said to be rather imperious and irritable. However, after a little reflection, he concluded it was his
duty, and accordingly he did it.

When the Southerner was informed that his servant was free, and that a lawyer had been consulted
on the subject, he was extremely angry, and used
very contemptuous language concerning people who
tampered with gentlemen's servants. The young
Quaker replied, "If thy son were a slave in Algiers,
thou wouldst thank me for tampering with *him* to
procure his liberty. But in the present case, I am
not obnoxious to the charge thou hast brought ; for
thy servant came of his own accord to consult me, I
merely made him acquainted with his legal rights;
and I intend to see that he is protected in them."

When Charles delivered the lawyer's note, and his

master saw that he no longer had any legal power over him, he proposed to hire him to drive the carriage home. But Charles was very well aware that Virginia would be a very dangerous place for him, and he positively refused. The incensed Southerner then claimed his servant's clothes as his property, and ordered him to strip instantly. Charles did as he was ordered, and proceeded to walk out of the room naked. Astonished to find him willing to leave the house in that condition, he seized him violently, thrust him back into the room, and ordered him to dress himself. When he had assumed his garments, he walked off; and the master and servant never met again.

Charles was shrewd and intelligent, and conducted himself in such a manner as to gain respect. He married an industrious, economical woman, who served in the family of Chief Justice Tilghman. In process of time, he built a neat two-story house, where they brought up reputably a family of fourteen children, who obtained quite a good education at the school established by Anthony Benezet.

BEN JACKSON.

Ben was born a slave in Virginia. When he was about sixteen years old, his mind became excited on the subject of slavery. He could not reconcile it with the justice and goodness of the Creator, that

one man should be born to toil for another without
wages, to be driven about, and treated like a beast
of the field. The older he grew, the more heavily
did these considerations press upon him. At last,
when he was about twenty-five years old, he resolved
to gain his liberty, if possible. He left his master,
and after encountering many difficulties, arrived in
Philadelphia, where he let himself on board a vessel
and went several voyages. When he was thirty
years of age, he married, and was employed as a
coachman by Dr. Benjamin Rush, one of the signers
of the Declaration of Independence. He lived with
him two years; and when he left, Dr. Rush gave
him a paper certifying that he was a free man, honest, sober, and capable.

In 1799, his master came to Philadelphia, and arrested him as his fugitive slave. Ben had an extraordinary degree of intelligence and tact. When his
master brought him before a magistrate, and demanded the usual certificate to authorize him to take his
human chattel back to Virginia, Ben neither admitted nor denied that he was a slave. He merely showed the certificate of Dr. Rush, and requested that
Isaac T. Hopper might be informed of his situation.
Joseph Bird, the justice before whom the case was
brought, detested slavery, and was a sincere friend
to the colored people. He committed Ben to prison
until morning, and despatched a note to Isaac T.

Hopper informing him of the circumstance, and requesting him to call upon Dr. Rush. When the doctor was questioned, he said he knew nothing about
Ben's early history; he lived with him two years,
and was *then* a free man.

When Friend Hopper went to the prison, he found
Ben in a state of great anxiety and distress. He admitted that he was the slave of the man who claimed
him, and that he saw no way of escape open for him.
His friend told him not to be discouraged, and promised to exert himself to the utmost in his behalf.
The constable who had arrested him, sympathized
with the poor victim of oppression, and promised to
do what he could for him. Finding him in such a
humane mood, Friend Hopper urged him to bring
Ben to the magistrate's office a short time *before* the
hour appointed for the trial. He did so, and found
Friend Hopper already there, watching the clock.
The moment the hand pointed to nine, he remarked
that the hour, of which the claimant had been apprized, had already arrived; no evidence had been
brought that the man was a slave; on the contrary,
Dr. Rush's certificate was strong presumptive evidence of his being a freeman; he therefore demanded that the prisoner should be discharged. Justice
Bird, having no desire to throw obstacles in the way,
promptly told Ben he was at liberty, and he lost no
time in profiting by the information. Just as he

passed out of the door, he saw his master coming, and ran full speed. He had sufficient presence of mind to take a zigzag course, and running through a house occupied by colored people, he succeeded in eluding pursuit.

When Friend Hopper went home, he found him at his house. He tried to impress upon his mind the peril he would incur by remaining in Philadelphia, and advised him by all means to go to sea. But his wife was strongly attached to him, and so unwilling to consent to this plan, that he concluded to run the risk of staying with her. He remained concealed about a week, and then returned to the house he had previously occupied. They lived in the second story, and there was a shed under their bed-room window. Ben placed a ladder under the window, to be ready for escape; but it was so short, that it did not reach the roof of the shed by five or six feet. His wife was an industrious, orderly woman, and kept their rooms as neat as a bee-hive. The only thing which marred their happiness was the continual dread that man-hunters might pounce upon them, in some unguarded hour, and separate them forever. About a fortnight after his arrest, they were sitting together in the dusk of the evening, when the door was suddenly burst open, and his master rushed in with a constable. Ben sprang out of the window, down the ladder, and made his escape. His master and the constable followed; but as soon as they were on the ladder, Ben's wife cut the cord that held it, and they tumbled heels over head upon the shed. This bruised them some, and frightened them still more. They scrambled upon their feet, cursing at a round rate.

Ben arrived safely at the house of Isaac T. Hopper, who induced him to quit the city immediately, and go to sea. His first voyage was to the East Indies. While he was gone, Friend Hopper negotiated with the master, who, finding there was little chance of regaining his slave, agreed to manumit him for one hundred and fifty dollars. As soon as Ben returned, he repaid from his wages the sum which had been advanced for his ransom. His wife's health was greatly impaired by the fear and anxiety she had endured on his account. She became a prey to melancholy, and never recovered her former cheerfulness.

THOMAS COOPER.

The person who assumed this name was called Notly, when he was a slave in Maryland. He was compelled to labor very hard, was scantily supplied with food and clothing, and lodged in a little ricketty hut, through which the cold winds of winter whistled freely. He was of a very religious turn of mind, and often, when alone in his little cabin at midnight, he

prayed earnestly to God to release him from his sufferings.

In the year 1800, he found a favorable opportunity to escape from his unfeeling master, and made his
way to Philadelphia, where he procured employment
in a lumber-yard, under the name of John Smith.
He was so diligent and faithful, that he soon gained
the good-will and confidence of his employers. He
married a worthy, industrious woman, with whom he
lived happily. By their united earnings they were
enabled to purchase a small house, where they enjoyed more comfort than many wealthy people, and
were much respected by neighbors and acquaintances.

Unfortunately, he confided his story to a colored
man, who, for the sake of reward, informed his master where he was to be found. Accordingly, he came
to Philadelphia, arrested him, and carried him before
a magistrate. Having brought forward satisfactory
evidence that he was a slave, an order was granted
to carry him back to Maryland. Isaac T. Hopper
was present at this decision, and was afflicted by it
beyond measure. John's employers pitied his condition, and sympathized with his afflicted wife and
children. They offered to pay a large sum for his
ransom; but his savage master refused to release
him on any terms. This sober, industrious man,
guiltless of any crime, was hand-cuffed and had his

arms tied behind him with a rope, to which another rope was appended, for his master to hold. While they were fastening his fetters, he spoke a few affectionate words to his weeping wife. "Take good care of the children," said he; "and don't let them forget their poor father. If you are industrious and frugal, I hope you will be enabled to keep them at school, till they are old enough to be placed at service in respectable families. Never allow them to be idle; for that will lead them into bad ways. And now don't forget my advice; for it is most likely you will never see me again."

Then addressing his children, he said, "You will have no father to take care of you now. Mind what your mother tells you, and be very careful not to do anything to grieve her. Be industrious and faithful in whatever you are set about; and never play in the streets with naughty children."

They all wept bitterly while he thus talked to them; but he restrained his sobs, though it was evident his heart was well nigh breaking. Isaac T. Hopper was present at this distressing scene, and suffered almost as acutely as the poor slave himself. In the midst of his parting words, his master seized the rope, mounted his horse, snapped his whip, and set off, driving poor John before him. This was done in a Christian country, and there was no law to protect the victim.

John was conveyed to Washington and offered for sale to speculators, who were buying up gangs for the Southern market. The sight of dejected and brutified slaves, chained together in coffles, was too common at the seat of our republican government to attract attention; but the barbarity of John's master was so conspicuous, that even there he was rebuked for his excessive cruelty. These expressions of sympathy were quite unexpected to the poor slave, and they kindled a faint hope of escape, which had been smouldering in his breast. Manacled as he was, he contrived to trip up his master, and leaving him prostrate on the ground, he ran for the woods. He was soon beyond the reach of his tyrant, and might have escaped easily if a company had not immediately formed to pursue him. They chased him from the shelter of the bushes to a swamp, where he was hunted like a fox, till night with friendly darkness overshadowed him. While his enemies were sleeping, he cautiously made his way by the light of the stars, to the house of an old acquaintance, who hastened to take off his fetters, ·and give him a good supper.

Thus refreshed, he hastened to bid his colored friend farewell, and with fear and trembling set off for Philadelphia. He had several rivers to cross, and he thought likely men would be stationed on the bridges to arrest him. Therefore, he hid himself in the deepest recesses of the woods in the day-time, and travelled only in the night. He suffered much with hunger and fatigue, but arrived home at last, to the great astonishment and joy of his family. He well knew that these precious moments of affectionate greeting were highly dangerous; for his own roof could afford no shelter from pursuers armed with the power of a wicked law. He accordingly hastened to Isaac T. Hopper for advice and assistance.

The yellow fever was then raging in Philadelphia, and the children had all been carried into the country by their mother. Business made it necessary for Friend Hopper to be in the city during the day-time, and a colored domestic remained with him to take charge of the house. This woman was alone when the fugitive arrived; but she showed him to an upper chamber secured by a strong fastening. He had been there but a short time, when his master came with two constables and proceeded to search the house. When they found a room with the door bolted, they demanded entrance; and receiving no answer, they began to consult together how to gain admittance. At this crisis, the master of the house came home, and received information of what was going on up-stairs. He hastened thither, and ordered the intruders to quit his house instantly. One of the constables said, "This gentleman's slave is here; and if you don't deliver him up immediately, we will get a warrant to search the house."

"Quit my premises," replied Friend Hopper. "The mayor dare not grant a warrant to search my house."

The men withdrew in no very good humor, and a message soon came from the mayor requesting to see Isaac T. Hopper. He obeyed the summons, and the magistrate said to him, "This gentleman informs me that his slave is in your house. Is it so?"

The wary Friend replied, "Thou hast just told me that this man *says* he is. Dost thou not believe him?"

"But I wish to know from yourself whether he is in your house or not," rejoined the magistrate.

"If the mayor reflects a little, I think he will see that he has no right to ask such a question; and that I am not bound to answer it," replied Friend Hopper. "If he is in my house, and if this man can prove it, I am liable to a heavy penalty; and no man is bound to inform against himself. These people have not behaved so civilly, that I feel myself under any especial obligations of courtesy toward them. Hast thou any further business with me?"

"Did you say I dared not grant a warrant to search your house?" asked the mayor.

He answered, "Indeed I did say so; and I now

repeat it. I mean no disrespect to anybody in authority; but neither thou nor any other magistrate would dare to grant a warrant to search my house. I am a man of established reputation. I am not a suspicious character."

The mayor smiled, as he replied, "I don't know about that, Mr. Hopper. In the present case, I am inclined to think you are a *very* suspicious character." And so they parted.

The master resorted to various stratagems to recapture his victim. He dressed himself in Quaker costume and went to his house. The once happy home was desolate now; and the anxious wife sat weeping, with her little ones clinging to her in childish sympathy. The visitor professed to be very friendly to her husband, and desirous to ascertain where he could be found, in order to render him advice and assistance in eluding the vigilance of his master. The wife prudently declined giving any information, but referred him to Isaac T. Hopper, as the most suitable person to consult in the case. Finding that he could not gain his object by deception, he forgot to sustain the quiet character he had assumed, but gave vent to his anger in a great deal of violent and profane language. He went off, finally, swearing that in spite of them all he would have his slave again, if he was to be found on the face of the earth.

John Smith remained under the protection of
Friend Isaac about a week. Spies were seen lurk-
ing round the house for several days; but they disappeared at last. Supposing this was only a trick
to put them off their guard, a colored man was employed to run out of the house after dark. The enemies who were lying in ambush, rushed out and laid
violent hands upon him. They released him as soon
as they discovered their mistake; but the next day
Friend Hopper had them arrested, and compelled
them to enter into bonds for their good behavior.
On the following evening the same man was employed to run out again; and this time he was not interrupted. The third evening, John Smith himself ventured forth from his hiding-place, and arrived safely
in New-Jersey.

He let himself to a worthy farmer, and soon gained the confidence and good will of all the family.
He ate at the same table with them, and sat with
them on Sunday afternoons, listening to their reading of the Scriptures and other religious books.
This system of equality did not diminish the modes-
ty of his deportment, but rather tended to increase
his habitual humility.

He remained there several months, during which
time he never dared to visit his family, though only
eight miles distant from them. This was a great
source of unhappiness · for he was naturally affec

tionate, and was strongly attached to his wife and children. At length, he ventured to hire a small house in a very secluded situation, not far from the village of Haddonfield: and once more he gathered his family around him. But his domestic comfort was constantly disturbed by fear of men-stealers. While at his work in the day-time, he sometimes started at the mere rustling of a leaf; and in the night time, he often woke up in agony from terrifying dreams.

The false friend, who betrayed him to his cruel master, likewise suffered greatly from fear. When he heard that John had again escaped, he was exceedingly alarmed for his own safety. He dreamed that his abused friend came with a knife in one hand and a torch in the other, threatening to murder him and burn the house. These ideas took such hold of his imagination, that he often started up in bed and screamed aloud. But John was too sincerely religious to cherish a revengeful spirit. The wrong done to him was as great as one mortal could inflict upon another; but he had learned the divine precept not to render evil for evil.

The event proved that John's uneasiness was too well founded. A few months after his family rejoined him, Isaac T. Hopper heard that his master had arrived in Philadelphia, and was going to New-Jersey to arrest him. He immediately apprised him of his danger; and the tidings were received with feelings of desperation amounting to phrensy. He loaded his gun and determined to defend himself Very early the next morning, he saw his master with two men coming up the narrow lane that led to his house. He stationed himself in the door-way, leveled his gun, and called out, "I will shoot the first man that crosses that fence!" They were alarmed, and turned back to procure assistance. John seized that opportunity to quit his retreat. He hastened to Philadelphia, and informed Isaac T. Hopper what had happened. His friend represented to him the unchristian character of such violent measures, and advised him not to bring remorse on his soul by the shedding of blood. The poor hunted fugitive seemed to be convinced, though it was a hard lesson to learn in his circumstances. Again he resolved to fly for safety; and his friend advised him to go to Boston. A vessel from that place was then lying in the Delaware, and the merchant who had charge of her, pitying his forlorn situation, offered him a passage free of expense. Kindness bestowed on him was always like good seed dropped into a rich soil. He was so obliging and diligent during the voyage, that he more than compensated the captain for his passage. He arrived safely in Boston, where his certificates of good character soon enabled him to procure employment. Not long after, he sent for his wife, who sold what little property they had in Philadelphia, and took her children to their new home.

When John left New-Jersey, he assumed the name of Thomas Cooper, by which he was ever afterward known. He had early in life manifested a religious turn of mind; and this was probably increased by his continual perils and narrow escapes. He mourned over every indication of dishonesty, profanity, or dissipation, among people of his own color; and this feeling grew upon him, until he felt as if it were a duty to devote his life to missionary labors. He became a popular preacher among the Methodists, and visited some of the West India Islands in that capacity. His christian example and fervid exhortations, warm from the heart, are said to have produced a powerful effect on his untutored hearers. After his return, he concluded to go to Africa as a missionary. For that purpose, he took shipping with his family for London, where he was received with much kindness by many persons to whom he took letters of introduction. His children were placed at a good school by a benevolent member of the Society of Friends; and from various quarters he received the most gratifying testimonials of respect and sympathy. But what was of more value than all else to the poor harassed fugitive, was the fact that he now, for the first time in his life, felt entirely safe from the fangs of the oppressor.

He remained in London about a year and a half. During that time he compiled a hymn book which his friends published with his portrait in front. He preached with great acceptance to large congregations: several thousand persons assembled to hear his farewell sermon on the eve of his departure fo Africa. He sailed for Sierra Leone, in the latte part of 1818, and was greeted there with much cordiality; for his fame had preceded him. All classes flocked to hear him preach, and his labors were highly useful. After several years spent in the discharge of religious duties, he died of the fever which so often proves fatal to strangers in Africa. His wife returned with her children to end her days in Philadelphia.

A CHILD KIDNAPPED.

In the year 1801, a Captain Dana engaged passage in a Philadelphia schooner bound to Charleston, South Carolina. The day he expected to sail, he called at the house of a colored woman, and told her he had a good suit of clothes, too small for his own son, but about the right size for her little boy. He proposed to take the child home to try the garments, and if they fitted him he would make him a present of them. The mother was much gratified by these friendly professions, and dressed the boy up as well as she could to accompany the captain, who gave him a piece of gingerbread, took him by the hand, and led him away. Instead of going to his lodgings, as he had promised, he proceeded directly to the schooner, and left the boy in care of the captain: saying that he himself would come on board while the vessel was on the way down the river. As they were about to sail, a sudden storm came on. The wind raged so violently, that the ship dragged her anchor, and they were obliged to haul to at a wharf in the district of Southwark. A respectable man, who lived in the neighborhood, was standing on the wharf at the time, and hearing a child crying very bitterly on board the vessel, he asked the colored cook whose child that was, and why he was in such distress. He replied that a passenger by the name of Dana brought him on board, and that the boy said he stole him from his mother.

A note was immediately despatched to Isaac T. Hopper, who, being away from home, did not receive it till ten o'clock at night. The moment he read it, he called for a constable, and proceeded directly to the schooner. In answer to his inquiries, the captain declared that all the hands had gone on shore, and that he was entirely alone in the vessel. Friend Hopper called for a light, and asked him to open the forecastle, that they might ascertain whether any person were there. He peremptorily refused; saying that his word ought to be sufficient to satisfy

them. Friend Hopper took up an axe that was lying
on the deck, and declared that he would break the
door, unless it was opened immediately. In this
dilemma, the captain, with great reluctance, unlocked the forecastle; and there they found the cook and
the boy. The constable took them all in custody,
and they proceeded to the mayor's. The rain fell in
torrents, and it was extremely dark; for in those
days, there were no lamps in that part of the city.
They went stumbling over cellar doors, and wading
through gutters, till they arrived in Front street,
where Mr. Inskeep, the mayor, lived. It was past
midnight, but when a servant informed him that Isaac
T. Hopper had been ringing at the door, and wished
to see him, he ordered him to be shown up into his
chamber. After apologizing for the unseasonable-
ness of the hour, he briefly stated the urgency of the
case, and asked for a verbal order to put the captain
and cook in prison to await their trial the next morning. The magistrate replied, "It is a matter of too
much importance to be disposed of in that way. I
will come down and hear the case." A large hicko-
ry log, which had been covered with ashes in the
parlor fire-place, was raked open, and they soon had
a blazing fire to dry their wet garments, and take
off the chill of a cold March storm. The magistrate
was surprised to find that the captain was an old acquaintance; and he expressed much regret at meet-

ing him under such unpleasant circumstances. After some investigation into the affair, he was required
to appear for trial the next morning, under penalty
of forfeiting three thousand dollars. The cook was
committed to prison, as a witness; and the colored
boy was sent home with Isaac T. Hopper, who
agreed to produce him at the time appointed.

Very early the next morning, he sent a messenger
to inform the mother that her child was in safety;
but she was off in search of him, and was not to be
found. On the way to the mayor's office, they met
her in the street, half distracted. As soon as she
perceived her child, she cried out, "My son! My
son!" threw her arms round him, and sobbed aloud.
She kissed him again and again, saying, "Oh my
child, I thought I had lost you forever."

When they all arrived at the mayor's office, at the
hour appointed for trial, the captain protested that
he had no knowledge of anything wrong in the business, having merely taken care of the boy at the re
quest of a passenger. When he was required to appear at the next court to answer to the charge of
kidnapping, he became alarmed, and told where Captain Dana could be arrested. His directions were
followed, and the delinquent was seized and taken to
Isaac T. Hopper's house. He was in a towering
passion, protesting his innocence, and threatening
vengeance against everybody who should attempt to

detain him.   Badly as Friend Hopper thought of the
man, he almost wished he had escaped, when he discovered that he had a wife and children to suffer for
his misdoings.   His tender heart would not allow
him to be present at the trial, lest his wife should be
there in distress.   She did not appear, however, and
Captain Dana made a full confession, alleging poverty as an excuse.   He was an educated man, and
had previously sustained a fair reputation.   He was
liberated on bail for fifteen hundred dollars, which
was forfeited; but the judgments were never enforc-
ed against his securities.

WAGELMA.

Wagelma was a lively intelligent colored boy of
ten years old, whom his mother had bound as an apprentice to a Frenchman in Philadelphia.   This man
being about to take his family to Baltimore, in the
summer of 1801, with the intention of going thence
to France, put his apprentice on board a Newcastle
packet bound to Baltimore, without having the consent of the boy or his mother, as the laws of Pennsylvania required.   The mother did not even know
of his intended departure, till she heard that her
child was on board the ship.   Fears that he might be
sold into slavery, either in Baltimore or the West Indies, seized upon her mind; and even if that dread-

ful fate did not await him, there was great probability that she would never see him again.

In her distress she called upon Isaac T. Hopper, immediately after sunrise. He hastened to the wharf, where the Newcastle packet generally lay, but had the mortification to find that she had already started, and that a gentle breeze was wafting her down the stream. He mounted a fleet horse, and in twenty minutes arrived at Gloucester Point, three miles below the city. The ferry at that place was kept by a highly respectable widow, with whom he had been long acquainted. He briefly stated the case to her, and she at once ordered one of her ferrymen to put him on board the Newcastle packet, which was in sight, and near the Jersey shore. They made all speed, for there was not a moment to lose.

When they came along-side the packet, the captain, supposing him to be a passenger for Baltimore, ordered the sailors to assist him on board. When his business was made known, he was told that the Frenchman was in the cabin. He sought him out, and stated that the laws of Pennsylvania did not allow apprentices to be carried out of the state without certain preliminaries, to which he had not attended. The Frenchman had six or eight friends with him, and as he was going out of the country, he put the laws at defiance. Meanwhile, the vessel was gliding down the river, carrying friend Hopper to Newcas-

tle. He summoned the captain, and requested him
to put the colored boy into the ferry-boat, which was
alongside ready to receive him. He was not disposed to interfere; but when Friend Hopper drew a
volume from his pocket and read to him the laws applicable to the case, he became alarmed, and said
the boy must be given up. Whereupon, Friend
Hopper directed the child to go on deck, which he
was ready enough to do; and the ferryman soon
helped him on board the boat.

The Frenchman and his friends were very noisy
and violent. They attempted to throw Friend Hopper overboard; and there were so many of them,
that they seemed likely to succeed in their efforts.
But he seized one of them fast by the coat; resolved
to have company in the water, if he were compelled
to take a plunge. They struck his hand with their
canes, and pulled the coat from his grasp. Then he
seized hold of another; and so the struggle continued for some minutes. The ferryman, who was watching the conflict, contrived to bring his boat into a favorable position; and Friend Hopper suddenly let go
the Frenchman's coat, and tumbled in.

When he returned to Philadelphia with the boy,
he found the mother waiting at his house, in a state
of intense anxiety. The meeting between mother
and son was joyful indeed; and Wagelma made them
all laugh by his animated description of his friend's

encounter with the Frenchmen, accompanied by a lively imitation of their gesticulations. In witnessing the happiness he had imparted, their benefactor found more than sufficient compensation for all the difficulties he had encountered.

JAMES POOVEY.

Slavery having been abolished by a gradual process in Pennsylvania, there were many individuals who still remained in bondage at the period of which I write. Among them was James Poovey, slave to a blacksmith in Pennsylvania. He had learned his master's trade, and being an athletic man, was very valuable. During several winters, he attended an evening school for the free instruction of colored people. He made very slow progress in learning, but by means of unremitting industry and application, he was at last able to accomplish the desire of his heart, which was to read the New Testament for himself.

The fact that colored men born a few years later than himself were free, by the act of gradual emancipation, while he was compelled to remain in bondage, had long been a source of uneasiness; and increase of knowledge by no means increased his contentment. Having come to the conclusion that slavery was utterly unjust, he resolved not to submit to it any longer. In the year 1802 when he was about thirty-three years of age, he took occasion to inform his master that he could read the New Testament. When he observed that he was glad to hear it, James replied, "But in the course of my reading I have discovered that it would be a sin for me to serve you as a slave any longer".

"Aye?" said his master. "Pray tell me how you made that discovery."

"Why, the New Testament says we must do as we would be done by," replied James. "Now if I submit to let you do by *me*, as you would not be willing I should do by *you*, I am as bad as you are. If you will give me a paper that will secure my freedom at the end of seven years, I will serve you faithfully during that time; but I cannot consent to be a slave any longer."

His master refused to consent to this proposition. James then asked permission to go to sea till he could earn money enough to buy his freedom; but this proposal was likewise promptly rejected.

"You will get nothing by trying to keep me in slavery," said James; "for I am determined to be free. I shall never make you another offer."

He walked off, and his master applied for a warrant to arrest him, and commit him to prison, as a disobedient and refractory slave. When he had been in jail a month, he called to see him, and inquired whether he were ready to return home and go to work.

"I *am* at home," replied James. "I expect to end my days here. I never will serve you again as a slave, or pay you one single cent. What do you come here for? There is no use in your coming."

The master was greatly provoked by this conduct, and requested the inspectors to have him put in the cells and kept on short allowance, till he learned to submit. Isaac T. Hopper was one of the board; and as the question was concerning a colored man, they referred it to him. Accordingly, the blacksmith sought an interview with him, and said, "Jim has been a faithful industrious fellow; but of late he has taken it into his head that he ought to be free. He strolled off and refused to work, and I had him put in prison. When I called to see him he insulted me grossly, and positively refused to return to his business. I have been referred to you to obtain an order to confine him to the cells on short allowance, till he submits."

Friend Hopper replied, "I have been long acquainted with Jim. I was one of his teachers; and I have often admired his punctuality in attending school, and his patient industry in trying to learn."

"It has done him no good to learn to read," rejoined the master. "On the contrary, it has made him worse."

"It has made him wiser," replied Isaac; "but I think it has not made him worse. I have scruples about ordering him to be punished; for he professes to be conscientious about submitting to serve as a slave. I have myself suffered because I could not conscientiously comply with military requisitions. The Society of Friends have suffered much in England on account of ecclesiastical demands. I have thus some cause to know how hateful are persecutors, in the sight of God and of men. I cannot therefore be active in persecuting James, or any other man, on account of conscientious scruples."

"It is your duty to have him punished," rejoined the blacksmith.

"I am the best judge of that," answered Friend Hopper; "and I do not feel justified in compelling him to submit to slavery."

The blacksmith was greatly exasperated, and went off, saying, "I hope to mercy your daughter will marry a negro."

At the expiration of the term of imprisonment allowed by law, James still refused to return to service, and he was committed for another thirty days. His master called to see him again, and told him if he would return home, and behave well, he should have a new suit of clothes and a Methodist hat. "I don't want your new clothes, nor your Methodist hat," replied James. "I tell you I never will serve you nor any other man as a slave. I had rather end my days in jail."

His master finding him so intractable, gave up the case as hopeless. When his second term of imprisonment expired, he was discharged, and no one attempted to molest him. He earned a comfortable living, and looked happy and respectable; but his personal appearance was not improved by leaving his beard unshaved. One day, when Friend Hopper met him in the street, he said, "Jim, why dost thou wear that long beard? It looks very ugly."

"I suppose it does," he replied, "but I wear it as a memorial of the Lord's goodness in setting me free; for it was Him that done it."

ROMAINE.

A Frenchman by the name of Anthony Salignac removed from St. Domingo to New-Jersey, and brought with him several slaves; among whom was Romaine. After remaining in New-Jersey several years, he concluded in 1802, to send Romaine and his wife and child back to the West Indies. Finding him extremely reluctant to go, he put them in prison some days previous, lest they should make an attempt to escape. From prison they were put into a carriage to be conveyed to Newcastle, under the custody of a Frenchman and a constable. They started from Trenton late in the evening, and arrived in Philadelphia about four o'clock in the morning. People at the inn where they stopped remarked that

Romaine and his wife appeared deeply dejected.
When food was offered they refused to eat. His
wife made some excuse to go out, and though sought
for immediately after, she was not to be found. Romaine was ordered to get into the carriage. The
Frenchman was on one side of him and the constable on the other. "*Must* I go?" cried he, in accents
of despair. They told him he must. "And alone?"
said he. "Yes, you must," was the stern reply.
The carriage was open to receive him, and they
would have pushed him in, but he suddenly took a
pruning knife from his pocket, and drew it three
times across his throat with such force that it severed
the jugular vein instantly, and he fell dead on the
pavement.

As the party had travelled all night, seemed in
great haste, and watched their colored companions
so closely some persons belonging to the prison
where they stopped suspected they might have nefa-
rious business on hand; accordingly, a message was
sent to Isaac T. Hopper, as the man most likely to
right all the wrongs of the oppressed. He obeyed
the summons immediately; but when he arrived, he
found the body of poor Romaine weltering in blood
on the pavement.

Speaking of this scene forty years later, he said,
"My whole soul was filled with horror, as I stood
viewing the corpse. Reflecting on that awful spec

tacle, I exclaimed within myself, How long, O Lord, how long shall this abominable system of slavery be permitted to curse the land! My mind was introduced into sympathy with the sufferer. I thought of the agony he must have endured before he could have resolved upon that desperate deed. He knew what he had to expect, from what he had experienced in the West Indies before, and he was determined not to submit to the same misery and degradation again. By his sufferings he was driven to desperation; and he preferred launching into the unknown regions of eternity to an endurance of slavery.

An inquest was summoned, and after a brief consultation, the coroner brought in the following verdict: "Suicide occasioned by the dread of slavery, to which the deceased knew himself devoted."

Romaine and his wife were very good looking. They gave indications of considerable intelligence, and had the character of having been very faithful servants. His violent death produced a good deal of excitement among the people generally, and much sympathy was manifested for the wife and child, who had escaped.

The master had procured a certificate from the mayor of Trenton authorizing him to remove his slaves to the West Indies; but the jury of inquest, and many others, were of opinion that his proceedings were not fully sanctioned by law. Accordingly,

Friend Hopper, and two other members of the Abolition Society, caused him to be arrested and brought before a magistrate; not so much with the view of punishing him, as with the hope of procuring manumission for the wife and child. In the course of the investigation, the friends of the Frenchman were somewhat violent in his defence. Upon one occasion, several of them took Friend Hopper up and put him out of the house by main force; while at the same time they let their friend out of a back door to avoid him. However, Friend Hopper met him a few minutes after in the street and seized him by the button. Alarmed by the popular excitement, and by the perseverance with which he was followed up, he exclaimed in agitated tones, "Mon Dieu! What is it you do want? I will do anything you do want."

I want thee to bestow freedom on that unfortunate woman and her child," replied Friend Hopper.

He promised that he would do so; and he soon after made out papers to that effect, which were duly recorded.

THE SLAVE HUNTER.

IN July, 1802, a man by the name of David Lea, went to Philadelphia to hunt up runaway slaves for their Southern masters. A few days after his arrival, he arrested a colored man, whom he claimed as the property of Nathan Peacock of Maryland. The man had lived several years in Philadelphia, had taken a lot of ground in the Northern Liberties, and erected a small house on it.

In the course of the investigation, the poor fellow, seeing no chance of escape, acknowledged that he was Mr. Peacock's slave, and had run away from him because he wanted to be free. His friends, being unwilling to see him torn from his wife and children, made an effort to purchase his freedom. After much intreaty, the master named a very large sum as his ransom; and the slave was committed to prison until the affair was settled.

David Lea was a filthy looking man, apparently addicted to intemperance. Friend Hopper asked him if he had any business in Philadelphia. He answered, "No." He inquired whether he had any money, and he answered, "*No.*" Friend Hopper then' said to the magistrate, "Here is a stranger without money, who admits that he has no regular means of obtaining a livelihood. Judging from his appearance, there is reason to conclude that he may be a dangerous man. I would suggest whether it be proper that he should be permitted to go at large."

The magistrate interrogated the suspicious looking stranger concerning his business in Philadelphia; and he, being ashamed to acknowledge himself a slave-catcher, returned very evasive and unsatis

factory answers. He was accordingly committed
to prison, to answer at the next court of Sessions.
It was customary to examine prisoners before they
were locked up, and take whatever was in their
pockets, to be restored to them whenever they were
discharged. David Lea strongly objected to this
proceeding; and when they searched him they found
more than fifty advertisements for runaway slaves;
a fact which made the nature of his business sufficiently obvious. Friend Hopper, had a serious
conversation with him in prison, during which he
stated that he was to have received forty-five dollars
for restoring the slave to his master. Friend Hopper told him if he would give an order upon Mr.
Peacock for that amount, to go toward buying the
slave's freedom, he should be released from confinement, on condition of leaving the city forthwith.
He agreed to do so, and the money was paid. But
the slave was found to be in debt more than his
small house was worth, and the price for his ransom
was so exorbitantly high, that it was impossible to
raise it. Under these circumstances, Friend Hopper thought it right to return the forty-five dollars to
David Lea; but he declined receiving it. He would
take only three dollars, to defray his expenses home;
and gave the following written document concerning
the remainder: "I request Isaac T. Hopper to pay
the money received from the order, which I gave

him upon Nathan Peacock, to the managers of the
Pennsylvania Hospital, or to any other charitable
institution he may judge proper.   His

DAVID × LEA.

Mark.

He was discharged from prison, and the money
paid to the Pennsylvania Hospital. Next year, the
following item was published in their accounts:
" Received of David Lea, a noted negro-catcher, by
the hands of Isaac T. Hopper, forty-two dollars; he
having received forty-five dollars for taking up a
runaway slave, of which he afterward repented, and
directed the sum to be paid to the Pennsylvania
Hospital, after deducting three dollars to pay his
expenses home."

The slave was carried back to the South, but
escaped again. After encountering many difficulties,
he was at last bought for a sum so small, that it was
merely nominal; and he afterward lived in Philadelphia unmolested.

WILLIAM BACHELOR.

IT was a common thing for speculators in slaves
to purchase runaways for much less than their original value, and take the risk of not being able to
catch them. In the language of the trade, this was
called buying them running. In April, 1802, Joseph
Ennells and Captain Frazer, of Maryland, dealers
in slaves, purchased a number in this way, and came

to Philadelphia in search of them. There they arrested, and claimed as their property, William Bachelor, a free colored man, about sixty years old. A colored man, whom the slave-dealers brought with them, swore before a magistrate that William Bachelor once belonged to a gang of slaves, of which he was overseer; that he had changed his name, but he knew him perfectly well. William affirmed in the most earnest manner, that he was a free man; but Mr. Ennells and Captain Frazer appeared to be such respectable men, and the colored witness swore so positively, that the magistrate granted a certificate authorizing them to take him to Maryland.

As they left the office, they were met by Dr. Kinley, who knew William Bachelor well, and had a great regard for him. Finding that his protestations had no effect with the Marylanders, he ran with all speed to Isaac T. Hopper, and entering his door almost out of breath, exclaimed, "They've got old William Bachelor, and are taking him to the South, as a slave. I know him to be a free man. Many years ago, he was a slave to my father, and he manumitted him. He used to carry me in his arms when I was an infant. He was a most faithful servant."

Friend Hopper inquired which way the party had gone, and was informed that they went toward "Gray's Ferry." He immediately started in pursuit,

and overtook them half a mile from the Schuylkill. He accosted Mr. Ennells politely, and told
him he had made a mistake in capturing William
Bachelor; for he was a free man. Ennells drew a
pistol from his pocket, and said, "We have had
him before a magistrate, and proved to his satisfaction that the fellow is my slave. I have got his
certificate, and that is all that is required to authorize me to take him home. I will blow your
brains out if you say another word on the subject,
or make any attempt to molest me."

"If thou wert not a coward, thou wouldst not try
to intimidate me with a pistol," replied Isaac. "I
do not believe thou hast the least intention of using
it in any other way; but thou art much agitated,
and may fire it accidentally; therefore I request
thee not to point it toward me, but to turn it the
other way. It is in vain for thee to think of taking
this old man to Maryland. If thou wilt not return
to the city voluntarily, I will certainly have thee
stopped at the bridge, where thou wilt be likely to
be handled much more roughly than I am disposed
to do."

While this controversy was going on, poor William
Bachelor was in the greatest anxiety of mind. "Oh,
Master Hopper," he exclaimed, "Don't let them take
me! I am not a slave. All the people in Philadel-

phia know I am a free man. I never was in Maryland in my life."

Ennells, hearing the name, said, "So your name
is Hopper, is it? I have heard of you. It's time
the world was rid of you. You have done too much
mischief already."

When Friend Hopper inquired what mischief he
had done, he replied, "You have robbed many people
of their slaves."

"Thou art mistaken," rejoined the Quaker. "I
only prevent Southern marauders from robbing people of their liberty."

After much altercation, it was agreed to return to
the city; and William was again brought before the
alderman, who had so hastily surrendered him. Dr.
Kinley, and so many other respectable citizens,
attended as witnesses, that even Ennells himself
was convinced that his captive was a free man.
He was accordingly set at liberty. It was, however, generally believed that Mr. Ennells knew he
was not a slave when he arrested him. It was
therefore concluded to prosecute him for attempting
to take forcibly a free man out of the state and carry
him into slavery.

When Friend Hopper went to his lodgings with
a warrant and two constables, for this purpose, he
found him writing, with a pistol on each side of him.
The moment they entered, he seized a pistol and

ordered them to withdraw, or he would shoot them. Friend Hopper replied, "These men are officers, and have a warrant to arrest thee for attempting to carry off a free man into slavery. I advise thee to lay down thy pistol and go with us. If not, a sufficient force will soon be brought to compel thee. Remember thou art in the heart of Philadelphia. It is both foolish and imprudent to attempt to resist the law. A pistol is a very unnecessary article here, whatever it may be elsewhere. According to appearances, thou dost not attempt to use it for any other purpose than to frighten people; and thou hast not succeeded in doing that."

Rage could do nothing in the presence of such imperturbable calmness; and Ennells consented to go with them to the magistrate. On the way, he quarrelled with one of the constables, and gave him a severe blow on the face with his cane. The officer knocked him down, and would have repeated the blow, if Friend Hopper had not interfered. Assisting Ennells to rise, he said, "Thou hadst better take my arm and walk with me. I think we can agree better."

When the transaction had been investigated before a magistrate, Mr. Ennells was bound over to appear at the next mayor's court and answer to the charge against him. The proprietor of the hotel where he lodged became his bail. Meanwhile, numerous let-

ters came from people of the first respectability in
Maryland and Virginia, testifying to his good character.   His lawyer showed these letters to Friend
Hopper, and proposed that the prosecution should
be abandoned.   He replied that he had no authority
to act in the matter himself; but he knew the Abolition Society had commenced the prosecution from
no vindictive feelings, but merely with the view of
teaching people to be careful how they infringed on
the rights of free men.   The committee of that
society met the same evening, and agreed to dismiss
the suit, Mr. Ennells paying the costs; to which he
readily assented.

LEVIN SMITH.

Levin was a slave in Maryland.   He married a
free woman and had several children.   In 1802, his
master sold him to a speculator, who was in the
habit of buying slaves for the Southern market.
His purchaser took him to his farm in Delaware,
and kept him at work till he could get a profitable
chance to sell him.   His new master was a desperate fellow, and Levin was uneasy with the constant
liability of being sold to the far South.   He opened
his heart to a neighbor, who advised him to escape
and gave him a letter to Isaac T. Hopper.   His wife
and children had removed to Philadelphia, and there
he rejoined them.   She took in washing, and he sup

ported himself by sawing wood. He had been there little more than a month, when his master heard where he was, and bargained with the captain of a small sloop to catch him and bring him back to Delaware.

The plan was to seize Levin in his bed, hurry him on board the sloop, and start off immediately, before his family could have time to give the alarm. They would probably have succeeded in this project, if the captain had not drank a little too freely the evening previous, and so forgotten to get some goods on board, as he had promised. Levin was seized and carried off; but the sloop was obliged to wait for the goods, and in the meantime messengers were sent to Isaac T. Hopper. He was in bed, but sprang up the instant he heard a violent knocking at the door. In his haste, he thrust on an old rough coat and hat, which he was accustomed to wear to fires; for, in addition to his various other employments, he belonged to a fire-company. He hurried to the scene of action as quickly as possible, and found that the slave had been conveyed to a small tavern near the wharf where the sloop lay. When the landlord was questioned where the men were who had him in custody, he refused to give any information. But there was a crowd of men and boys; and one of them said, "They are up-stairs in the back room." The landlord stood in the door-way, and tried to prevent Friend Hopper from passing in; but he pushed him aside, and went up to the chamber, where he found Levin with his hands tied, and guarded by five or six men. "What are you going to do with this man?" said he. The words were scarcely out of his mouth, before they seized him violently and pitched him out of the chamber window. He fell upon empty casks, and his mind was so excited, that h was not aware of being hurt. There was no time to be lost; for unless there was an immediate rescue, the man would be forced on board the sloop and carried off. As soon as he could get upon his feet, he went round again to the front door and ascended the stairs; but the door of the chamber was locked. He then returned to the back yard, mounted upon the pent-house, by means of a high board fence, and clambered into the window of a chamber, that opened into the room where the slave was. He entered with an open penknife in his hand, exclaiming, " Let us see if you will get me out so soon again!" Speaking thus, he instantly cut the cords that bound the slave, and called out, "Follow me!" He rushed down stairs as fast as he could go, and the slave after him. The guard were utterly astonished at seeing the man return, whom they had just tossed out of an upper window, and the whole thing was done so suddenly, that Friend Hopper and the liberated captive were in the street before they had time to recover their wits.

A rowdy looking crowd of men and boys followed the fugitive and his protector, shouting, "Stop thief! Stop thief!" until they came to the office of a justice of the peace, half a mile from where they started. The astonished magistrate exclaimed, "Good heavens, Mr. Hopper, what brings you here this time of the morning, in such a trim, and with such a rabble at your heels!" When the circumstances were briefly explained, he laughed heartily, and said, "I don't think they would have treated you so roughly, if they had known who you were." He was informed that Levin was a slave in Maryland, but had been living in Delaware with a man who bought him, and had thus become legally free. Measures were taken to protect him from further aggression, and he was never after molested.

Friend Hopper went home to a late breakfast; and when he attempted to rise from the table, he was seized with violent pains in the back, in consequence of his fall. He never after entirely recovered from the effects of it.

ETIENNE LAMAIRE.

This man was a slave to a Frenchman of the same name, in the Island of Guadaloupe. In consideration of faithful services, his master gave him his freedom, and he opened a barber's shop on his own account. Some time after, he was appointed an officer

in the French army, against Victor Hughes. He
had command of a fort, and remained in the army
until the close of the war. After that period, there
were symptoms of insurrection among the colored
people, because the French government revoked the
decree abolishing slavery in their West India Islands.
Etienne was a man of talent, and had acquired considerable influence, particularly among people of his
own color. He exerted this influence on the side of
mercy, and was the means of saving the lives of
several white people who had rendered themselves
obnoxious by their efforts to restore slavery.

Affairs were so unsettled in Guadaloupe, that Etienne determined to seek refuge in the United States;
and an old friend of his master procured a passport
for him. A man by the name of Anslong, then at
Guadaloupe, had two slaves, whom he was about to
send to the care of Dennis Cottineau, of Philadelphia, with directions to place them on a farm he
owned, near Princeton, New-Jersey. When it was
proposed that Etienne should take passage in the
same vessel, Anslong manifested much interest in
his behalf. He promised that he should have his
passage free, for services that he might render on
board; and he took charge of his passport, saying
that he would give it to the captain for safe keeping.

When the vessel arrived at Philadelphia, in March,
1803, Etienne was astonished to find that Anslong

had paid his passage, and claimed him as his slave. Dennis Cottineau showed the receipts for the passage money, and written directions to forward the *three* slaves to New-Jersey. In this dilemma, he asked counsel of a colored man, whom he had formerly known in Guadaloupe; and he immediately conducted him to Isaac T. Hopper. He related the particulars of his case very circumstantially, and the two colored men, who were really the slaves of Anslong, confirmed his statement. When Friend Hopper had cautiously examined them, and cross-examined them, he became perfectly satisfied that Etienne was free. He advised him not to leave the city, and told him to let him know in case Dennis Cottineau attempted to compel him to do so. He accordingly waited upon that gentleman and told him he had resolved not to submit to his orders to go to New-Jersey. Whereupon Cottineau took possession of his trunk, containing his papers and clothing, and caused him to be committed to prison.

A writ of *habeas corpus* was procured, and the case was brought before Judge Inskeep, of the Court of Common Pleas. It was found to be involved in considerable difficulty. For while several witnesses swore that they knew Etienne in Guadaloupe, as a free man, in business for himself, others testified that they had known him as the slave of Anslong. It was finally referred to the Supreme Court, and Etienne was detained in prison several months to await his trial. Eminent counsel were employed on both sides; Jared Ingersoll for the claimant, and Joseph Hopkinson for the defendant. A certificate was produced from the municipality of Guadaloupe, showing that Etienne had been an officer in the French army for several years, and had filled the station in a manner to command respect. The National Decree abolishing slavery in that Island was also read; but Mr. Ingersoll contended that when the decree was revoked, Etienne again became a slave. In his charge, Judge Shippen said that the evidence for and against freedom was about equally balanced; and in that case, it was always a duty to decide in favor of liberty. The jury accordingly brought in a unanimous verdict that Etienne was free. The court ordered him to refund the twenty dollars, which Anslong had paid for his passage; and he was discharged.

He was a dark mulatto, tall, well-proportioned, and stylish-looking. His handsome countenance had a remarkably bright, frank expression, and there was a degree of courteous dignity in his manner, probably acquired by companionship with military officers. But he belonged to a caste which society has forbidden to develop the faculties bestowed by nature. Such a man might have performed some higher use than cutting hair, if he had lived in a wisely organized state of society. However, he made the best of such advantages as he had. He opened a barber's shop in Philadelphia, and attracted many of the most highly respectable citizens by his perfect politeness and punctuality. The colored people had various benevolent societies in that city, for the relief of the poor, the sick, and the aged, of their own complexion. Etienne Lamaire was appointed treasurer of several of these societies, and discharged his trust with scrupulous integrity.

Isaac T. Hopper had been very active and vigilant in assisting him to regain his freedom; and afterward, when he became involved in some difficulty on account of stolen goods left on his premises without his knowledge, he readily became bail for him. His confidence had not been misplaced; for when the affair had been fully investigated, the recorder declared that Mr. Lamaire had acted like an honest and prudent man, throughout the whole transaction.

His gratitude to Friend Hopper was unbounded, and he missed no opportunity to manifest it. To the day of his death, some fourteen or fifteen years ago, he never would charge a cent for shaving, or cutting the hair of any of the family, children, or grand-children; and on New Year's day, he frequently sent a box of figs, or raisins, or bon-bons, in token of grateful remembrance.

SAMUEL JOHNSON.

Samuel Johnson was a free colored man in the state of Delaware. He married a woman who was slave to George Black. They had several children, and when they became old enough to be of some value as property, their parents were continually anxious lest Mr. Black should sell them to some Georgia speculator, to relieve himself from pecuniary embarrassment; an expedient which was very often resorted to under such circumstances. When Johnson visited his wife, they often talked together on the subject; and at last they concluded to escape to a free state. They went to Philadelphia and hired a small house. He sawed wood, and she took in washing. Being industrious and frugal, they managed to live very comfortably, except the continual dread of being discovered.

In December, 1804, when they had been thus situated about two years, her master obtained some tidings of them, and immediately went in pursuit. A friend happened to become aware of the fact, and hastened to inform them that Mr. Black was in the city. Samuel forthwith sent his wife and children to a place of safety; but he remained at home, not supposing that he could be in any danger. The master arrived shortly after, with two constables, and was greatly exasperated when he found that his property had absconded. They arrested the husband, and vowed they would hold him as a hostage, till he informed them where they could find his wife and children. When he refused to accompany them, they beat him severely, and swore they would carry him to the South and sell him. He told them they might carry him into slavery, or murder him, if they pleased, but no torture they could inflict would ever induce him to betray his family. Finding they could not break his resolution, they tied his hands behind his back, and dragged him to a tavern kept by Peter Fritz, in Sassafras-street. There they left him, guarded by the landlord and several men, while they went in search of the fugitives.

Some of Johnson's colored neighbors informed Isaac T. Hopper of these proceedings; and he went to the tavern, accompanied by a friend. They attempted to enter the room occupied by Samuel and his guard, but found the door fastened, and the landlord refused to unlock it. When they inquired by what authority he made his tavern a prison, he replied that the man was placed in his custody by two constables, and should not be released till they came for him.

"Open the door!" said Friend Hopper; "or we will soon have it opened in a way that will cost something to repair it. Thou hast already made thyself liable to an action for false imprisonment.

If thou art not very careful, thou wilt find thyself involved in trouble for this business."

The landlord swore a good deal, but finding them so resolute, he concluded it was best to open the door. After obtaining the particulars of the case from Johnson himself, Friend Hopper cut the cord that bound his hands, and said, "Follow me!"

The men on guard poured forth a volley of threats and curses. One of them sprang forward in great fury, siezed Johnson by the collar, and swore by his Maker that he should not leave the room till the constables arrived. Friend Hopper stepped up to him, and said, "Release that man immediately! or thou wilt be made to repent of thy conduct." The ruffian quailed under the influence of that calm bold manner, and after some slight altercation let go his grasp.

Johnson followed his protector in a state of intense anxiety concerning his wife and children. But they had been conveyed to a place of safety, and the man-hunters never afterward discovered their retreat.

PIERCE BUTLER'S BEN.

In August, 1804, a colored man about thirty-six years old waited upon the committee of the Abolition Society, and stated that he was born a slave to Pierce Butler, Esq., of South Carolina, and had

always lived in his family.   During the last eleven
years, he had resided most of the time in Pennsylvania.   Mr. Butler now proposed taking him to Georgia; but he was very unwilling to leave his wife, she
being in delicate health and needing his support.
After mature consideration of the case, the commit-
ee, believing Ben was legally entitled to freedom,
agreed to apply to Judge Inskeep for a writ of *habeas
corpus;* and Isaac T. Hopper was sent to serve it
upon Pierce Butler, Esq., at his house in Chestnut-
street.

Being told that Mr. Butler was at dinner, he said
he would wait in the hall until it suited his convenience to attend to him.   Mr. Butler was a tall, lord-
ly looking man, somewhat imperious in his manners,
as slaveholders are wont to be.   When he came into
the hall after dinner, Friend Hopper gave him a nod
of recognition, and said, "How art thou, Pierce Butler?   I have here a writ of *habeas corpus* for thy
Ben."

Mr. Butler glanced over the paper, and exclaimed,
"Get out of my house, you scoundrel!"

Feigning not to hear him, Friend Hopper looked
round at the pictures and rich furniture, and said
with a smile, "Why, thou livest like a nabob here!"

"Get out of my house, I say!" repeated Mr. Butler, stamping violently.

"This paper on the walls is the handsomest I ever

saw," continued Isaac. "Is it French, or English?
It surely cannot have been manufactured in this
country." Talking thus, and looking leisurely about
him as he went, he moved deliberately toward the
door; the slaveholder railing at him furiously all the
while.

"I am a citizen of South Carolina," said he
"The laws of Pennsylvania have nothing to do with
me. May the devil take all those who come between masters and their slaves; interfering with
what is none of their business." Supposing that his
troublesome guest was deaf, he put his head close to
his ear, and roared out his maledictions in stentorian
tones.

Friend Hopper appeared unconscious of all this.
When he reached the threshold, he turned round
and said, "Farewell. We shall expect to see thee
at Judge Inskeep's."

This imperturbable manner irritated the hot-blood-
ed slave-holder beyond endurance. He repeated
more vociferously than ever, "Get out of my house,
you scoundrel! If you don't, I'll kick you out."
The Quaker walked quietly away, as if he didn't
hear a word.

At the appointed time, Mr. Butler waited upon
the Judge, where he found Friend Hopper in attendance. The sight of him renewed his wrath. He
cursed those who interfered with his property; and

taking up the Bible, said he was willing to swear upon that book that he would not take fifteen hundred dollars for Ben. Friend Hopper charged him with injustice in wishing to deprive the man of his legal right to freedom. Mr. Butler maintained that he was as benevolent as any other man.

"Thou benevolent!" exclaimed Friend Hopper. "Why, thou art not even just. Thou hast already sent back into bondage two men, who were legally entitled to freedom by staying in Philadelphia during the term prescribed by law. If thou hadst a proper sense of justice, thou wouldst bring those men back, and let them take the liberty that rightfully belongs to them."

"If you were in a different walk of life, I would treat your insult as it deserves," replied the haughty Southerner.

"What dost thou mean by that? asked Isaac. Wouldst thou shoot me, as Burr did Hamilton? I assure thee I should consider it no honor to be killed by a member of Congress; and surely there would be neither honor nor comfort in killing thee; for in thy present state of mind thou art not fit to die."

Mr. Butler told the judge he believed that man was either deaf or crazy when he served the writ of *habeas corpus;* for he did not take the slightest notice of anything that was said to him. Judge Ins-

keep smiled as he answered, "You don't know **Mr.
Hopper** as well as we do."

A lawyer was procured for Ben; but Mr. Butler
chose to manage his own cause. He maintained
that he was only a sojourner in Pennsylvania; that
Ben had never resided six months at any one time in
that State, except while he was a member of Congress; and in that case, the law allowed him to keep
his slave in Pennsylvania as long as he pleased.
The case was deemed an important one, and was
twice adjourned for further investigation. In the
course of the argument, Mr. Butler admitted that he
returned from Congress to Philadelphia, with Ben,
on the second of January, 1804, and had remained
there with him until the writ of *habeas corpus* was
served, on the third of August, the same year. The
lawyers gave it as their opinion that Ben's legal
right to freedom was too plain to admit of any
doubt. They said the law to which Mr. Butler had
alluded was made for the convenience of Southern
gentlemen, who might need the attendance of their
personal slaves, when Congress met in Philadelphia;
but since the seat of government was removed, it by
no means authorized members to come into Pennsylvania with their slaves, and keep them there as
long as they chose. After much debate, the judge
gave an order discharging Ben from all restraint,
and he walked off rejoicing.

His master was very indignant at the decision, and complained loudly that a Pennsylvania court should presume to discharge a Carolinian slave.

When Ben was set at liberty, he let himself to Isaac W. Morris, then living at his country seat called Cedar Grove, three miles from Philadelphia. Being sent to the city soon after, on some business for his employer, he was attached by the marshall of the United States, on a writ *De homine replegiando*, at the suit of Mr. Butler, and two thousand dollars were demanded for bail. The idea was probably entertained that so large an amount could not be procured, and thus Ben would again come into his master's possession. But Isaac T. Hopper and Thomas Harrison signed the bail-bond, and Ben was again set at liberty, to await his trial before the Circuit Court of the United States. Bushrod Washington, himself a slaveholder, presided in that court, and Mr. Butler was sanguine that he should succeed in having Judge Inskeep's decision reversed. The case was brought in October, 1806, before Judges Bushrod Washington and Richard Peters. It was ably argued by counsel on both sides. The court discharged Ben, and he enjoyed his liberty thenceforth without interruption.

DANIEL BENSON.

Daniel and his mother were slaves to Perry Boots, of Delaware. His master was in the habit of letting him out to neighboring farmers and receiving the wages himself. Daniel had married a free woman, and they had several children, mostly supported by her industry. His mother was old and helpless; and the master, finding it rather burdensome to support her, told Daniel that if he would take charge of her, and pay him forty dollars a year, he might go where he pleased.

The offer was gladly accepted; and in 1805 he removed to Philadelphia, with his mother and family. He sawed wood for a living, and soon established such a character for industry and honesty, that many of the citizens were in the habit of employing him to purchase their wood and prepare it for the winter. Upon one occasion, when he brought in a bill to Alderman Todd, that gentleman asked if he had not charged rather high. Daniel excused himself by saying he had an aged mother to support, in addition to his own family; and that he punctually paid his master twenty dollars every six months, according to an agreement he had made with him. When the alderman heard the particulars, his sympathy was excited, and he wrote a note to Isaac T. Hopper, requesting him to examine into the case; stating his own opinion that Daniel had a legal right to freedom.

The wood-sawyer started off with the note with great alacrity, and delivered it to Friend Hopper, saying in very animated tones, "Squire Todd thinks I am free!" He was in a state of great agitation between hope and fear. When he had told his story, he was sent home to get receipts for all the money he had paid his master since his arrival in Philadelphia. It was easy to prove from these that he had been a resident in Pennsylvania, with his owner's consent, a much longer time than the law required to make him a free man. When Friend Hopper gave him this information, he was overjoyed. He could hardly believe it. The tidings seemed too good to be true. When assured that he was certainly free, beyond all dispute, and that he need not pay any more of his hard earnings to a master, the tears came to his eyes, and he started off to bring his wife, that she also might hear the glad news. When Friend Hopper was an old man, he often used to remark how well he remembered their beaming countenances on that occasion, and their warm expressions of gratitude to God.

Soon after this interview, a letter was addressed to Perry Boots, informing him that his slave was legally free, and that he need not expect to receive any more of his wages. He came to Philadelphia immediately, to answer the letter in person. His first salutation was, "Where can I find that ungrateful villain Dan? I will take him home in irons."

Friend Hopper replied, "Thou wilt find thyself relieved from such an unpleasant task; for I can easily convince thee that the law sustains thy slave in taking his freedom."

Reading the law did not satisfy him. He said he would consult a lawyer, and call again. When he returned, he found Daniel waiting to see him; and he immediately began to upbraid him for being so ungrateful. Daniel replied, "Master Perry, it was not *justice* that made me your slave. It was the *law;* and you took advantage of it. Now, the law makes me free; and ought you to blame me for taking the advantage which it offers me? But suppose I were not free, what would you be willing to take to manumit me?"

His master, somewhat softened, said, "Why, Dan, I always intended to set you free some time or other."

"I am nearly forty years old," rejoined his bondsman, "and if I am ever to be free, I think it is high time now. What would you be willing to take for a deed of manumission?"

Mr. Boots answered, "Why I think you ought to give me a hundred dollars."

"Would that satisfy you, master Perry? Well, I can pay you a hundred dollars," said Daniel.

Here Friend Hopper interfered, and observed there was nothing rightfully due to the master; that if justice were done in the case, he ought to pay Daniel for his labor ever since he was twenty-one years old.

The colored man replied, "I was a slave to master Perry's father; and he was kind to me. Master Perry and I are about the same age. We were brought up more like two brothers, than like master and slave. I can better afford to give him a hundred dollars, than he can afford to do without it. I will go home and get the money, if you will make out the necessary papers while I am gone."

Surprised and gratified by the nobility of soul manifested in these words, Friend Hopper said no more to dissuade him from his generous purpose. He brought one hundred silver dollars, and Perry Boots signed a receipt for it, accompanied by a deed of manumission. He wished to have it inserted in the deed that he was not to be responsible for the support of the old woman. But Daniel objected; saying, "Such an agreement would imply that I would not voluntarily support my poor old mother."

When the business was concluded, he invited his former master and Friend Hopper to dine with him; saying, "We are going to have a pretty good dinner, in honor of the day." Mr. Boots accepted the invitation; but Friend Hopper excused himself, on account of an engagement that would detain him till

after dinner. When he called, he found they had
not yet risen from the table, on which were the remains of a roasted turkey, a variety of vegetables,
and a decanter of wine. Friend Hopper smiled when
Daniel remarked, "I know master Perry loves a little brandy; but I did not like to get brandy; so I
bought a quart of Mr. Morris' best wine, and thought
perhaps that would do instead. I never drink anything but water myself."

Soon after Daniel Benson became a free man, he
gave up sawing wood, and opened a shop for the sale
of second-hand clothing. He was successful in business, brought up his family very reputably, and
supported his mother comfortably to the end of her
days. For many years, he was class-leader in a
Methodist church for colored people, and his correct
deportment gained the respect of all who knew him.

If slavery were *ever* justifiable, under *any* circumstances, which of these two characters ought to have
been the master, and which the slave ?

THE QUICK-WITTED SLAVE.

About the year 1805, a colored man, who belonged
to Colonel Hopper, of Maryland, escaped with his
wife and children, who were also slaves. He went
to Philadelphia and hired a small house in Green's
Court, where he lived several months before his
master discovered his retreat. As soon as he ob-

tained tidings of him, he went to Philadelphia, and applied to Richard Hunt, a constable who was much employed as a slave hunter. Having procured a warrant, they went together, in search of the fugitives. It was about dusk, and the poor man just returned from daily toil, was sitting peacefully with his wife and children, when in rushed his old master, accompanied by the constable.

With extraordinary presence of mind, the colored man sprang up, and throwing his arms round his master's neck, exclaimed, "O, my dear master, how glad I am to see you! I *thought* I should like to be free; but I had a great deal rather be a slave. I can't get work, and we have almost starved. I would have returned home, but I was afraid you would sell me to the Georgia men. I beg your pardon a thousand times. If you will only forgive me, I will go back with you, and never leave you again."

The master was very agreeably surprised by this reception, and readily promised forgiveness. He was about to dismiss the constable, but the slave urged him to stay a few minutes. "I have earned a little money to-day, for a rarity," said he; "and I want to go out and buy something to drink; for I suppose old master must be tired." He stepped out, and soon returned with a quantity of gin, with which he liberally supplied his guests. He knew full well that they were both men of intemperate habits; so he talked gaily about affairs in Maryland, making various inquiries concerning what had happened since he left ; and ever and anon he replenished their glasses with gin. It was not long before they were completely insensible to all that was going on around them. The colored man and his family then made speedy preparations for departure. While Colonel Hopper and the constable lay in the profound stupor of intoxication, they were on the way to New Jersey, with all their household goods, where they found a safe place of refuge before the rising of the sun.

When consciousness returned to the sleepers, they were astonished to find themselves alone in the house ; and as soon as they could rally their wits, they set off in search of the fugitives. After spending several days without finding any track of them, the master called upon Isaac T. Hopper. He complained bitterly of his servant's ingratitude in absconding from him, and of the trick he had played to deceive him. He said he and his family had always been extremely comfortable in Maryland, and it was a great piece of folly in them to have quitted such a happy condition. He concluded by asking for assistance in tracing them ; promising to treat them as kindly as if they were his own children, if they would return to him.

Friend Hopper replied, "If the man were as happy with thee as thou hast represented. he will doubtless return voluntarily, and my assistance will be quite unnecessary. I do not justify falsehood and deception; but I am by no means surprised at them in one who has always been a slave, and had before him the example of slaveholders. Why thou shouldst accuse him of ingratitude, is more than I can comprehend. It seems to me that he owes thee nothing. On the contrary, I should suppose that thou wert indebted to him; for I understand that he has served thee more than thirty years without wages. So far from helping thee to hunt the poor fugitives, I will, with all my heart, do my utmost to keep them out of thy grasp."

"Have you seen my man?" inquired the slaveholder.

"He came to me when he left his own house in Green's Court," replied Friend Hopper; "and I gave him such advice on that occasion, as I thought proper. Thou art the first slaveholder I ever met with bearing my name. Perhaps thou hast assumed it, as a means of gaining the confidence of colored people, to aid thee in recapturing the objects of thy avarice."

The Colonel replied that it was really his name, and departed without having gained much satisfaction from the interview. He remained in Philadelphia a week or ten days, where he was seized with *mania a potu*. He was carried home in a straight jacket, where he soon after died.

A few months after these transactions, the slave called to see Friend Hopper. He laughed till he could hardly stand, while he described the method he had taken to elude his old master, and the comical scene that followed with him and the constable. "I knew his weak side," said he. "I knew where to touch him."

Friend Hopper inquired whether he was not aware that it was wrong to tell falsehoods, and to get men drunk.

"I suppose it *was* wrong," he replied. "But liberty is sweet; and none of us know what we would do to secure it, till we are tried."

He afterward returned to Philadelphia, where he supported his family comfortably, and remained unmolested.

JAMES DAVIS.

In 1795, James escaped from bondage in Maryland, and went to Philadelphia, where he soon after married. He remained undisturbed for ten years, during which time he supported himself and family comfortably by sawing wood. But one day, in the year 1805, his master called to see him, accompanied by two other men, who were city constables. He appeared to be very friendly, asked James how he was getting along, and said he was glad to see him doing so well. At last, he remarked, "As you left my service without leave, I think you ought to make me some compensation for your time. Autumn is now coming on, and as that is always a busy season for wood-sawyers, perhaps you can make me a small payment at that time."

This insidious conversation threw James completely off his guard, and he promised to make an effort to raise some money for his master. As soon as he had said enough to prove that he was his bondsman, the slaveholder threw off the mask of kindness, and ordered the constables to seize and hand-cuff him. His wife and children shrieked aloud, and Isaac T. Hopper, who happened to be walking through the street at the time, hastened to ascertain the cause of such alarming sounds. Entering the house, he found the colored man hand-cuffed, and his wife and children making the loud lamentations, which had arrested his attention. The poor woman told how her husband had been duped by friendly words, and now he was to be torn from his family and carried off into slavery. Friend Hopper's feelings were deeply affected at witnessing such a heart-rending scene, and he exerted his utmost eloquence to turn the master from his cruel purpose. The wife and children wept and entreated also ; but it was all in vain. He replied to their expostulations by ridicule, and proceeded to hurry his victim off to prison. The children clung round Friend Hopper's knees, crying and sobbing, and begging that he would not let those men take away their father. But the fact that the poor fellow had acknowledged himself a slave rendered resistance hopeless. He was taken before a magistrate, and thence to prison.

Friend Hopper was with him when his master came the next day to carry him away. With a countenance expressive of deepest anguish, the unhappy creature begged to speak a word in private, before his master entered. When Friend Hopper took him into an adjoining room, he exclaimed in an imploring tone, "Can't you give me some advice?" Agitated by most painful sympathy, the Friend knew not what to answer. After a moment's hesitation, he said, "Don't try to run away till thou art sure thou hast a good chance." This was all he could do for the poor fellow. He was obliged to submit to seeing him bound with cords, put into a carriage, and driven off like a sheep to the slaughter-house.

He was conveyed to Maryland and lodged in jail. Several weeks after, he was taken thence and sold to a speculator, who was making up a coffle of slaves for the far South. After crossing the Susquehanna, they stopped at a miserable tavern, where the speculator and his companions drank pretty freely, and then began to amuse themselves by shooting at a mark. They placed the slave by the tavern door, where they could see him. While he sat there, thinking of his wife and children, feeling sad and forlorn beyond description, he noticed that a fisherman drew near the shore with a small boat, to which was fastened a rope and a heavy stone, to supply the place of an anchor. When he saw the man step out of the boat and throw the stone on the ground, Friend Hopper's parting advice instantly flashed through his mind. Hardship, scanty food, and above all, continual distress of mind, had considerably reduced his flesh. He looked at his emaciated hands, and thought it might be possible to slip them through his iron cuffs. He proceeded cautiously, and when he saw that his guard were too busy loading their pistols to watch him, he released himself from his irons by a violent effort, ran to the river, threw the stone anchor into the boat, jumped in, and pushed for the opposite shore. The noise attracted the attention of his guard, who threatened him with instant death if he did not return. They loaded their pistols as quickly as possible, and fired after him, but luckily missed their aim. James succeeded in reaching the opposite side of the river, where he set the boat adrift, lest some one should take it back and enable them to pursue him. He bent his course toward Philadelphia, and on arriving there, went directly to Friend Hopper's house. He had become so haggard and emaciated, that his friend could hardly believe it was James Davis who stood before him. He said he dared not go near his old home, and begged that some place might be provided where he could meet his wife and children in safety. This was accomplished, and Friend Hopper was present when the poor harassed fugitive was restored to his family. He described the scene as affecting beyond description. The children, some of whom were very small, twined their little arms round him, eagerly inquiring, "Where have you been? How did you get away?" and his wife sobbed aloud, while she hugged the lost one to her heart.

The next morning he was sent to Bucks County in a market wagon. Some friends there procured a small house for him, and his family soon joined him. He was enabled to earn a comfortable living, and his place of retreat was never afterward discovered by enemies of the human family.

MARY HOLLIDAY.

A very light mulatto girl, named Fanny, was slave to the widow of John Sears, in Maryland. When about twenty-four years old, she escaped to Philadelphia, and lived in the family of Isaac W. Morris, where she was known by the assumed name of Mary Holliday. She was honest, prudent, and industrious, and the family became much attached to her. She had not been there many months when her mistress obtained tidings of her, and went to Philadelphia, accompanied by a man named Dutton. She was arrested on the seventh of June, 1805, and taken before Matthew Lawler, who was then mayor. Isaac W. Morris immediately waited on Isaac T. Hopper to inform him of the circumstance, and they proceeded together to the mayor's office.

Dutton, being examined as a witness, testified that he knew a mulatto named Fanny, who belonged to Mrs. Sears, and he believed the woman present, called Mary Holliday, was that person. Mary denied that she was the slave of the claimant, or that her name was Fanny; but her agitation was very evident, though she tried hard to conceal it.

Friend Hopper remarked to the mayor, "This case requires testimony as strong as if the woman were on trial for her life, which is of less value than liberty. I object to the testimony as insufficient; for the witness cannot say positively that he *knows* she is the same person, but only that he *believes* so. Wouldst thou consider such evidence satisfactory in the case of a white person?"

The mayor who was not friendly to colored people, replied, "I should not; but I consider it sufficient in such cases as these."

"How dark must the complexion be, to justify thee in receiving such uncertain evidence?" inquired Friend Hopper.

The mayor pointed to the prisoner and said, "As dark as that woman."

"What wouldst thou think of such testimony in case of thy own daughter?" rejoined Friend Hopper. "There is very little difference between her complexion and that of the woman now standing before thee."

He made no reply, but over-ruled the objection to the evidence. He consented, however, to postpone the case three days, to give time to procure testimony in her favor.

Isaac W. Morris soon after called upon Friend Hopper and said, "Mary has acknowledged to us that her name is Fanny, and that she belongs to Mrs. Sears. My family are all very much attached to her, and they cannot bear the thought of her being carried away into slavery. I will advance three hundred dollars, if thou wilt obtain her freedom."

Friend Hopper accordingly called upon Mrs. Sears, and after stipulating that nothing said on either side should be made use of in the trial, he offered two hundred dollars for a deed of manumission. The offer was promptly rejected. After considerable discussion, three hundred and fifty dollars were offered; for it was very desirable to have the case settled without being obliged to resort to an expensive and uncertain process of law. Mrs. Sears replied, "It is in vain to treat with me on the subject; for I am

determined not to sell the woman on any terms. I
will take her back to Maryland, and make an example of her."

"I hope thou wilt find thyself disappointed," rejoined Friend Hopper. The slaveholder merely answered with a malicious smile, as if perfectly sure of
her triumph.

Finding himself disappointed in his attempts to
purchase the woman, Friend Hopper resolved to
carry the case to a higher court, and accumulate
as many legal obstructions as possible. For that
purpose, he obtained a writ *De homine replegiando,*
and when the suitable occasion arrived, he accompanied Mary Holliday to the mayor's office, with a
deputy sheriff to serve the writ. When the trial
came on, he again urged the insufficiency of proof
brought by the claimant. The mayor replied, in a
tone somewhat peremptory, "I have already decided that matter. I shall deliver the slave to her
mistress."

Friend Hopper gave the sheriff a signal to serve
the writ. He was a novice in the business, but in
obedience to the instructions given him, he laid his
hand on Mary's shoulder, and said, "By virtue of
this writ, I replevin this woman, and deliver her to
Mr. Hopper."

Her protector immediately said to her, "Thou
canst now go home with me." But her mistress

seized her by the arm, and said she should *not* go.
The mayor was little acquainted with legal forms,
beyond the usual routine of city business. He seemed much surprised, and inquired what the writ was.

"It is a *homine replegiando*," replied Friend Hopper.

"I don't understand what that means," said the
mayor.

"It is none the less powerful on that account,"
rejoined Friend Hopper. "It has taken the woman
out of thy power, and delivered her to another tribunal."

During this conversation, the mistress kept her
grasp upon Mary. Friend Hopper appealed to the
mayor, again repeating that the girl was now to
await the decision of another court. He accordingly
told Mrs. Sears it was necessary to let her go. She
asked what was to be done in such a case. The
mayor, completely puzzled, and somewhat vexed,
replied impatiently, "I don't know. You must ask
Mr. Hopper. His laws are above mine. I thought
I knew something about the business ; but it seems
I don't."

Mary went home with her protector, and Mrs.
Sears employed Alexander J. Dallas as counsel.
The case was kept pending in the Supreme Court a
long time ; for no man understood better than Friend
Hopper how to multiply difficulties. Mrs. Sears fre-

quently attended, bringing witnesses with her from
Maryland; which of course involved much trouble
and expense. After several years, the trial came on;
but it was found she had left some of her principal
witnesses at home. Most of the forenoon was spent
in disputes about points of law, and the admissibility
of certain evidence. The court then adjourned to
three in the afternoon.

Mrs. Sears was informed that even if the court
adjudged Mary to be her slave, Friend Hopper would
doubtless fail to produce her, and they would be
compelled to go through another process to recover
from him the penalty of the bond. She had become
exceedingly weary of the law, the trouble and expense of which had far exceeded her expectations.
She therefore instructed her lawyer to try to effect a
compromise. Friend Hopper, being consulted for
this purpose, offered to pay two hundred and fifty
dollars for Mary, if the claimant would pay the costs.
She accepted the terms, well pleased to escape from
further litigation.

When the court met in the afternoon, they were
informed that the matter was settled; and the jury
with consent of parties, rendered a verdict that Mary
was free. By her own earnings, and donations from
sympathizing friends, she gradually repaid Isaac W.
Morris three hundred dollars toward the sum he had
advanced for the expenses of her trial.

In his efforts to protect the rights and redress the wrongs of colored people, Friend Hopper had a zealous and faithful ally in Thomas Harrison, also a member of the Society of Friends. When recounting the adventures they had together, he used to say, "That name excites pleasant emotions whenever it occurs to me. I shall always reverence his memory. He was my precursor in Philadelphia, as the friend of the slave, and my coadjutor in scores of cases for their relief. His soul was always alive to the sufferings of his fellow creatures, and dipped into sympathy with the oppressed; not that idle sympathy that can be satisfied with lamenting their condition, and make no exertions for their relief; but sympathy, like the apostle's faith, manifesting itself in works, and extending its influence to all within its reach."

Thomas Harrison was a lively, bustling man, with a roguish twinkle in his eye, and a humorous style of talking. Some Friends, of more quiet temperaments than himself, thought he had more activity than was consistent with dignity. They reminded him that Mary sat still at the feet of Jesus, while Martha was "troubled about many things."

"All that is very well," replied Thomas; "but Mary would have had a late breakfast, after all, if it had not been for Martha."

From among various anecdotes in which Friend Harrison's name occurs, I select the following :

JAMES LAWLER.

James was a slave to Mr. Mc Calmont of Delaware. In 1805, when he was about thirty years old, he escaped to New-Jersey and let himself out to a farmer. After he had been there a few months, several runaway slaves in his neighborhood were arrested and carried back to the South. This alarmed him, and he became very anxious that some person should advance a sum of money sufficient to redeem him from bondage, which he would bind himself to repay by labor. Finding that his employer abhorred slavery, and was very friendly to colored people, he ventured to open his heart to him; and Isaac T. Hopper was consulted on the subject.

The first step was to write to Mr. Mc Calmont to ascertain what were the lowest terms on which he would manumit his slave. The master soon came in person, accompanied by a Philadelphia merchant, who testified that his friend Mc Calmont was a highly respectable man, and treated his slaves with great kindness. He said James would be much happier with his master than he could be in any other situation, and strongly urged Friend Hopper to tell where he might be found.

He replied, "It does not appear that James *thought*

himself so happy, or he would not have left his service. Even if I had no objection to slavery, I should still be bound by every principle of honor not to betray the confidence reposed in me. But feeling as it is well known I do on that subject, I am surprised thou shouldst make such a proposition to me."

They then called upon Thomas Harrison, and tried to enlist him in their favor by repeating how well James had been treated, and how happy he was in slavery. Friend Harrison replied, in his ironical way, "O, I know very well that slaves sleep on feather beds, while their master's children sleep on straw; that they eat white bread, and their master's children eat brown. But enclose ten acres with a high wall, plant it with Lombardy poplars and the most beautiful shrubbery, build a magnificent castle in the midst of it, give thee pen, ink, and paper, to write about the political elections in which thou art so much interested, load thee with the best of everything thy heart could desire, still I think thou wouldst want to get out beyond the wall."

The master, being unable to ascertain where his slave could be found, finally informed Friend Hopper that he would manumit him on the receipt of one hundred and fifty dollars. Mr. John Hart, a druggist, generously advanced the sum, and James was indentured to him for the term of five years. Before the contract was concluded, somebody remarked

that perhaps he would repeat his old trick of running away. "I am not afraid of that," replied Mr.
Hart. "I will tie him by the teeth;" meaning he
would feed him well.

In fact, James now appeared quite satisfied. His
new master and mistress were kind to him, and·he
was faithful and diligent in their service. When a
year or two had elapsed, he asked permission to
visit his old master and fellow servants. Mr. Hart
kept a carriage, which he seldom used in the winter,
and he told James he might take one of the horses.
This suited his taste exactly. He mounted a noble
looking animal, with handsome saddle and bridle,
and trotted off to Delaware. When he arrived,
he tied the horse and went into the kitchen. Mr.
Mc Calmont coming home soon after, and observing
a very fine horse in his yard, supposed he must have
some distinguished visitor. Upon inquiry, he was
informed that Jim rode the horse there, and was
then·in the kitchen. He went out and spoke very
pleasantly to his former slave, and said he was glad
to see him. Being informed that the horse belonged
to his new master, Mr. Hart, who had kindly permitted him to use it, he ordered the animal to be
taken to the stable and supplied with hay and oats.
James was treated kindly by all the family, and
spent two days very agreeably. When about to
take leave, Mr. Mc Calmont said to him, "Well,

Jim, I am glad to find that you have a good master, and are happy. But I had rather you would not come here again in the style you now have; for it will make my people dissatisfied."

James returned much pleased with his excursion, and soon went to give Friend Hopper an account of it. He served out his time faithfully, and remained afterward in the same family, as a hired servant.

WILLIAM ANDERSON.

WILLIAM was a slave in Virginia. When about twenty-five years old, he left his master and went to Philadelphia with two of his fellow slaves; giving as a reason that he wanted to try whether he could n't do something for himself. When they had been absent a few months, their master "sold them running" to Mr. Joseph Ennells, a speculator in slaves, who procured a warrant and constable, and repaired to Philadelphia in search of his newly acquired property. They arrived on Saturday, a day when many people congregated at the horse-market. Ennells soon espied the three fugitives among the crowd, and made an attempt to pounce upon them. Luckily, they saw the movement, and dodging quickly among the multitude, they escaped.

After spending some days in search of them, Ennells called upon Isaac T. Hopper and Thomas Harrison, and offered to sell them very cheap if they would hunt them up. Friend Hopper immediately recognized him as the man who had threatened to blow out his brains, when he went to the rescue of old William Bachelor; and he thus addressed him: "I would advise thee to go home and obtain thy living in some more honorable way; for the trade in which thou art engaged is a most odious one. On a former occasion *thou* wert treated with leniency; and I recommend a similar course to thee with regard to these poor fugitives."

The speculator finally agreed to sell the three men for two hundred and fifty dollars. The money was paid, and he returned home. In the course of a few days William Anderson called upon Isaac T. Hopper for advice. He informed him that Thomas Harrison had bought him and his companions, and told him he had better find the other two, and go and make a bargain with Friend Harrison concerning the payment. He called accordingly, and offered to bind himself as a servant until he had earned enough to repay the money that had been advanced; but he said he had searched in vain for the two companions of his flight. They had left the city abruptly, and he could not ascertain where they had gone. Thomas Harrison said to him, "Perhaps thou art not aware that thou hast a legal claim to thy freedom already; for I am a citizen of Pennsylvania, and the laws here do not allow any man to hold a slave."

William replied, "I am too grateful for the kindness you have shown me, to feel any disposition to take advantage of that circumstance. If I live, you shall never lose a single cent on my account."

He was soon after indentured to Mr. Jacob Downing a respectable merchant of Philadelphia, who agreed to pay one hundred and twenty-five dollars for his services. This was half of the money advanced for all of them. William served the stipulated time faithfully. His master said he never had a more honest and useful servant; and he on his part always spoke of the family with great respect and affection.

When the time of his indenture had expired, he called upon his old benefactor, Thomas Harrison. After renewing his grateful acknowledgments for the service rendered to him in extremity, he inquired whether anything had ever been heard from the two other fugitives. Being answered in the negative, he replied, "Well, Mr. Harrison, you paid two hundred and fifty dollars for us, and you have not been able to find my companions. You have received only one hundred and twenty-five dollars. It is not right that you should lose by your kindness to us. I am willing you should bind me again to make up the balance."

"Honest fellow! Honest fellow!" exclaimed Thomas Harrison. "Go about thy business. Thou hast

paid thy share, and I have no further claim upon
thee. Conduct as well as thou hast done since I
have known thee, and thou wilt surely prosper."

Friend Hopper happened to be present at this interview; and he used to say, many years afterward,
that he should never forget how it made his heart
glow to witness such honorable and disinterested
conduct. The two other fugitives were never heard
of, and Friend Harrison of course lost one hundred
and twenty-five dollars. William frequently called
upon his benefactors, and always conducted in the
most exemplary manner.

SARAH ROACH.

Sarah Roach, a light mulatto, was sold by her
master in Maryland to a man residing in Delaware.
The laws of Delaware prohibit the introduction of
slaves, unless brought into the state by persons intending to reside there permanently. If brought
under other circumstances they become free. Sarah
remained with her new master several years before
she was made aware of this fact. Meanwhile, she
gave birth to a daughter, who was of course free, if
the mother was free at the time she was born. At
last, some one informed the bondwoman that her
master had no legal claim to her services. She then
left him and went to Philadelphia. But she remained ignorant of the fact that her daughter was

free, in consequence of the universal maxim of slave law, that "the child follows the condition of the mother."

When the girl was about sixteen years old, she absconded from Delaware, and went to her mother, who inquired of Isaac T. Hopper what was the best method of eluding the vigilance of her master. After ascertaining the circumstances, he told her that her daughter was legally free, and instructed her to inform him in case any person attempted to arrest her.

Her claimant soon discovered her place of abode, and in the summer of 1806 went in pursuit of her. Being aware that his claim had no foundation in law, he did not attempt to establish it before any magistrate, but seized the girl and hurried her on board a sloop, that lay near Spruce-street wharf, unloading staves. Fearing she would be wrested from him by the city authorities, he removed the vessel from the wharf and anchored near an island between Philadelphia and New-Jersey. A boat was placed alongside the sloop, into which the cargo was unloaded and carried to the wharf they had left.

The mother went to Isaac T. Hopper in great distress, and informed him of the transaction. He immediately made application to an alderman, who issued a process to have the girl brought before him. Guided by two colored men, who had followed her when she was carried off, he immediately proceeded to the sloop, accompanied by an officer. When the claimant saw them appoaching, he went into the cabin for his gun, and threatened them with instant death if they came near his vessel. Friend Hopper quietly told the men to go ahead and pay no attention to his threats. When they moored their boat alongside of the one into which they were unloading staves, he became very vociferous, and pointing his gun at Friend Hopper's breast, swore he should not enter the vessel.

He replied, "I have an officer with me, and I have authority from a magistrate to bring before him a girl now in thy vessel. I think we are prepared to show that she is free."

The man still kept his gun pointed, and told them to beware how they attempted to come on board.

"If thou shouldst injure any person, it would be impossible for thee to escape," replied Friend Hopper; "for thou art a hundred and twenty miles from the Capes, with hundreds of people on the wharf to witness thy deed."

While speaking thus, he advanced toward him until he came near enough to sieze hold of the gun and turn it aside. The man made a violent jerk to wrest the weapon from him, and still clinging fast hold of it he was pulled on board. In the scuffle to regain possession of his gun, the man trod upon a

roller on the deck, lost his balance, and fell sprawling
on his back.   Friend Hopper seized that opportunity
to throw the gun overboard. Whereupon, a sailor
near by siezed an axe and came toward him in a
great rage.   Even if the courageous Quaker had
wished to escape, there was no chance to do so.
He advanced to meet the sailor, and looking him
full in the face said, "Thou foolish fellow, dost thou
think to frighten me with that axe, when thy companion could not do it with his gun? Put the axe
down.   Thou art resisting legal authority, and liable
to suffer severely for thy conduct."

In a short time they became more moderate, but
denied that the girl was on board.   The vessel was
nearly emptied of her cargo, and Friend Hopper
peeping into the hold found her stowed away in a
remote part of it.   He brought her on deck and
took her with him into the boat, of which his companions, including the constable, had retained possession.

The girl was uncommonly handsome, with straight
hair and regular European features.   No one could
have guessed from her countenance that any of her
remote ancestors were Africans.

The claimant did not make his appearance at the
alderman's office.   A warrant was obtained charging
him and the sailor with having resisted an officer in
the discharge of his duty.   Isaac T. Hopper returned

to the sloop with a constable and brought the two
men before a magistrate to answer to this charge.
They did not attempt to deny the truth of it, but
tried to excuse themselves on the plea that they resisted an attempt to take away their property. Of
course, this was of no avail, and they were obliged
to enter into bonds for their appearance at court.
Being strangers in the city, it was difficult to obtain
bail, and there seemed to be no alternative but a
prison.   However, as there must unavoidably be
considerable trouble and delay in procuring all the
necessary evidence concerning the birth of the alleged slave, her friends agreed to dismiss them, if
they would pay all expenses, give each of the officers
five dollars, and manumit the girl. Under existing
circumstances, they were glad to avail themselves of
the offer; and so the affair was settled.

ZEKE.

A man by the name of Daniel Godwin, in the
lower part of Delaware, made a business of buying
slaves running; taking the risk of losing the small
sums paid for them under such circumstances. In
the year 1806, he purchased in this way a slave
amed Ezekiel, familiarly called Zeke. He went to
Philadelphia, and called on Isaac T. Hopper; thinking if he knew where the man was, he would be
glad to have his freedom secured on moderate terms.

While they were talking together, a black man hap
pened to walk in, and leaning on the counter looked
up in Mr. Godwin's face all the time he was telling
the story of his bargain. When he had done speaking, he said, "How do you do, Mr. Godwin? Don't
you know me?"

The speculator answered that he did not.

"Then you don't remember a man that lived with
your neighbor, Mr. —— ?" continued he.

Mr. Godwin was at first puzzled to recollect whom
he meant; but when he had specified the time, and
various other particulars, he said he did remember
such a person.

"Well," answered the black man, "I am he; and
I am Zeke's brother."

The speculator inquired whether he knew where
he was.

He replied, "O yes, Mr. Godwin, I know where
he is, well enough. But I'm sorry you've bought
Zeke. You'll never make anything out of him. A
bad speculation, Mr. Godwin."

"Why, what's the matter with Zeke?" asked the
trader.

"O, these blacks 'come to Philadelphia and they
get into bad company," replied he. "They are
afraid to be seen in the day-time, and so they go
prowling about in the night. I'm very sorry you've

bought Zeke. He'll never do you one cent's worth of good. A bad speculation, Mr. Godwin."

The prospect seemed rather discouraging, and the trader said, "Come now, suppose you buy Zeke yourself? I'll sell him low."

"If I bought him, I should only have to maintain him into the bargain," replied the black man. "He's my brother, to be sure; but then he'll never be good for anything."

"Perhaps he would behave better if he was free," urged Mr. Godwin.

"That's the only chance there is of his ever doing any better," responded the colored man. "But I'm very doubtful about it. If I should make up my mind to give him a chance, what would you be willing to sell him for?"

The speculator named one hundred and fifty dollars.

"Poh! Poh!" exclaimed the other. "I tell you Zeke will never be worth a cent to you or anybody else. A hundred and fifty dollars, indeed!"

The parley continued some time longer, and the case seemed such a hopeless one, that Mr. Godwin finally agreed to take sixty dollars. The colored nan went off, and soon returned with the required sum. Isaac T. Hopper drew up a deed of manumission, in which the purchaser requested him to insert that Zeke was now commonly called Samuel

Johnson. The money was paid, and the deed signed
with all necessary formalities. When the business
was entirely completed, the colored man said, "Zeke
is now free, is he?" When Mr. Godwin answered,
"Yes," he turned to Friend Hopper and repeated the
question: "Zeke is free, and nobody can take him;
can they, Mr. Hopper? If he was here, he would
be in no danger; would he?"

Friend Hopper replied, "Wherever Zeke may
now be, I assure thee he is free."

Being thus assured, the black man made a low
bow, and with a droll expression of countenance said,
"I hope you are very well, Mr. Godwin. I am happy to see you, sir. I am Zeke!"

The speculator, finding himself thus outwitted,
flew into a violent rage. He seized Zeke by the
collar, and began to threaten and abuse him. But
the colored man shook his fist at him, and said, "If
you don't let me go, Mr. Godwin, I'll knock you
down. I'm a free citizen of these United States;
and I won't be insulted in this way by anybody."

Friend Hopper interfered between them, and Mr.
Godwin agreed to go before a magistrate to have the
case examined. When the particulars had been recounted, the magistrate answered, "You have been
outwitted, sir. Zeke is now as free as any man in
this room."

There was something so exhilarating in the consciousness of being his own man, that Zeke began to "feel his oats," as the saying is. He said to the magistrate, "May it please your honor to grant me a warrant against Mr. Godwin? He violently seized me by the collar; thus committing assault and battery on a free citizen of these United States."

Friend Hopper told him he had better be satisfied with that day's work, and let Mr. Godwin go home. He yielded to this expostulation, though he might have made considerable trouble by insisting upon retaliation.

POOR AMY.

A Frenchman named M. Bouilla resided in Spring Garden, Philadelphia, in the year 1806. He and a woman, who had lived with him some time, had in their employ a mulatto girl of nine years old, called Amy. Dreadful stories were in circulation concerning their cruel treatment to this child; and compassionate neighbors had frequently solicited Friend Hopper's interference. After a while, he heard they were about to send her into the country; and fearing she might be sold into slavery, he called upon M. Bouilla to inquire whither she was going. As soon as he made known his business, the door wa unceremoniously slammed in his face and locked. A note was then sent to the Frenchman, asking for a friendly interview; but he returned a verbal answer. "Tell Mr. Hopper to mind his own business."

Considering it his business to protect an abused child, he applied to a magistrate for a warrant, and proceeded to the house, accompanied by his friend Thomas Harrison and a constable. As soon as they entered the door, M. Bouilla ran up-stairs, and arming himself with a gun, threatened to shoot whoever advanced toward him. Being blind, however, he could only point the gun at random in the direction of their voices, or of any noise which might reach his ear. The officer refused to attempt his arrest under such peril; saying, he was under no obligation to risk his life. Friend Hopper expostulated with the Frenchman, explained the nature of their errand, and urged him to come down and have the matter inquired into in an amicable way. But he would not listen, and persisted in swearing he would shoot the first person who attempted to come near him. At last, Friend Hopper took off his shoes, stepped up-stairs very softly and quickly, and just as the Frenchman became aware of his near approach, he seized the gun and held it over his shoulder. It discharged instantly, and shattered the plastering of the stairway, making it fly in all directions. There arose a loud cry, "Mr. Hopper's killed! Mr. Hopper's killed!"

The gun being thus rendered harmless, the Frenchman was soon arrested, and they all proceeded to the the magistrate's office, accompanied by several of the neighbors. There was abundant evidence that the child had been half starved, unmercifully beaten, and tortured in various ways. Indeed, she was such a poor, emaciated, miserable looking object, that her appearance was of itself enough to prove the cruel treatment she had received. When the case had been fully investigated, the magistrate ordered her to be consigned to the care of Isaac T. Hopper, who hastened home with her, being anxious lest his wife should accidentally hear the rumor that he had been shot.

He afterwards ascertained that Amy was daughter of the white woman who had aided in thus shamefully abusing her. He kept her in his family till she became well and strong, and then bound her to one of his friends in the country to serve till she was eighteen. She grew up a very pretty girl, and deported herself to the entire satisfaction of the family. When her period of service had expired, she returned to Philadelphia, where her conduct continued very exemplary. She frequently called to see Friend Hopper, and often expressed gratitude to him for having rescued her from such a miserable condition.

MANUEL.

Manuel was an active, intelligent slave in North Carolina. His master, Mr. Joseph Spear, a tar manufacturer, employed him to transport tar, and

other produce of the place, down Tar river to Tarborough. After laboring several years for another's
benefit, Manuel began to feel anxious to derive some
advantage from his own earnings. He had children,
and it troubled him to think that they must live and
die in slavery. He was acquainted with a colored
man in the neighborhood, named Samuel Curtis, who
had a certificate of freedom drawn up by the clerk
of the county, and duly authenticated, with the
county seal attached to it. Manuel thought he could
easily pass for Samuel Curtis, and make his way to
Philadelphia, if he could only obtain possession of
this valuable paper. He accordingly made him a
confidant of his plans, and he bought the certificate
for two dollars.

The next time Manuel was sent to Tarborough,
he delivered the cargo as usual, then left the boat
and started for the North. He arrived safely in
Philadelphia, where he assumed the name of Samuel
Curtis, and earned a living by sweeping chimneys.
In a short time, he had several boys in his employ,
and laid by money. When he had been going on
thus for about two years, he was suddenly met in the
street by one of the neighbors of his old master, who
immediately arrested him as a fugitive from slavery.
He was taken before Robert Wharton, then mayor.
The stranger declared that the colored man he had
seized was a slave, belonging to one of his near

neighbors in North Carolina. Samuel denied that
he was a slave, and showed his certificate of freedom. The stranger admitted that the document was
authentic, but he insisted that the real name of the
person who had possession of the paper was Manuel.
He said he knew him perfectly well, and also knew
Samuel Curtis, who was a free colored man in his
neighborhood. The mayor decided that he could
not receive parole evidence in contradiction to a public record; and Samuel Curtis was set at liberty.

To the honor of this worthy magistrate be it recorded that during forty years whilst he was alderman in Philadelphia, and twenty years that he
was mayor, he never once surrendered a fugitive
slave to his claimant, though frequently called upon
to do so. He used to tell Friend Hopper that he
could not conscientiously do it; that he would rather
resign his office. He often remarked that the Declaration, "All men are created equal; they are endowed by their Creator with certain inalienable
rights; among these are life, liberty, and the pursuit
of happiness;" appeared to him based on a sacred
principle, paramount to all law.

When Samuel Curtis was discharged, he deemed
it expedient to go to Boston; thinking he might be
safer there than in Philadelphia. But he had not
been there many days, before he met the same man
who had previously arrested him; and he by no

means felt sure that the mayor of that city would prove as friendly to the colored people as was Robert Wharton. To add to his troubles, some villain broke open his trunk while he was absent from his lodgings, and stole a hundred and fifty dollars of his hard earnings. The poor fugitive began to think there was no safe resting-place for him on the face of the earth. He returned to Philadelphia disconsolate and anxious. He was extremely diligent and frugal, and every year he contrived to save some money, which he put out at interest in safe hands. At last, he was able to purchase a small lot in Powell-street, on which he built a good three-story brick house, where he lived with his apprentices, and let some of the rooms at a good profit.

In 1807, he called upon Friend Hopper and told him that his eagerness to make money had chiefly arisen from a strong desire to redeem his children from bondage. But being a slave himself, he said it was impossible for him to go in search of them, unless his own manumission could be obtained. It happened that a friend of Isaac T. Hopper was going to North Carolina. He agreed to see the master and ascertain what could be done. Mr. Spear never expected to hear from his slave again, and the proposition to buy him after so many years had elapsed, seemed like finding a sum of money. He readily agreed to make out a bill of sale for one hundred dollars, which was immediately paid.

The first use Samuel Curtis made of the freedom he had purchased was to set off for the South in search of his children. To protect himself as much as possible from the perils of such an undertaking, he obtained a certificate of good character, signed by the mayor of Philadelphia, and several of the most respectable citizens. They also gave him "a pass" stating the object of his journey, and commending him to the protecting kindness of those among whom he might find it necessary to travel. With these he carefully packed his deed of manumission, and set forth on his errand of paternal love. When he went to take leave of Friend Hopper, he was much agitated. He clasped his hand fervently, and the tears flowed fast down his weather-beaten cheeks. "I know I am going into the midst of danger," said he. "Perhaps I may be seized and sold into slavery. But I am willing to hazard everything, even my own liberty, if I can only secure the freedom of my children. I have been a slave myself, and I know what slaves suffer. Farewell! Farewell, my good friend. May God bless you, and may he restore to me my children. Then I shall be a happy man."

He started on his journey, and went directly to his former master to obtain information. He did not at first recognize his old servant. But when he became convinced that the person before him was the identical Manuel, who had formerly been his slave, he seemed pleased to see him, entertained him kindly, and inquired how he had managed to get money enough to buy his children.

The real Samuel Curtis, who sold him the certificate of freedom, was dead; and since he could no longer be endangered by a statement of particulars, the spurious Samuel related the whole story of his escape, and of his subsequent struggles; concluding the whole by expressing an earnest wish to find his children.

Mr. Spear had sold them, some years before, to a man in South Carolina; and thither the father went in search of them. On arriving at the designated place, he found they had been sold into Georgia. He went to Georgia, and was told they had been sold to a man in Tennessee. He followed them into Tennessee, but there he lost all track of them. After the most patient and diligent search, he was compelled to return home without further tidings of them.

As soon as he arrived in Philadelphia, he went to Isaac T. Hopper to tell how the cherished plan of his life had been frustrated. He seemed greatly dejected, and wept bitterly. "I have deprived myself of almost every comfort," said he; "that I might save money to buy my poor children. But now they are

not to be found, and my money gives me no satisfaction. The only consolation I have is the hope
that they are all dead."

The bereaved old man never afterward seemed to
take comfort in anything. He sunk. into a settled
melancholy, and did not long survive his disappoint-
ment.

SLAVEHOLDERS MOLLIFIED.

In the winter of 1808, several Virginia planters
went to Philadelphia to search for eleven slaves, who
had absconded. Most of these colored people had
been there several years, and some of them had acquired a little property. Their masters had ascertained where they lived, and one evening, when they
returned from their acustomed labors, unconscious
of danger impending over them, they were pounced
upon suddenly and conveyed to prison. It was late
at night when this took place, and Friend Hopper
did not hear of it till the next morning.

He had risen very early, according to his usual
custom, and upon opening his front door he found a
letter slipped under it, addressed to him. This
anonymous epistle informed him that eleven slaves
had been arrested, and were to be tried before Alderman Douglass that morning; that the owners
were gentlemen of wealth and high standing, and
could produce the most satisfactory evidence that

the persons arrested were their slaves; consequently
Friend Hopper's attendance could be of no possible
benefit to them. It went on to say that the magistrate understood his business, and could do justice
without his assistance; but if, notwithstanding this
warning, he did attend at the magistrate's office, for
the purpose of wresting from these gentlemen their
property, his house would be burned while himself
and family were asleep in it, and his life would certainly be taken. The writer invoked the most awful imprecations upon himself if he did not carry
these threats into execution.

Friend Hopper was too much accustomed to such
epistles to be disturbed by them. He put it in his
pocket, and said nothing about it, lest his wife should
be alarmed. A few minutes afterward, he received
a message from some colored people begging him to
go to the assistance of the fugitives; and when the
trial came on, he was at the alderman's office, of
course. Richard Rush was counsel for the claimants. The colored prisoners had no lawyer. This
examination was carried on with much earnestness
and excitement. One of the Virginians failed in
proof as to the identity of the person he claimed. In
the case of several others, the power of attorney was
pronounced informal by the magistrate. After a
long protracted controversy, during which Friend
Hopper threw as many difficulties in the way as

possible, it was decided that four of the persons in custody were proved to be slaves, and the other seven were discharged. This decision greatly exas perated the Southerners, and they vented their anger in very violent expressions. The constables em- ployed were unprincipled men, ready for any low business, provided it were profitable. The man-hun- ters had engaged to give them fifty dollars for each slave they were enabled to take back to Virginia; but they were to receive nothing for those who were discharged. Hence, their extreme anxiety to avoid Friend Hopper's interference. When they found that more than half of their destined prey had slip- ped through their fingers, they were furious. One of them especially raved like a madman. He had written the anonymous letter, and was truly "a lewd fellow of the baser sort."

Friend Hopper's feelings were too much interested for those who had been decreed slaves, to think any- thing of the abuse bestowed on himself. All of them, three men and one woman, were married to free persons ; and it was heart-breaking to hear their lamentations at the prospect of being separated for- ever. There was a general manifestation of sympa- thy, and even the slaveholders were moved to com- passion. Friend Hopper opened a negotiation with them in behalf of the Abolition Society, and they finally consented to manumit them all for seven hun-

dred dollars. The money was advanced by a Friend
named Thomas Phipps, and the poor slaves returned
to their humble homes rejoicing. They repaid every
farthing of the money, and ever after manifested the
liveliest gratitude to their benefactors.

When the anger of the Southerners had somewhat
cooled, Friend Hopper invited them to come and see
him. They called, and spent the evening in discuss-
ing the subject of slavery. When they parted from
the veteran abolitionist, it was with mutual courtesy
and kindliness. They said they respected him for
acting so consistently with his own principles; and
if they held the same opinions, they should doubtless
pursue the same course.

This was a polite concession, but it was based on
a false foundation; for it assumed that it was a
mere matter of *opinion* whether slavery were right
or wrong; whereas it is a palpable violation of im-
mutable principles of justice. They might as well
have made the same remark about murder or robbery, if they had lived where a selfish majority were
strong enough to get those crimes sanctioned by law
and custom. The Bedouin considers himself no rob-
ber because he forcibly takes as much toll as he
pleases from all who pass through the desert. His
ancestors established the custom, and he is not one
whit the less an Arab gentleman, because he perpe-
tuates their peculiar institution. Perhaps he also

would say that if he held the same opinions as more
honest Mahometans, he would do as they do.   In
former days, custom made it honorable to steal a
neighbor's cattle, on the Scottish border; as many
Americans now deem it respectable to take children
from poor defenceless neighbors, and sell them like
sheep in the market.   Sir Walter Scott says playfully, "I have my quarters and emblazonments free
of all stain but Border Theft and High Treason,
which I hope are *gentlemanlike crimes*." Yet the
stealing of cattle does not now seem a very noble
achievement in the eyes of honorable Scotchmen
How will the stealing of children, within bounds
prescribed by law and custom, appear to future gene-
rations of Americans?

THE UNITED STATES BOND.

A planter in Virginia, being pressed for money,
sold one of his bondwomen, of sixteen years old, to
a speculator who was buying up slaves for the markets of the South and South-west.   The girl was
uncommonly handsome, with smooth hair, and a
complexion as light as most white people.   Her new
owner, allured by her beauty, treated her with great
kindness, and made many flattering promises.   She
understood his motives, and wished to escape 'from
the degradation of such a destiny as he had in store
for her.   In order to conciliate her good will, he im-

posed few restraints upon her.   The liberty thus allowed gave her a favorable opportunity to abscond,
which she did not fail to improve.   She travelled to
Philadelphia without encountering any difficulties on
the road; for her features and complexion excited
no suspicion of her being a fugitive slave.   She maintained herself very comfortably by her own industry,
and after a time married a light mulatto, who was a
very sober industrious man.   He was for many years
employed by Joshua Humphreys, a ship-carpenter of
great respectability in the District of Southwark.
By united industry and frugality they were enabled
to build a small house on a lot they had taken on
ground rent.   The furniture was simple, but extremely neat, and all the floors were carpeted.   Every thing indicated good management and domestic
comfort.

     She had been in Philadelphia thirteen years, and
was the mother of a promising family, when in 1808 she
was arrested by her last master, as a fugitive slave.
The Virginian who sold her, and two other persons
from the South, attended as witnesses.   Isaac T.
Hopper also attended, with his trusty friend Thomas
Harrison.   When the witnesses were examined, her
case appeared utterly hopeless; and in private conversation with Friend Hopper she admitted that she
was a slave to the man who claimed her.   Mr. Humphreys, pitying the distress of his honest, industrious

workman, offered to advance one hundred dollars
toward purchasing her freedom. But when Isaac
T. Hopper and Thomas Harrison attempted to nego
tiate with the claimant for that purpose, he treated
all their offers with the rudest contempt. They tried
to work upon his feelings, by representing the misery
he would inflict on her worthy husband and innocent
children; but he turned a deaf ear to all their entreaties. They finally offered to pay him four hundred
dollars for a deed of manumission, which at that
time was considered a very high price; but he stopped all further discussion by declaring, with a violent oath, that he would not sell her on *any* terms.
Of course, there was nothing to be done, but to
await the issue of the trial.

When the magistrate asked the woman whether
she were a slave, Friend Hopper promptly objected
to her answering that question, unless he would agree
to receive as evidence *all* she might say. He declined doing that. Friend Hopper then made some
remarks, in the course of which he said, "The most
honest witnesses are often mistaken as to the identity of persons. It surprises me that the witnesses in
this case should be so very positive, when the woman was but sixteen years old at the time they say
she eloped, and such a long period has since elapsed.

The question at stake is as important as life itself
to this woman, to her honest husband, and to her

poor little innocent children. For my own part, I
conscientiously believe she has a *just* claim to her
freedom."

All this time, the woman stood holding her little
girl and boy by the hand. She was deeply dejected,
but her manners were as calm and dignified, as if
she had been one of the best educated ladies in the
land. The children were too young to understand
the terrible doom that threatened their mother, but
they perceived that their parents were in some great
trouble, and the little creatures wept in sympathy.

When Friend Hopper described this scene forty
years afterward, he used to say, "I shall never forget the anguish expressed in her handsome countenance, as she looked down upon her children. I see
it as plainly as if it all happened yesterday."

At the time, it was almost too much for his sympathizing heart to endure. He felt like moving hea
ven and earth to rescue her. The trial came on in
the afternoon, and it happened that the presiding
magistrate was accustomed to drink rather freely of
wine after dinner. Friend Hopper perceived that
his mental faculties were slightly confused, and that
the claimant was a heavy, stupid-looking fellow.
With these thoughts there suddenly flashed through
his brain the plan of eluding an iniquitous law, in
order to sustain a higher law of justice and humanity. He asked to have the case adjourned till the

next day, that there might be further opportunity to inquire into it; adding, "Thomas Harrison and myself will be responsible to the United States for this woman's appearance to-morrow. In case of forfeiture, we will agree to pay any sum that may be deemed reasonable."

The claimant felt perfectly sure of his prey, and made no objection to the proposed arrangement. It was accordingly entered on the docket that Thomas Harrison and Isaac T. Hopper were bound to the United States, in the sum of one thousand dollars, to produce the woman for further trial at nine o'clock the next morning.

When Friend Hopper had obtained a copy of the recognizance, signed by the magistrate, he chuckled inwardly and marched out of the office. If there was a flaw in anything, Thomas Harrison had a jocose way of saying, "There is a hole in the ballad." As they went into the street together, his friend said, "Thomas, there's a hole in the ballad. The recognizance we have just signed is good for nothing. The United States have not the slightest claim upon that woman."

The next morning, at nine o'clock all parties, except the woman, were at the mayor's office. After waiting for her about an hour, the magistrate said, "Well gentlemen, the woman does not make her appearance, and I shall be obliged to forfeit your recognizance."

"A thousand dollars is a large sum to lose," rejoined Friend Hopper. "But if it comes to the worst, I suppose we must make up our minds to pay the United States all the claim they have upon us."

"The United States! The United States!" exclaimed the magistrate quickly. He turned to look at his docket, and after a slight pause he said to the claimant, "There is difficulty here. You had better employ counsel."

Thomas Ross, a respectable lawyer, who lived a few doors above, was summoned, and soon made his appearance. Having heard the particulars of the case briefly stated, he also examined the docket; then turning to Isaac T. Hopper, with a comical gesture and tone, he exclaimed, "Eh!" To the claimant he said, "You must catch your slave again if you can; for you can do nothing with these securities."

Of course, the master was very angry, and so was the magistrate, who had inadvertently written the recognizance just as it was dictated to him. They charged Friend Hopper with playing a trick upon them, and threatened to prosecute him. He told them he had no fears concerning a prosecution; and if he *had* played a trick, he thought it was better than to see a helpless woman torn from husband and children and sent into slavery.

The magistrate asked, "How could you say you believed the woman had a right to her freedom? You have brought forward no evidence whatever to prove your assertion."

He replied, "I did not say I believed she had a *legal* right to her freedom. That she had a *just* right to it, I did believe; for I think every human being has a just claim to freedom, unless guilty of some crime. The system of slavery is founded on the grossest and most manifest injustice."

"It is sanctioned by the law of the land, answered the claimant; "and you have no right to fly in the face of the laws."

Friend Hopper contented himself with saying, "If I have broken any law, I stand ready to meet the consequences. But no law can make wrong right."

The speculator spent several days in fruitless search after the fugitive. When he had relinquished all hopes of finding her, he called on Isaac T. Hopper and offered to manumit her for four hundred dollars. He replied, "At one time, we would gladly have given that sum; but now the circumstances of the case are greatly changed, and we cannot consent to give half that amount." After considerable controversy he finally agreed to take one hundred and fifty dollars. The money was paid, and the deed of manumission made out in due form. At parting, the claimant said, with a very bitter smile, "I hope I may live to see you south of the Potomac some day."

Friend Hopper replied, "Thou hadst better go home and repent of sins already committed, instead of meditating the commission of more."

When telling this story in after years, he was wont to say, "I am aware that some will disapprove of the part I acted in that case; because they will regard it as inconsistent with the candor which men ought always to practice toward each other. I can only say that my own conscience has never condemned me for it. I could devise no other means to save the poor victim."

Before we decide to blame Friend Hopper more than he blamed himself in this matter, it would be well to imagine how we ourselves should have felt, if we had been witnesses of the painful scene, instead of reading it in cool blood, after a lapse of years. If a handsome and modest woman stood before us with her weeping little ones, asking permission to lead a quiet and virtuous life, and a pitiless law was about to tear her from husband and children and consig her to the licentious tyrant from whom she had es caped, should we not be strongly tempted to evade such a law by any means that offered at the moment?

It would be wiser to expend our moral indignation on statesmen who sanction and sustain laws so wicked, that just and kind-hearted citizens are compelled either to elude them, or to violate their own honest convictions and the best emotions of their hearts.

THE TENDER MERCIES OF A SLAVE-HOLDER.

In the year of 1808 a Southerner arrested a fugitive slave in Philadelphia and committed him to prison. When he called for him, with authority to take him back to the South, the poor fellow seemed dreadfully distressed. He told the keeper that his master was very severe, and he knew that terrible sufferings awaited him if he was again placed in his power. He hesitated long before he followed the keeper to the iron gate, through which he was to pass out of prison. When he saw his oppressor standing there with fetters in his hand, ready to take him away, he stopped and pleaded in the most piteous tones for permission to find a purchaser in Philadelphia. His owner took not the slightest notice of these humble entreaties, but in a peremptory manner ordered him to come out. The slave trembled all over, and said in the fainting accents of despair, "Master, I *can't* go with you!"

"Come out, you black rascal!" exclaimed the inexorable tyrant. "Come out immediately!"

The poor wretch advanced timidly a few steps, then turned back suddenly, as if overcome with mortal fear. The master became very impatient, and in angry vociferous tones commanded the keeper to bring him out by force.

All this time, the keeper had stood with his hand on the key of the iron door, very reluctant to open it. But at last he unlocked it, and told the poor terrified creature that he must go. He rushed to the door in the frenzy of desperation, gazed in his master's face for an instant, then flew back, took a sharp knife, which he had concealed about him, and drew it across his throat with such force, that he fell senseless near his master's feet, spattering his garments with blood. All those who witnessed this awful scene, supposed the man was dead. Dr. Church, physician of the prison, examined the wound, and said there was scarcely a possibility that he could survive, though the wind-pipe was not entirely separated. But even the terrible admonition of that ghastly spectacle produced no relenting feelings in the hard heart of the slaveholder. He still demanded to have his victim delivered up to him. When the keeper declined doing it, and urged the reason that the physician said he could not be moved without imminent danger to his life, the brutal tyrant exclaimed, " Damn him ! He's my property; and I

will have him, dead or alive. If he dies, it's nobody's loss but mine."

As he had the mayor's warrant for taking him,
the keeper dared not incur the responsibility of diso-
beying his requisitions. He convened the inspectors
for consultation ; and they all agreed that any attempt to remove the wounded man would render
them accessory to his death. They laid the case
before the mayor, who ordered that the prisoner
should remain undisturbed till the physician pronounced him out of danger. When the master was
informed of this, he swore that nobody had any right
to interfere between him and his property. He cursed the mayor, threatened to prosecute the keeper,
and was in a furious rage with every body.

Meanwhile, the sympathy of Isaac T. Hopper was
strongly excited in the case, and he obtained a promise from the physician that he would let him know
if there was any chance that the slave would recover. Contrary to all expectation, he lingered along
day after day ; and in about a week, the humane
physician signified to Friend Hopper, and Joseph
Price, one of the inspectors, that a favorable result
might now be anticipated. Of course, none of them
considered it a duty to inform the master of their
hopes. They undertook to negotiate for the purchase of the prisoner, and obtained him for a moderate price. The owner was fully impressed with the

belief that he would die before long, and therefore regarded the purchase of him as a mere freak of humanity, by which he was willing enough to profit. When he heard soon afterward that the doctor pronounced him out of danger, he was greatly enraged. But his suffering victim was beyond the reach of his fury, which vented itself in harmless execrations.

The colored man lived many years, to enjoy the liberty for which he had been willing to sacrifice his life. He was a sober, honest, simple-hearted person, and always conducted in a manner entirely satisfactory to those who had befriended him in his hour of utmost need.

THE FOREIGN SLAVE.

Early in the year of 1808, a Frenchman arrived in Philadelphia from one of the West India Islands, bringing with him a slave, whom he took before one of the aldermen, and had him bound to serve him seven years in Virginia. When the indenture was executed, he committed his bondman to prison, for safe-keeping, until he was ready to leave the city. One of the keepers informed Isaac T. Hopper of the circumstance, and told him the slave was to be carried South the next morning.

Congress had passed an Act prohibiting the importation of slaves, which was to begin to take effect at the commencement of the year 1808. It immediately occurred to Friend Hopper that the present case came within the act; and if so, the colored man was of course legally entitled to freedom. In order to detain him till he could examine the law, and take advice on the subject, he procured a warrant for debt and lodged it at the prison, telling the keeper not to let the colored man go till he had paid his demand of a hundred dollars.

When the Frenchman called for his slave next morning, they refused to discharge him; and he obtained a writ of *habeas corpus*, to bring the case before the mayor's court. Friend Hopper was informed that the slave was on trial, that the Recorder did not think it necessary to notify him, and had made very severe remarks concerning the fictitious debt assumed for the occasion. He proceeded directly to the court, which was thronged with people, who watched him with lively curiosity, and made a lane for him to pass through. Mahlon Dickinson, the Recorder, was in the act of giving his decision on the case, and he closed his remarks by saying, "The conduct of Mr. Hopper has been highly reprehensible. The man is not his debtor; and the pretence that he was so could have been made for no other reason but to cause unnecessary delay, vexation, and expense." The lawyers smiled at each other, and seemed not a little pleased at hearing him so roughly rebuked; for many of them had been more or less annoyed by his skill and ready wit in tangling their skein, in cases where questions of freedom were involved. Friend Hopper stood before the Recorder, looking him steadfastly in the face, while he was making animadversions on his conduct; and when he had finished, he respectfully asked leave to address the court for a few minutes.

"Well, Mr. Hopper," said the Recorder, "what have you to say in justification of your very extraordinary proceedings?"

He replied, "It is true the man is not my debtor; but the court has greatly erred in supposing that the step I have taken was merely intended to produce unnecessary delay and expense. The Recorder will doubtless recollect that Congress has passed an act prohibiting the introduction of foreign slaves into this country. It is my belief that the case now before the court is embraced within the provisions of that act. But I needed time to ascertain the point; and I assumed that the man was my debtor merely to detain him until the Act of Congress could be examined."

Jared Ingersoll, an old and highly respectable lawyer, rose to say, "May it please your honors, I believe Mr. Hopper is correct in his opinion. A National Intelligencer containing the Act of Congress is at my office, and I will send for it if you wish." The paper was soon brought, and Friend Hopper read aloud the section which Mr. Ingersoll pointed out; placing strong emphasis on such portions as bore upon the case then pending. When he had concluded, he observed, "I presume the court must now be convinced that the censures so liberally bestowed on my conduct are altogether unmerited."

The counsel for the claimant said a newspaper was not legal evidence of the existence of a law. Friend Hopper replied, "The court is well aware that I am no lawyer. But I have heard lawyers talk about *prima facie* evidence; and I should suppose the National Intelligencer amounted at least to that sort of evidence, for it is the acknowledged organ of government, in which the laws are published for the information of citizens. But if that is not satisfactory, I presume the court will detain the man until an authenticated copy of the law can be obtained."

After some discussion, the court ordered a copy of the law to be procured; but the attorney abandoned the case, and the slave was set at liberty.

As soon as this decision was announced, the throng of spectators, white and colored, began to shout, "Hurra for Mr. Hopper!" The populace were so accustomed to see him come off victorious from such contests, that they began to consider his judgment infallible.

Many years afterward, when Friend Hopper met

Mahlon Dickinson on board a steam-boat, he inquired
whether he recollected the scolding he gave him on
a certain occasion. He replied pleasantly, "Indeed
I do. I thought I *had* you that time, and I intended
to give it to you; but you slipped through my fingers, as usual."

THE NEW-JERSEY SLAVE.

In the year 1809, a gentleman from East New-
Jersey visited Philadelphia, and brought a young slave
to wait upon him. When they had been in that city
four or five months, the lad called upon Isaac T.
Hopper to inquire whether his residence in Philadelphia had made him free. He was informed that he
would not have a legal claim to freedom till he had
been there six months. Just as the term expired,
somebody told the master that the laws of Pennsylvania conferred freedom on slaves under such circumstances. He had been ignorant of the fact, or
had forgotten it, and as soon as he received the information he became alarmed lest he should lose his
locomotive property. He sent for a constable, who
came to his door with a carriage. The lad had just
come up from the cellar with an armful of wood.
When he entered the parlor, the constable ordered
him to put it down and go with him. He threw the
wood directly at the legs of the officer, and ran down
cellar full speed, slamming the door after him. As

soon as the constable could recover from the blow he had received, he followed the lad into the cellar; but he had escaped by another door, and gone to Isaac T. Hopper.

It was snowing fast, and when he arrived there in his shirt sleeves, his black wool plentifully powdered with snow, he was a laughable object to look upon. But his countenance showed that he was too thoroughly frightened and distressed to be a subject of mirth to any compassionate heart. Friend Hopper tried to comfort him by promising that he would protect him, and assuring him that he was now legally free. His agitation subsided in a short time, and he began to laugh heartily to think how he had upset the constable. The master soon came to Friend Hopper's house, described the lad's dress and appearance, and inquired whether he had seen him. He admitted that he had, but declined telling where he was. The master made some severe remarks about the meanness of tampering with gentlemen's servants, and went away. In about half an hour he returned with the constable and said Alderman Kepler desired his respects to Isaac T. Hopper, and wished to see him at his office. He replied, "I think it likely that Alderman Kepler has not much more respect for me than I have for him. If he has more *business* with me than I have with him, I am at home, and can be spoken with."

The master went away, but soon returned with two constables and a lawyer, who was very clamorous in his threats of what would be the consequences if the slave was not at once surrendered to the gentleman. One of the officers said he had a warrant to search the house. "Very well," replied Friend Hopper, "execute it."

"I have great respect for you," rejoined the officer. "I should be sorry to search your house by virtue of the warrant. I hope you will consent to my doing so without."

"There is no need of delicacy on this occasion," replied Friend Hopper. "Thou hadst better proceed to the extent of thy authority."

"You give your consent, do you?" inquired the officer.

He answered, "No, I do not. If thou hast a warrant, of course my consent is not necessary. Proceed to the full extent of thy authority. But if thou goest one inch beyond, thou wilt have reason to repent of it."

The party left the house utterly discomfited. He afterward learned that they had applied for a search-warrant, but could not procure one.

The first step in the process of securing the lad's freedom was to obtain proof that he had been in Philadelphia six months. The landlord of the hotel where the master lodged, refused to say anything on

the subject, being unwilling to offend his lodger.
But the servants were under no such prudential restraint; and from them Friend Hopper obtained testimony sufficient for his purpose. He then wrote a
note to the alderman that he would be at his office
with the lad at nine o'clock next morning, and re-
uesting him to inform the claimant. In the mean
time, he procured a writ of *habeas corpus*, to have it
in readiness in case circumstances required it. The
claimant made his appearance at the appointed hour,
and stated how he had come to Philadelphia on a
visit, and brought a slave to attend upon him. He
descanted quite largely upon the courtesy due from
citizens of one state to those of another state.

Friend Hopper was about to reply, when the
magistrate interrupted him by saying, "I shall not
interfere with the citizens of other states. I shall
surrender the boy to his master. If he thinks he has
a legal claim to his freedom, let him prosecute it in
New-Jersey."

Friend Hopper said nothing, but gave a signal to
have the writ served. The magistrate was highly
offended, and asked in an angry tone, "What was
your object in procuring a writ of *habeas corpus?*"

Friend Hopper replied, "From my knowledge of
thee, I anticipated the result that has just occurred;
and I determined to remove the case to a tribunal

where I had confidence that justice would be done in the premises."

The Court of Common Pleas was then in session. The case was brought before it the next day, and after the examination of two or three witnesses, the lad was declared free.

A SLAVE HUNTER DEFEATED.

In 1810, a slave escaped from Virginia to Philadelphia. In a few months, his master heard where he was, and caused him to be arrested. He was a fine looking young man, apparently about thirty years old. When he was brought before Alderman Shoemaker, that magistrate's sympathy was so much excited, that he refused to try the case unless some one was present to defend the slave. Isaac T. Hopper was accordingly sent for. When he had heard a statement of the case, he asked the agent of the slaveholder to let him examine the Power of Attorney by which he had been authorized to arrest a "fugitive from labor," and carry him to Virginia. The agent denied his right to interfere, but Alderman Shoemaker informed him that Mr. Hopper was a member of the Emancipation Society, and had a right to be satisfied.

The Power of Attorney was correctly drawn, and had been acknowledged in Washington, before Bushrod Washington, one of the judges of the Supreme

Court of the United States.   Friend Hopper's keen
eye could detect no available flaw in it.   When the
agent had been sworn to answer truly all questions
relating to the case, he inquired whether the fugitive
he was in search of had been advertised; if so, he
wished to see the advertisement.   It was handed to
him, and he instantly noticed that it was headed
"Sixty Dollars Reward."

"Art thou to receive sixty dollars for apprehend-
ing the man mentioned in this advertisement?" said
he.

The agent replied, "I am to receive that sum provided I take him home to Virginia."

"How canst thou prove that the man thou hast
arrested is the one here advertised?" inquired he.

The agent answered that he could swear to the
fact.

"That may be," rejoined Friend Hopper; "but in
Philadelphia we do not allow any person, especially
a stranger, to swear sixty dollars into his own
pocket.   Unless there is better evidence than thy
oath, the man must be set at liberty."

The agent became extremely irritated, and said
indignantly, "Do you think I would swear to a
lie?"

"Thou art a stranger to me," replied Friend Hopper.   "I don't know whether thou wouldst swear

falsely or not. But there is one thing I do know, and that is, I am not willing to trust thee."

The agent reiterated, "I know the man standing there as well as I know any man living. I am perfectly sure he is the slave described in the advertisement. I was overseer for the gentleman who owns him. If you examine his back, you will find scars of the whip."

"And perhaps thou art the man who made the scars, if he has any," rejoined the Friend.

Without replying to this suggestion, the slave-hunter ordered the colored man to strip, that his back might be examined by the court. Friend Hopper objected to such a proceeding. "Thou hast produced no evidence that the man thou hast arrested is a slave," said he. "Thou and he are on the same footing before this court. We have as good a right to examine thy back, as we have to examine his." He added, with a very significant tone, "In some places, they whip for kidnapping."

This remark put the slave-hunter in a violent rage. The magistrate decided that his evidence was not admissible, on the ground that he was interested. He then proposed to summon two witnesses from a Virginian vessel lying at one of the wharves.

"Of course thou art at liberty to go for witnesses," replied Friend Hopper. "But I appeal to the magistrate to discharge this man. Under present circumstances, he ought not to be detained a single moment." The alderman needed no urging on that point. He very promptly discharged the prisoner. As soon as he left the office, the slave-hunter siezed hold of him, and swore he would keep him till witnesses were brought. But Friend Hopper walked up to him, and said in his resolute way, "Let go thy hold! or I will take such measures as will make thee repent of thy rashness. How darest thou lay a finger upon the man after the magistrate has discharged him?"

Thus admonished, he reluctlantly relinquished his grasp, and went off swearing vengeance against "the meddlesome Quaker."

Friend Hopper hastened home with the colored man, and wrote a brief letter to his friend William Reeve, in New-Jersey, concluding with these words: "Verily I say unto you, inasmuch as ye have done it unto the least of these my brethren, ye have done it unto me." This letter was given to the fugitive with directions how to proceed. His friend accompanied him to the ferry, saw him safely across the river, and then returned home.

In an hour or two the slave-hunter came to the house, accompanied by a constable and two witnesses from Virginia. "The slave I arrested was seen to come here," said he. "Where is he? Produce him."

Friend Hopper replied very quietly, "The man has been here; but he is gone now."

This answer made the agent perfectly furious. After discharging a volley of oaths, he said he had a search warrant, and swore he would have the house searched from garret to cellar. "Very well," replied Friend Hopper, "thou art at liberty to proceed according to law; but be careful not to overstep that boundary. If thou dost, it will be at thy peril."

After the slave-hunter had vented his rage in a torrent of abuse, the constable proposed to speak a few words in private. With many friendly professions, he acknowledged that they had no search-warrant. "The gentleman was about to obtain one from the mayor," said he; "but I wished to save your feelings. I told him you were well acquainted with me, and I had no doubt you would permit me to search your house without any legal process."

Friend Hopper listened patiently, perfectly well aware that the whole statement was a sham. When the constable paused for a reply, he opened the door, and said very concisely, "Thou art at liberty to go about thy business."

They spent several days searching for the fugitive, but their efforts were unavailing.

MARY MORRIS.

A WOMAN, who was born too early to derive benefit from the gradual emancipation law of Pennsylvania, escaped from bondage in Lancaster County to Philadelphia.   There she married a free colored man by the name of Abraham Morris.   They lived together very comfortably for several years, and seemed to enjoy life as much as many of their more wealthy neighbors.   But in the year 1810, it unfortunately happened that Mary's master ascertained where she lived, and sent a man to arrest her, with directions either to sell her, or bring her back to him.

Abraham Morris was a very intelligent, industrious man, and had laid up some money.   He offered one hundred and fifty dollars of his earnings to purchase the freedom of his wife.   The sum was accepted, and the parties applied to Daniel Bussier, a magistrate in the District of Southwark, to draw up a deed of manumission.   The money was paid, and the deed given; but the agent employed to sell the woman absconded with the money.   The master, after waiting several months and not hearing from him, sent to Philadelphia and caused Mary Morris to be arrested again.   She was taken to the office of Daniel Bussier, and notwithstanding he had witnessed her deed of manumission a few months before, he committed her to prison as a fugitive slave.   When her

husband called upon Isaac T. Hopper and related all
the circumstances, he thought there must be some
mistake; for he could not believe that any magistrate would be so unjust and arbitrary, as to commit
a woman to prison as a fugitive, when he had seen
the money paid for her ransom, and the deed of
manumission given.   He went to Mr. Bussier immediately, and very civilly told him that he had called
to make inquiry concerning a colored woman committed to prison as a fugitive slave on the evening
previous.

"Go out of my office !" said the undignified magistrate.   "I want nothing to do with you."

He replied, "I come here as the friend and adviser of the woman's husband. My request is reasonable, and I trust thou wilt not refuse it."

In answer to this appeal, Mr. Bussier merely repeated, "Go out of my office !"

Friend Hopper offered him half a dollar, saying,
"I want an extract from thy docket. Here is the
lawful fee."

All this time, Mr. Bussier had been under the
hands of a barber, who was cutting his hair. He
became extremely irritated, and said, "If you won't
leave this office, I will put you out, as soon as I have
taken the seat of justice."

"I wish thou wouldst take the seat of justice,"
replied Friend Hopper; "for then I should obtain

what I want; but if thou dost, I apprehend it will be for the first time."

Mr. Bussier sprang hastily from his chair, and seated himself at the magisterial desk, which was raised about a foot from the floor, and surrounded by a railing. Conceiving himself now armed with the thunders of the law, he called out, in tones of authority, "Mr. Hopper, I command you to quit this office !"

The impassive Quaker stood perfectly still, and pointing to Abraham Morris, he again tendered the half dollar, saying, "I want an extract from thy docket, in the case of this man's wife. Here is the lawful fee for it. Please give it to me."

This quiet perseverance deprived the excited magistrate of what little patience he had left. He took the importunate petitioner by the shoulders, pushed him into the street, and shut the door.

Friend Hopper then applied to Jacob Rush, President of the Court of Common Pleas for a writ of *habeas corpus*. The woman was brought before him, and when he had heard the particulars of the case, and examined her deed of manumission, he immediately discharged her, to the great joy of herself and husband.

Friend Hopper thought it might be a useful lesson for Mr. Bussier to learn that his "little brief authority" had boundaries which could not be passed with impunity. He accordingly had him indicted for assault and battery. He and his political friends were a good deal ashamed of his conduct, and finally, after many delays in bringing on the trial, and various attempts to hush up the matter, Mr. Bussier called upon Friend Hopper to say that he deeply regretted the course he had pursued. His apology was readily accepted, and the case dismissed; he agreeing to pay the costs.

THE SLAVE MOTHER.

Cassy was slave to a merchant in Baltimore, by the name of Claggett. She had reason to believe that her master was about to sell her to a speculator, who was making up a coffle for the markets of the far South. The terror felt in view of such a prospect can be understood by slaves only. She resolved to escape; and watching a favorable opportunity, she succeeded in reaching the neighborhood of Haddonfield, New-Jersey. There she obtained service in a very respectable family. She was honest, steady, and industrious, and made many friends by her cheerful, obliging manners. But her heart was never at rest; for she had left in Baltimore a babe little more than a year old. She had not belonged to an unusually severe master; but she had experienced quite enough of the sufferings of slavery to dread it for her child. Her thoughts dwelt so much on this painful subject, that her naturally cheerful character became extremely saddened. She at last determined to make a bold effort to save her little one from the liability of being sold, like a calf or pig in the shambles. She went to see Isaac T. Hopper and communicated to him her plan. He tried to dissuade her; for he considered the project extremely danger ous, and well nigh hopeless. But the mother's heart yearned for her babe, and the incessant longing stimulated her courage to incur all hazards. To Baltimore she went; her pulses throbbing hard and fast, with the double excitement of hope and fear. She arrived safely, and went directly to the house of a colored family, old friends of hers, in whom she could confide with perfect safety. To her great joy, she found that they approved her plan, and were ready to assist her. Arrangements were soon made to convey the child to a place about twenty miles from Baltimore, where it would be well taken care of, till the mother could find a safe opportunity to remove it to New-Jersey.

Before she had time to take all the steps necessary to insure success in this undertaking, her master was informed of her being in the city, and sent constables in pursuit of her. Luckily, her friends were apprized of this in season to give her warning; and her own courage and ingenuity proved adequate to the emergency. She disguised herself in sailor's

clothes, and walked boldly to the Philadelphia boat.
There she walked up and down the deck, with her
arms folded, smoking a cigar, and occasionally passing and repassing the constables who had been sent
on board in search of her. These men, having
watched till the last moment for the arrival of a colored woman answering to her description, took their
departure. The boat started, and brought the courageous mother safely to Philadelphia, where Friend
Hopper and others rejoiced over the history of her
hair-breadth escape.

A few weeks after, she went to the place where
her child had been left, and succeeded in bringing it
safely away. For a short time, her happiness seemed to be complete; but when the first flush of joy
and thankfulness had subsided, she began to be
harassed with continual fears lest she and her child
should be arrested in some evil hour, and carried
back into slavery. By unremitting industry, and
very strict economy, she strove to lay by money
enough to purchase their freedom. She had made
friends by her good conduct and obliging ways, while
her maternal affection and enterprising character excited a good deal of interest among those acquainted
with her history. Donations were occasionally added
to her earnings, and a sum was soon raised sufficient
to accomplish her favorite project. Isaac T. Hopper entered into negotiation with her master, and suc-

ceeded in obtaining manumission for her and her child.

COLONEL RIDGELEY'S SLAVE.

A slave escaped from Colonel Ridgeley, who resided in the southern part of Virginia. He went to Philadelphia, and remained there undiscovered for several years. But he was never quite free from anxiety, lest in some unlucky hour, he should be arrested and carried back to bondage. When he had laid up some money, he called upon Isaac T. Hopper to assist him in buying the free use of his own limbs. A negotiation was opened with Col. Ridgeley, who agreed to take two hundred dollars for the fugitive, and appointed a time to come to Philadelphia to arrange the business. But instead of keeping his agreement honorably, he went to that city several weeks before the specified time, watched for his bondman, seized him, and conveyed him to Friend Hopper's office. When the promised two hundred dollars were offered, he refused to accept them.

"Why, that is the sum thou hast agreed upon," said Friend Hopper.

"I know that," replied the Colonel; "but I won't take it now. He was the best servant I ever had. I can sell him for one thousand dollars in Virginia.

Under present circumstances, I will take five hundred dollars for him, and not one cent less."

After considerable discussion, Friend Hopper urged him to allow his bondman until ten o'clock next morning, to see what could be done among his friends; and he himself gave a written obligation that the man should be delivered up to him at that hour, in case he could not procure five hundred dollars to purchase his freedom.

When the master was gone, Friend Hopper said to the alarmed fugitive, "There now remains but one way for thee to obtain thy freedom. As to raising five hundred dollars, that is out of the question. But if thou wilt be prompt and resolute, and do precisely as I tell thee, I think thou canst get off safely."

"I will do anything for freedom," replied the bondman; "for I have made up my mind, come what may, that I never will go back into slavery."

"Very well then," rejoined his friend. "Don't get frightened when the right moment comes to act; but keep thy wits about thee, and do as I tell thee. Thy master will come here to-morrow at ten o'clock, according to appointment. I must deliver thee up to him, and receive back the obligation for one thousand dollars, which I have given him. Do thou stand with thy back against the door, which opens from this room into the parlor. When he has re-

turned the paper to me, open the door quickly, lock
it on the inside, and run through the parlor into the
back-yard. There is a wall there eight feet high,
with spikes at the top. Thou wilt find a clothes-
horse leaning against it, to help thee up. When
thou hast mounted, kick the clothes-horse down behind thee, drop on the other side of the wall, and be
off." The premises were then shown to him, and he
received minute directions through what alleys and
streets he had better pass, and at what house he
could find a temporary refuge.

Col. Ridgeley came the next morning, at the appointed hour, and brought a friend to stand sentinel
at the street door, lest the slave should attempt to
rush out. It did not occur to him that there was
any danger of his running *in*.

"We have not been able to raise the five hundred
dollars," said Friend Hopper; "and here is thy man,
according to agreement."

The Colonel gave back his obligation for one
thousand dollars; and the instant it left his hand,
the fugitive passed into the parlor. The master
sprang over the counter after him, but found the
door locked. Before he could get to the back yard
by another door, the wall was scaled, the clothes-
horse thrown down, and the fugitive was beyond his
reach. Of course, he returned very much disappointed and enraged; declaring his firm belief that a

trick had been played upon him purposely. After
he had given vent to his anger some little time,
Friend Hopper asked for a private interview with
him. When they were alone together in the parlor,
he said, "I admit this was an intentional trick; but
I had what seemed to me good reasons for resorting
to it. In the first place, thou didst not keep the
agreement made with me, but sought to gain an un-
fair advantage. In the next place, I knew that man
was thy own son; and I think any person who is so
unfeeling as to make traffic of his own flesh and
blood, deserves to be tricked out of the chance to do
it."

"What if he is my son?" rejoined the Virginian.
"I've as good a right to sell my own flesh and blood
as that of any other person. If I choose to do it, it
is none of your business." He opened the door, and
beckoning to his friend, who was in waiting, he said,
"Hopper admits this was all a trick to set the slave
free." Then turning to Friend Hopper, he added,
"You admit it was a trick, don't you?"

"Thou and I will talk that matter over by ourselves," he replied. "The presence of a third person
is not always convenient."

The Colonel went off in a violent passion, and
forgetting that he was not in Virginia, he rushed into
the houses of several colored people, knocked them
about, overturned their beds, and broke their furni-

ture, in search of the fugitive. Being unable to obtain any information concerning him, he cooled down considerably, and went to inform Friend Hopper that he would give a deed of manumission for two hundred dollars; but his offer was rejected.

"Why that was your own proposal!" vociferated the Colonel.

"Very true," he replied; "and I offered thee the money; but thou refused to take it."

After storming awhile, the master went off to obtain legal advice from the Hon. John Sergeant. Meanwhile, several of the colored people had entered a complaint against him for personal abuse, and damage done to their furniture. He was obliged to give bonds for his appearance at the next court, to answer their accusations. This was a grievous humiliation for a proud Virginian, who had been educated to think that colored people had no civil rights. In this unpleasant dilemma, his lawyer advised him to give a deed of manumission for one hundred and fifty dollars; promising to exert his influence to have the mortifying suits withdrawn.

The proposed terms were accepted, and the money promptly paid by the slave from his own earnings. But when Mr. Sergeant proposed that the suits for assault and battery should be withdrawn, Friend Hopper replied, "I have no authority to dismiss them."

"They will be dismissed if you advise it," rejoined the lawyer; "and if you will promise to do it, I shall be perfectly satisfied."

"These colored people have been very badly treated," answered Friend Hopper. "If the aggressor wants to settle the affair, he had better go to them and offer some equivolent for the trouble he has given."

The lawyer replied, "When he agreed to manumit the man for one hundred and fifty dollars, he expected these suits would be dismissed, of course, as a part of the bargain. What sum do you think these people will take to withdraw them?"

Friend Hopper said he thought they would do it for one hundred and fifty dollars.

"I will pay it," replied Mr. Sergeant; "for Colonel Ridgeley is very anxious to return home."

Thus the money paid for the deed of manumission was returned. Forty dollars were distributed among the colored people, to repay the damage done to their property. After some trifling incidental expenses had been deducted, the remainder was returned to the emancipated slave; who thus obtained his freedom for about fifty dollars, instead of the sum originally offered.

STOP THIEF!

About the year 1826, a Marylander, by the name
of Solomon Low, arrested a fugitive slave in Philadelphia, and took him to the office of an alderman to
obtain the necessary authority for carrying him back
into bondage. Finding the magistrate gone to dinner, they placed the colored man in the entry, while
Mr. Low and his companions guarded the door.
Some of the colored people soon informed Isaac T.
Hopper of these circumstances, and he hastened to
the office. Observing the state of things there, he
concluded it would be no difficult matter to give the
colored man a chance to escape. He stepped up to
the men at the door, and demanded in a peremptory
manner by what authority they were holding that
man in duress. Mr. Low replied, "He is my slave."

"This is strange conduct," rejoined Friend Hopper. "Who can tell whether he is thy slave or not?
What proof is there that you are not a band of kidnappers? Dost thou suppose the laws of Pennsylvania tolerate such proceedings?"

These charges arrested the attention of Mr. Low
and his companions, who turned round to answer the
speaker. The slave, seeing their backs toward him
for an instant, seized that opportunity to rush out;
and he had run two or three rods before they missed
him. They immediately raised the cry of "Stop

Thief! Stop Thief!" An Irishman, who joined in the pursuit, arrested the fugitive and brought him back to his master.

Friend Hopper remonstrated with him; saying, "The man is not a thief. They claim him for a slave, and he was running for liberty. How wouldst thou like to be made a slave?"

The kind-hearted Hibernian replied, "Then they lied; for they said he was a thief. If he is a slave, I'm sorry I stopped him. However, I will put him in as good a condition as I found him." So saying, he went near the man who had the fugitive in custody, and seized him by the collar with a sudden jerk, that threw him on the pavement. The slave instantly started, and ran at his utmost speed, again followed by the cry of "Stop Thief!" Having run some distance, and being nearly out of breath, he darted into the shop of a watch-maker, named Samuel Mason, who immediately closed and fastened his door, so that the crowd could not follow him. The fugitive passed out of the back door, and was never afterward recaptured.

The disappointed master brought an action against Samuel Mason for rescuing his slave. Charles J. Ingersoll and his brother Joseph, two accomplished lawyers of Philadelphia, conducted the trial for him, with zeal and ingenuity worthy of a better cause. Isaac T. Hopper was summoned as a witness, and in the course of examination he was asked what course members of the Society of Friends adopted when a fugitive slave came to them. He replied, "I am not willing to answer for any one but myself."

"Well," said Mr. Ingersoll, "what would *you* do in such a case? Would you deliver him to his master?"

"Indeed I would not!" answered the Friend. "My conscience would not permit me to do it. It would be a great crime; because it would be disobedience to my own dearest convictions of right. I should never expect to enjoy an hour of peace afterward. I would do for a fugitive slave whatever I should like to have done for myself, under similar circumstances. If he asked my protection, I would extend it to him to the utmost of my power. If he was hungry, I would feed him. If he was naked, I would clothe him. If he needed advice, I would give such as I thought would be most beneficial to him."

The cause was tried before Judge Bushrod Washington, nephew of General Washington. Though a slaveholder himself, he manifested no partiality during the trial, which continued several days, with able arguments on both sides. The counsel for the claimant maintained that Samuel Mason prevented the master from regaining his slave, by shutting his door, and refusing to open it. The counsel for the defendant replied that there was much valuable and brittle property in the watchmaker's shop, which would have been liable to robbery and destruction, if a promiscuous mob had been allowed to rush in. Judge Washington summed up the evidence very clearly to the jury, who after retiring for deliberation a considerable time, returned into court, declaring that they could not agree upon a verdict, and probably never should agree. They were ordered out again, and kept together till the court adjourned, when they were dismissed.

At the succeeding term, the case was tried again, with renewed energy and zeal. But the jury, after being kept together ten days, were discharged without being able to agree upon a verdict. Some, who were originally in favor of the defendant, became weary of their long confinement, and consented to go over to the slaveholder's side; but one of them, named Benjamin Thaw, declared that he would eat his Christmas dinner in the jury-room, before he would consent to such a flagrant act of injustice.

His patience held out till the court adjourned. Consequently a third trial became necessary; and the third jury brought in a verdict in favor of the watchmaker.

The expenses of these suits were estimated at seventeen hundred dollars. Solomon Low was in limited circumstances; and this expenditure in prosecuting an innocent man was said to have caused his failure soon after.

THE DISGUISED SLAVEHOLDER.

A colored woman and her son were slaves to a man in East-Jersey. She had two sons in Philadelphia, who had been free several years, and her present master was unacquainted with them. In 1827, she and her younger son escaped, and went to live in Philadelphia. Her owner, knowing she had free sons in that city, concluded as a matter of course that she had sought their protection. A few weeks after her flight, he followed her, and having assumed Quaker costume, went to the house of one of her sons. He expressed great interest for the woman, and said he wished to obtain an interview with her for her benefit. His friendly garb and kind language completely deceived her son, and he told him that his mother was then staying at his brother's house, which was not far off. Having obtained this information, the slaveholder procured a constable and immediately went to the place described. Fortunately, the son was at home, and it being warm weather he sat near the open door. The mother was seated at a chamber window, and saw a constable approaching the house, with a gentleman in Quaker costume, whom she at once recognized as her master. She gave the alarm to her son, who instantly shut the door and fastened it. The master, being refused admittance, placed a guard there, while he went to procure a search-warrant. These proceedings attracted the attention of colored neighbors, and a crowd soon gathered about the house. They seized the man who guarded the door, and held him fast, while the woman and her fugitive son rushed out. It was dusk, and the uncertain light favored their escape. They ran about a mile, and took refuge with a colored family in Locust-street. The watchman soon got released from the colored people who held him, and succeeded in tracing the woman to her new retreat, where he again mounted guard. The master returned meanwhile, and having learned the circumstances, went to the magistrate to obtain another warrant to search the house in Locust-street.

At this stage of the affair, Friend Hopper was summoned, and immediately went to the rescue, accompanied by one of his sons, about sixteen years old. He found the woman and her son stowed away in a closet, exceedingly terrified. He assured them they would be quite as safe on the mantel-piece, as they would be in that closet; that their being found concealed would be regarded as the best evidence that they were the persons sought for. Knowing it was dangerous for them to remain in that house, he told them of a plan he had formed, on the spur of the moment. After giving them careful instructions how to proceed, he left them and requested that the street door might be opened for him. A crowd immediately rushed in, as he had foreseen would be the case. He affected to be greatly displeased, and ordered the men of the house to turn all the intruders out. They obeyed him; and among the number turned out were the two fugitives. It was dark, and in the confusion, the watchman on guard could not distingush them among the multitude.

Friend Hopper had hastily consigned them to his son, with instructions to take them to his house; and the watchman, seeing that he himself remained about the premises, took it for granted that the fugitives had not escaped.

As soon as it was practicable, Friend Hopper returned home, where he found the woman and her son in a state of great agitation. He immediately sent her to a place of greater safety, and gave the son a letter to a farmer thirty miles up in the country. He went directly to the river Schuylkill, but was afraid to cross the bridge, lest some person should be stationed there to arrest him. He accordingly walked along the margin of the river till he found a small boat, in which he crossed the stream. Following the directions he had received, he arrived at the farmer's house, where he had a kindly welcome, and obtained employment.

The master being unable to recapture his slaves,

called upon Isaac T. Hopper to inquire if he knew anything about them. He coolly replied, "I believe they are doing very well. From what I hear, I judge it will not be necessary to give thyself any further trouble on their account."

"There is no use in trying to capture a runaway slave in Philadelphia," rejoined the master. "I believe the devil himself could not catch them when they once get here."

"That is very likely," answered Friend Hopper. "But I think he would have less difficulty in catching the masters ; being so much more familiar with them."

Sixty dollars had already been expended in vain ; and the slave-holder, having relinquished all hope of tracing the fugitives, finally agreed to manumit the woman for fifty dollars, and her son for seventy-five dollars. These sums were advanced by two citizens friendly to the colored people, and the emancipated slaves repaid them by faithful service.

THE SLAVE OF DR. RICH.

In the autumn of 1828, Dr. Rich of Maryland came to Philadelphia with his wife, who was the daughter of an Episcopal clergyman in that city, by the name of Wiltbank. She brought a slave to wait upon her, intending to remain at her father's until after the birth of her child, which was soon expected to take place. When they had been there a few months, the slave was informed by some colored acquaintance that she was free in consequence of being brought to Philadelphia. She called to consult with Isaac T. Hopper, and seemed very much disappointed to hear that a residence of six months was necessary to entitle her to freedom; that her master was doubtless aware of that circumstance, and would probably guard against it.

After some minutes of anxious reflection, she said, "Then there is nothing left for me to do but to run away; for I am determined never to go back to Maryland."

Friend Hopper inquired whether she thought it would be right to leave her mistress without any one to attend upon her, in the situation she then was. She replied that she felt no scruples on that point, for her master was wealthy, and could hire as many servants as he pleased. Finding her mind entirely made up on the subject, he gave her such instructions as seemed suited to the occasion.

The next morning she was not to be found; and Dr. Rich went in search of her, with his father-in-law, Mr. Wiltbank. Having frightened some ignorant colored people where she visited, by threats of prosecuting them for harboring a runaway, they confessed that she had gone from their house to Isaac T. Hopper. Mr. Wiltbank accordingly waited upon him, and after relating the circumstances of the case, inquired whether he had seen the fugitive. In reply, he made a frank statement of the interview he had with her, and of her fixed determination to obtain her freedom. The clergyman reproached her with ingratitude, and said she had always been treated with great kindness.

"The woman herself gives a very different account of her treatment," replied Friend Hopper; "but be that as it may, I cannot blame her for wishing to obtain her liberty."

He asked if Friend Hopper knew where she then was; and he answered that he did not. "Could you find her, if you tried?" inquired he.

"I presume I could do it very easily," rejoined the Quaker. "The colored people never wish to secrete themselves from me; for they know I am their true friend."

Mr. Wiltbank then said, "If you will cause her to be brought to your house, Dr. Rich and myself will come here at eight o'clock this evening. You will then hear her ask her master's pardon, acknowledge the kindness with which she has always been treated, and express her readiness to go home with him."

Friend Hopper indignantly replied, "I have no doubt that fear might induce her to profess all thou hast said. But what trait hast thou discovered in my character, that leads thee to suppose I would be such a hypocrite as to betray the confidence this poor woman has reposed in me, by placing her in the power of her master, in the way thou hast proposed ?"

Mr. Wiltbank then requested that a message might be conveyed to the woman, exhorting her to return, and promising that no notice whatever would be taken of her offence.

"She shall be informed of thy message, if that will be any satisfaction to thee," replied Friend Hopper; "but I am perfectly sure she will never voluntarily return into slavery."

Dr. Rich and Mr. Wiltbank called in the evening, and were told the message had been delivered to the woman, but she refused to return. "She is in your house now," exclaimed Dr. Rich. "I can prove it; and if you don't let me see her, I will commence a suit against you to-morrow, for harboring my slave."

"I believe Solomon Low resides in thy neighborhood," said Friend Hopper. "Art thou acquainted with him ?"

Being answered in the affirmative, he said, "Solomon Low brought three such suits as thou hast threatened. They cost him seventeen hundred dollars, which I heard he was unable to pay. But perhaps thou hast seventeen hundred dollars to spare ?"

Dr. Rich answered that he could well afford to lose that sum.

"Very well," rejoined his opponent. "There are lawyers enough who need it, and still more who would be glad to have it."

Finding it alike impossible to coax or intimidate the resolute Quaker, they withdrew. About eleven o'clock at night, some of the family informed Friend Hopper that there was a man continually walking back and forth in front of the house. He went out and accosted him thus: "Friend, art thou watching my house?" When the stranger replied that he was, he said, "It is very kind in thee; but I really do not think there is any occasion for thy services. I am quite satisfied with the watchmen employed by the public."

The man answered gruffly, "I have taken my stand, and I intend to keep it."

Friend Hopper told him he had no objection; and he was about to re-enter the house, when he observed Dr. Rich, who was so wrapped up in a large cloak, that at first he did not recognize him. He exclaimed, "Why doctor, art thou here! Is it possible thou art parading the streets so late in th night, at this cold season of the year? Now, from motives of kindness, I do assure thee thy slave is not in my house. To save thee from exposing thy health

by watching at this inclement season, I will give thee
leave to search the house."

The doctor replied, "I shall obtain a warrant in
the morning, and search it with the proper officer."

"There appear to be several on the watch," said
Friend Hopper ; "and it surely is not necessary for all
of them to be out in the cold at the same time. If
thou wilt be responsible that nothing shall be stolen,
thou art welcome to use my parlor as a watch-
house." This offer was declined with freezing civili-
ty, and Friend Hopper returned to his dwelling.
Passing through the kitchen, he observed two colored domestics talking together in an under tone,
apparently planning something which made them
very merry. Judging from some words he over-
heard, that they had a mischievous scheme on
foot, he resolved to watch their movements without
letting them know that he noticed them. One of
them put on an old cloak and bonnet, opened the
front door cautiously, looked up the street and down
the street, but saw nobody. The watchers had seen
the dark face the moment it peeped out, and they
were lying in ambush to observe her closely. After
a minute of apparent hesitation, she rushed into the
street and ran with all speed. They joined in hot
pursuit, and soon overtook her. She pretended to
be greatly alarmed, and called aloud for a watchman. The offenders were arrested and brought back

to the house with the girl. Friend Hopper explained
that these men had been watching his house, supposing a fugitive slave to be secreted there; and that
they had mistaken one of his domestics for the person they were in search of. After laughing a little
at the joke practised upon them, he proposed that
they should be set at liberty; and they were accordingly released.

The next morning, a soon as it was light, he invited the watchers to come in and warm themselves;
but they declined. After sunrise, they all dispersed,
except two. When breakfast was ready, he urged
them to come in and partake; telling them that one
could keep guard while the other was eating. But
they replied that Dr. Rich had ordered them to hold
no communication with him.

Being firmly persuaded that the slave was in the
house, they kept sentry several days and nights.
For fear she might escape by the back way, a messenger was sent to Mr. Warrence, who occupied a
building in the rear, offering to pay him for his trouble if he would watch the premises in that direction.
His wife happened to overhear the conversation; and
having a pitcher of scalding water in her hand, she
ran out saying, "Do you propose to hire my husband to watch neighbor Hopper's premises for a runaway slave? Go about your business! or I will
throw this in your face."

When Dr. Rich called again, he was received politely, and the first inquiry was how he had succeeded in his efforts to procure a search-warrant. He replied, "The magistrate refused to grant one."

"Perhaps Joseph Reed, the Recorder, would oblige thee in that matter," said Friend Hopper.

The answer was, "I have been to him, and he declines to interfere."

It was then suggested that it might be well to retain a lawyer with a portion of the seventeen hundred dollars he said he had to spare.

"I have been to Mr. Broome," rejoined the doctor. "He tells me that you understand the law in such cases as well as he does; and he advises me to let the matter alone."

"I will give thee permission to search my house," said Friend Hopper; "and I have more authority in that matter than any magistrate, judge, or lawyer, in the city."

"That is very gentlemanly," replied the doctor; "but I infer from it that the woman is not in your house."

He was again assured that she was not; and they fell into some general discourse on the subject of slavery. "Suppose you came to Maryland and lost your horse," said the Doctor. "If you called upon me, and I told you that I knew where he was, but would not inform you, would you consider yourself

treated kindly ?"   "In such a case, I should not consider myself well treated," replied Friend Hopper.
" But in this part of the country, we make a distinction between horses and men.   We believe that human beings have souls."

"That makes no difference," rejoined the Doctor.
"You confess that you could find my slave if you
were so disposed; and I consider it your duty to tell
me where she is."   "I will do it when I am of the
same opinion," replied Friend Hopper; "but till
then thou must excuse me."

The fugitive was protected by a colored man named Hill, who soon obtained a situation for her as servant in a respectable country family, where she was
kindly treated.   In the course of a year or two, she
returned to Philadelphia, married a steady industrious man, and lived very comfortably.

Mr. Hill had a very revengeful temper.   One of
his colored neighbors brought suits against him for
criminal conduct, and recovered heavy damages.
From that time he seemed to hate people of his own
complexion, and omitted no opportunity to injure
them.   The woman he befriended, when he was in a
better state of mind, had been married nine or ten
years, and had long ceased to think of danger, when
he formed the wicked project of making a little
money by betraying her to her master.   Accordingly
he sought her residence accompanied by one of those

wretches who make a business of capturing slaves. When he entered her humble abode, he found her busy at the wash-tub. Rejoiced to see the man who had rendered her such essential service in time of need, she threw her arms about his neck, exclaiming, "O, uncle Hill, how glad I am to see you!" She hastily set aside her tub, wiped up the floor, and thinking there was nothing in the house good enough for her benefacter, she went out to purchase some little luxuries. Hill recommended a particular shop, and proposed to accompany her. The slave-hunter, who had been left in the street, received a private signal, and the moment she entered the shop, he pounced upon her. Before her situation could be made known to Isaac T. Hopper, she was removed to Baltimore. The last he ever heard of her she was in prison there, awaiting her day of sale, when she was to be transported to New-Orleans.

He used to say he did not know which was the most dificult for his mind to conceive of, the cruel depravity manifested by the ignorant colored man, or the unscrupulous selfishness of the slaveholder, a man of education, a husband and a father, who could consent to use such a tool for such a purpose.

Many more naratives of similar character might be added; for I think he estimated at more than one thousand the number of cases in which he had been employed for fugitives, in one way or another, during his forty years' residence in Philadelphia. But enough have been told to illustrate the active benevolence, uncompromising boldness, and ready wit, which characterized this friend of humanity. His accurate knowledge of all laws connected with slavery was so proverbial, that magistrates and lawyers were generally averse to any collision with him on such subjects.

In 1810, Benjamin Donahue of Delaware applied to Mr. Barker, mayor of Philadelphia, to assist him in recovering a fugitive, with whose place of residence he was perfectly sure Isaac T. Hopper was acquainted. After a brief correspondence with Friend Hopper, the mayor said to Mr. Donahue, "We had better drop this business, like a hot potato; for Mr. Hopper knows more law in such cases as this, than you and I put together."

He would often resort to the most unexpected expedients. Upon one occasion, a slave case was brought before Judge Rush, brother of Dr. Benjamin Rush. It seemed likely to terminate in favor of the slaveholder; but Friend Hopper thought he observed that the judge wavered a little. He seized that moment to inquire, "Hast thou not recently published a legal opinion, in which it is distinctly stated that thou wouldst never seek to sustain a human law, if thou wert convinced that it conflicted with any law in the Bible?"

"I did publish such a statement," replied Judge Rush; "and I am ready to abide by it; for in all cases, I consider the divine law above the human."

Friend Hopper drew from his pocket a small Bible, which he had brought into court for the express purpose, and read in loud distinct tones the following verses: "Thou shalt not deliver unto his master the servant which is escaped from his master unto thee: He shall dwell with thee, even among you, in that place which he shall choose, in one of thy gates, where it liketh him best: thou shalt not oppress him." Deut. 23: 15, 16.

The slaveholder smiled; supposing this appeal to old Hebrew law would be considered as little applicable to modern times, as the command to stone a man to death for picking up sticks on the Sabbath. But when the judge asked for the book, read the sentence for himself, seemed impressed by it, and adjourned the decision of the case, he walked out of the court-house muttering, "I believe in my soul the old fool *will* let him off on that ground." And sure enough, the slave was discharged.

Friend Hopper's quickness in slipping through loop-holes, and dodging round corners, rendered him exceedingly troublesome and provoking to slaveholders. He often kept cases pending in court three or four years, till the claimants were completely wearied out, and ready to settle on any terms. His acute perception of the slightest flaw in a document, or imperfection in evidence, always attracted notice in the courts he attended. Judges and lawyers often remarked to him, "Mr. Hopper, it is a great pity you were not educated for the legal profession. You have such a judicial mind." Mr. William Lewis, an eminent lawyer, offered him every facility for studying the profession. "Come to my office and use my library whenever you please," said he ; "or I will obtain a clerkship in the courts for you, if you prefer that. Your mind is peculiarly adapted to legal investigation, and if you would devote yourself to it, you might become a judge before long."

But Friend Hopper could never overcome his scruples about entering on a career of worldly ambition. He thought he had better keep humble, and resist temptations that might lead him out of the plainness and simplicity of the religious Society to which he belonged.

As for the colored people of Philadelphia, they believed in his infallibility, as devout Catholics believe in the Pope. They trusted him, and he trusted them ; and it is remarkable in how few instances he found his confidence misplaced. The following anec dote will illustrate the nature of the relation ex isting between him and that much abused race. Prince Hopkins, a wood-sawyer of Philadelphia, was claimed as a fugitive slave by John Kinsmore of Baltimore. When Friend Hopper went to the magistrate's office to inquire into the affair, he found the poor fellow in tears. He asked for a private interview, and the alderman gave his consent. When they were alone, Prince confessed that he was the slave in question. In the course of his narrative, it appeared that he had been sent into Pennsylvania by his mistress, and had resided there with a relative of hers two years. Friend Hopper told him to dry up his tears, for it was in his power to protect him. When he returned to the office, he informed the magistrate that Prince Hopkins was a free man; having resided in Pennsylvania, with the consent of his mistress, a much longer time than the law required. Mr. Kinsmore was irritated, and demanded that the colored man should be imprisoned till he could obtain legal advice.

"Let him go and finish the wood he was sawing," said Friend Hopper. "I will be responsible for his appearance whenever he is wanted. If the magistrate will give me a commitment, Prince will call at my house after he has finished sawing his wood, and I will send him to jail with it. He can remain there, until the facts I have stated are clearly proved."

The slave-holder and his lawyer seemed to regard this proposition as an insult. They railed at Friend Hopper for his "impertinent interference," and for the absurd idea of trusting "that nigger" under such circumstances.

He replied, "I would rather trust 'that nigger,' as you call him, than either of you." So saying, he marched off with the magistrate's mittimus in his pocket.

When Prince Hopkins had finished his job of sawing, he called for the commitment, and carried it to the jailor, who locked him up. Satisfactory evidence of his freedom was soon obtained, and he was discharged.

The colored people appeared to better advantage with their undoubted friend, than they possibly could have done where a barrier of prejudice existed. They were not afraid to tell him their experiences in their own way, with natural pathos, here and there dashed with fun. A fine-looking, athletic fugitive, telling him his story one day, said, "When I first run away, I met some people who were dreadful afraid I could n't take care of myself. But thinks I to myself I took care of master and myself too for a long spell; and I guess I can make out." With a roguish expression laughing all over his face, he added, "I don't look as if I was suffering for a master; do I, Mr. Hopper?"

Though slaveholders had abundant reason to dread Isaac T. Hopper, as they would a blister of Spanish flies, yet he had no hardness of feeling toward them, or even toward kidnappers; hateful as he deemed the system, which produced them both.

In 1801, a sober industrious family of free colored people, living in Pennsylvania on the borders of Maryland, were attacked in the night by a band of kidnappers. The parents were aged, and needed the services of their children for support. Knowing that the object of the marauders was to carry them off and sell them to slave speculators, the old father defended them to the utmost of his power. In the struggle, he was wounded by a pistol, and one of his daughters received a shot, which caused her death. One of the sons, who was very ill in bed, was beaten and bruised till he was covered with blood. But mangled and crippled as he was, he contrived to drag himself to a neighboring barn, and hide himself under the straw.

If such lawless violence had been practised upon any white citizens, the Executive of Pennsylvania would have immediately offered a high reward for the apprehension of the aggressors; but the victims belonged to a despised caste, and nothing was done to repair their wrongs. Friend Hopper felt the blood boil in his veins when he heard of this cruel outrage, and his first wish was to have the offenders punished; but as soon as he had time to reflect, he said, "I cannot find it in my heart to urge this subject upon the notice of the Executive; for death

would be the penalty if those wretches were con
victed."

There were many highly respectable individuals
among the colored people of Philadelphia. Richard
Allen, who had been a slave, purchased freedom
with the proceeds of his own industry. He married
and established himself as a shoemaker in that city
where he acquired considerable property, and built a
three-story brick house. He was the principal agent
in organizing the first congregation of colored people
in Philadelphia, and was their pastor to the day of
his death, without asking or receiving any compensation. During the latter part of his life, he was
Bishop of their Methodist Episcopal Church. Ab-
salom Jones, a much respected colored man, was
his colleague. In 1793, when the yellow fever was
raging, it was extremely difficult to procure at-
tendants for the sick on any terms; and the few
who would consent to render service, demanded ex-
orbitant prices. But Bishop Allen and Rev. Mr.
Jones never hesitated to go wherever they could be
useful; and with them the compensation was always
a secondary consideration. When the pestilence had
abated, the mayor sent them a certificate expressing
his approbation of their conduct. But even these
men, whose worth commanded respect, were not safe
from the legalized curse that rests upon their hunted
race. A Southern speculator arrested Bishop Allen,

and claimed him as a fugitive slave, whom he had
bought running. The constable employed to serve
the warrant was ashamed to drag the good man
through the streets; and he merely said, in a respectful tone, "Mr. Allen, you will soon come down
to Alderman Todd's office, will you?"

The fugitive, whom they were seeking, had absconded only four years previous; and everybody in
Philadelphia knew that Richard Allen had been
living there more than twenty years. Yet the speculator and his sons swore unblushingly that he was
the identical slave they had purchased. Mr. Allen
thought he ought to have some redress for this outrage; "For," said he, "if it had not been for the
kindness of the officer, I might have been dragged
through the streets like a felon."

Isaac T. Hopper was consulted, and a civil suit
commenced. Eight hundred dollars bail was demanded, and the speculator, being unable to procure
it, was lodged in the debtor's prison. When he had
been there three months, Mr. Allen caused him to be
discharged; saying he did not wish to persecute the
man, but merely to teach him not to take up free
people again, for the purpose of carrying them into
slavery.

The numerous instances of respectability among
the colored people were doubtless to be attributed in
part to the protecting influence extended over them

by the Quakers. But even in those days, the Society of Friends were by no means all free from prejudice against color; and in later times, I think they have not proved themselves at all superior to other sects in their feelings and practice on this subject. Friend Hopper, Joseph Carpenter, and the few wh resemble them in this respect, are *exceptions* to th general character of modern Quakers, not the *rule*. The following very characteristic anecdote shows how completely Isaac was free from prejudice on account of complexion. It is an unusual thing to see a colored Quaker; for the African temperament is fervid and impressible, and requires more exciting forms of religion. David Maps and his wife, a very worthy couple, were the only colored members of the Yearly Meeting to which Isaac T. Hopper belonged. On the occasion of the annual gathering in Philadelphia, they came with other members of the Society to share the hospitality of his house. A question arose in the family whether Friends of white complexion would object to eating with them. "Leave that to me," said the master of the household. Accordingly when the time arrived, he announced it thus: "Friends, dinner is now ready David Maps and his wife will come with me; and a I like to have all accommodated, those who object to dining with them can wait till they have done." The guests smiled, and all seated themselves at the table.

The conscientiousness so observable in several anecdotes of Isaac's boyhood was strikingly manifested in his treatment of a colored printer, named Kane. This man was noted for his profane swearing. Friend Hopper had expostulated with him concerning this bad habit, without producing the least effect. One day, he encountered him in the street, pouring forth a volley of terrible oaths, enough to make one shudder. Believing him incurable by gentler means, he took him before a magistrate, who fined him for blasphemy.

He did not see the man again for a long time; but twenty years afterward, when he was standing at his door, Kane passed by. The Friend's heart was touched by his appearance; for he looked old, feeble, and poor. He stepped out, shook hands with him, and said in kindly tones, "Dost thou remember me, and how I caused thee to be fined for swearing?"

"Yes, indeed I do," he replied. "I remember how many dollars I paid, as well as if it were but yesterday."

"Did it do thee any good;" inquired Friend Hopper.

"Never a bit," answered he. "It only made me mad to have my money taken from me."

The poor man was invited to walk into the house. The interest was calculated on the fine, and every

cent repaid to him. "I meant it for thy good," said
the benevolent Quaker; "and I am sorry that I only
provoked thee." Kane's countenance changed at
once, and tears began to flow. He took the money
with many thanks, and was never again heard to
swear.

Friend Hopper's benevolence was by no means
confined to colored people. Wherever there was
good to be done, his heart and hand were ready.
From various anecdotes in proof of this, I select the
following.

JOHN Mc GRIER.

John was an Irish orphan, whose parents died of
yellow fever, when he was very young. He obtained a scanty living by doing errands for cartmen. In
the year 1800, when he was about fourteen years
old, there was a long period during which he could
obtain scarcely any employment. Being without
friends, and in a state of extreme destitution, he was
tempted to enter a shop and steal two dollars from
the drawer. He was pursued and taken. Isaac T.
Hopper, who was one of the inspectors of the prison
at that time, saw a crowd gathered, and went to inquire the cause. The poor boy's history was soon
told. Friend Hopper liked the expression of his
countenance, and pitied his forlorn condition. When
he was brought up for trial, he accompanied him,

and pleaded with the judge in his favor. He urged
that the poor child's education had been entirely
neglected, and consequently he was more to be pitied
than blamed. If sent to prison, he would in all probability become hardened, if not utterly ruined. He
said if the judge would allow him to take charge of
the lad, he would promise to place him in good
hands, where he would be out of the way of temptation. The judge granted his request, and John was
placed in prison merely for a few days, till Friend
Hopper could provide for him. He proposed to his
father to have the boy bound to him. The old gentleman hesitated at first, on account of his neglected
education and wild way of living; but pity for the
orphan overcame his scruples, and he agreed to take
him. John lived with him till he was twenty-one
years of age, and was remarkably faithful and industrious. But about two years after, a neighbor
came one night to arrest him for stealing a horse.
Old Mr. Hopper assured him it was not possible
John had done such a thing; that during all the time
he had lived in his family he had proved himself entirely honest and trustworthy. The neighbor replied
that his horse had been taken to Philadelphia and
sold; and the ferryman from Woodbury was ready
to swear that the animal was brought over by Hopper's John, as he was generally called. John was in
bed, but was called up to answer the accusation

He did not attempt to deny it, but gave up the money at once, and kept repeating that he did know what made him do it. He was dreadfully ashamed and distressed. He begged that Friend Isaac would not come to see him in prison, for he could not look him the face. His anguish of mind was so great, that when the trial came on, he was emaciated almost to a skeleton. Old Mr. Hopper went into court and stated the adverse circumstances of his early life, and his exemplary conduct during nine years that he had lived in his family. He begged that he might be fined instead of imprisoned, and offered to pay the fine himself. The proposition was accepted, and the kind old man took the culprit home.

This lenient treatment completely subdued the last vestige of evil habits acquired in childhood. He was humble and grateful in the extreme, and always steady and industrious. He conducted with great propriety ever afterward, and established such a character for honesty, that the neighbors far and wide trusted him to carry their produce to market, receiving a small commission for his trouble. Eventually, he came to own a small house and farm, where he lived in much comfort and respectability. He always looked up to Isaac as the friend who had early raised him from a downward and slippery path; and he was never weary of manifesting gratitude by every little attention he could devise.

LEVI BUTLER.

Some one having told Friend Hopper of an apprentice who was cruelly treated, he caused investigation to be made, and took the lad under his own protection. As he was much bent upon going to sea, he was placed in a respectable boarding-house for sailors, till a fitting opportunity could be found to gratify his inclination. One day, a man in the employ of this boarding-house brought a bill to be paid for the lad. He was very ragged, but his manners were those of a gentleman, and his conversation showed that he had been well educated. His appearance excited interest in Friend Hopper's mind, and he inquired into his history. He said his name was Levi Butler; that he was of German extraction, and had been a wealthy merchant in Baltimore, of the firm of Butler and Magruder. He married a widow, who had considerable property, and several children. After her death, he failed in business, and gave up all his own property, but took the precaution to secure all her property to her children. His creditors were angry, and tried various ways to compel him to pay them with his wife's money. He was mprisoned a long time. He petitioned the Legislature for release, and the committee before whom the case was brought made a report in his favor, highly applauding his integrity in not involving his own affairs with the property belonging to his wife's children, who had been intrusted to his care. Poverty and persecution had broken down his spirits, and when he was discharged from prison he left Baltimore and tried to obtain a situation as clerk in Philadelphia. He did not succeed in procuring employment. His clothes became thread-bare, and he had no money to purchase a new suit. In this situation, some people to whom he applied for employment treated him as if he were an impostor. In a state of despair he went one day to drown himself. But when he had put some heavy stones in his pocket to make him sink rapidly, he seemed to hear a voice calling to him to forbear; and looking up, he saw a man watching him. He hurried away to avoid questions, and passing by a sailor's boarding-house, he went in and offered to wait upon the boarders for his food. They took him upon those terms; and the gentleman who had been accustomed to ride in his own carriage, and be waited upon by servants, now roasted oysters and went of errands for common seamen. He was in this forlorn situation, when accident introduced him to Friend Hopper's notice. He immediately furnished him with a suit of warm clothes; for the weather was cold, and his garments thin. He employed him to post up his account-books, and finding that he did it in a very perfect manner, he induced several of his friends to employ him in a similar way.

A brighter day was dawning for the unfortunate man, and perhaps he might have attained to comfortable independence, if his health had not failed. But he had taken severe colds by thin clothing and exposure to inclement weather. A rapid consumption came on, and he was soon entirely unable to work. Under these circumstances, the best Friend Hopper could do for him was to secure peculiar privileges at the alms-house, and surround him with all the little comforts that help to alleviate illness. He visited him very often, until the day of his death, and his sympathy and kind attentions were always received with heartfelt gratitude.

THE MUSICAL BOY.

ONE day when Friend Hopper visited the prison, he found a dark-eyed lad with a very bright expressive countenance His right side was palsied, so that the arm hung down useless. Attracted by his intelligent face, he entered into conversation with him, and found that he had been palsied from infancy. He had been sent forth friendless into the world rom an alms-house in Maryland. In Philadelphia, he had been committed to prison as a vagrant, because he drew crowds about him in the street by his wonderful talent of imitating a hand-organ, merely by whistling tunes through his fingers. Friend Hopper, who had imbibed the Quaker idea that music was a useless and frivolous pursuit, said to the boy, "Didst thou not know it was wrong to spend thy time in that idle manner?"

With ready frankness the young prisoner replied, "No, I did not; and I should like to hear how *you* can prove it to be wrong. God has given you sound limbs. Half of my body is paralyzed, and it is impossible for me to work as others do. It has pleased God to give me a talent for music. I do no harm with it. It gives pleasure to myself and others, and enables me to gain a few coppers to buy my bread. I should like to have you show me wherein it is wrong."

Without attempting to do so, Friend Hopper suggested that perhaps he had been committed to prison on account of producing noise and confusion in the streets.

"I make no riot," rejoined the youth. "I try to please people by my tunes; and if the crowd around me begin to be noisy, I quietly walk off."

Struck with the good sense and sincerity of these answers, Friend Hopper said to the jailor, "Thou mayest set this lad at liberty. I will be responsible for it."

The jailer relying on his well-known character, and his intimacy with Robert Wharton, the mayor, did not hesitate to comply with his request. At that moment, the mayor himself came in sight, and Friend Hopper said to the lad, "Step into the next room, and play some of thy best tunes till I come."

"What's this?" said Mr. Wharton. "Have you got a hand-organ here!"

"Yes," replied Friend Hopper; "and I will show it to thee. It is quite curious."

At first, the mayor could not believe that the sounds he had heard were produced by a lad merely whistling through his fingers. He thought them highly agreeable, and asked to have the tunes repeated.

"The lad was committed to prison for no other offence than making that noise, which seems to thee so pleasant," said Friend Hopper. "I dare say thou wouldst like to make it thyself, if thou couldst. I have taken the liberty to discharge him."

"Very well," rejoined the mayor, with a smile. "You have done quite right, Friend Isaac. You may go, my lad. I shall not trouble you. But try not to collect crowds about the streets."

"That I cannot help," replied the youth. "The crowds *will* come, when I whistle for them; and I get coppers by collecting crowds. But I promise you I will try to avoid their making any riot or confusion."

MARY NORRIS.

A stout healthy woman, named Mary Norris was continually taken up as a vagrant, or committed for petty larceny. As soon as she was discharged from the penalty of one misdemeanor, she was committed for another. One day, Friend Hopper, who was then inspector, said to her, "Well, Mary, thy time is out next week. Dost thou think thou shalt come back again?"

"Yes," she replied sullenly.

"Dost thou *like* to come back?" inquired he.

"No, to be sure I don't," rejoined the prisoner. "But I've no doubt I *shall* come back before the month is out."

"Why dost thou not make a resolution to behave better?" said the kindly inspector.

"What use would it be?" she replied. "You would n't take me into your family. The doctor would n't take me into his family. No respectable person would have anything to do with me. My associates *must* be such acquaintances as I make here. If they steal, I am taken up for it; no matter whether I am guilty or not. I am an old convict, and nobody believes what I say. O, yes, I shall come back again. To be sure I shall come back," she repeated bitterly.

Her voice and manner excited Friend Hopper's

compassion, and he thus addressed her : "If I will get a place for thee in some respectable family where they will be kind to thee, wilt thou give me thy word that thou wilt be honest and steady, and try to do thy duty."

Her countenance brightened, and she eagerly anwered, "Yes I *will!* And thank God and you too, the longest day I have to live."

He exerted his influence in her behalf, and procured a situation for her as head-nurse at the almshouse. She was well contented there, and behaved with great propriety. Seventeen years afterward, when Friend Hopper had not seen her for a long time, he called to inquire about her, and was informed that during all those years, she had been an honest, sober, and useful woman. She was rejoiced to see him again, and expressed lively gratitude, for the quiet and comfortable life she enjoyed through his agency.

THE MAGDALEN.

Upon one occasion, Friend Hopper entered a complaint against an old woman, who had presided over an infamous house for many years. She was tried, and sentenced to several months imprisonment. He went to see her several times, and talked very seriously with her concerning the errors of her life. Finding that his expostulations made some impression, he asked if she felt willing to amend her ways. "Oh, I should be thankful to do it!" she exclaimed. "But who would trust me? What can I do to earn an honest living? Everybody curses me, or makes game of me. How *can* I be a better woman, if I try ever so hard?"

"I will give thee a chance to amend thy life," he replied; "and if thou dost not, it shall be thy own fault."

He went round among the wealthy Quakers, and by dint of great persuasion he induced one to let her a small tenement at very low rent. A few others agreed to purchase some humble furniture, and a quantity of thread, needles, tape, and buttons, to furnish a small shop. The poor old creature's heart overflowed with gratitude, and it was her pride to keep everything very neat and orderly. There she lived contented and comfortable the remainder of her days, and became much respected in the neighborhood. The tears often came to her eyes when she saw Friend Hopper. "God bless that good man!" she would say. "He has been the salvation of me."

THE UNCOMPLIMENTARY INVITATION.

A preacher of the Society of Friends felt impressed with the duty of calling a meeting for vicious people; and Isaac T. Hopper was appointed to collect an audience. In the course of this mission, he knocked at the door of a very infamous house. A gentleman who was acquainted with him was passing by, and he stopped to say, "Friend Hopper, you have mistaken the house."

"No, I have not," he replied.

"But that is a house of notorious ill fame," said the gentleman.

"I know it," rejoined he; "but nevertheless I have business here."

His acquaintance looked surprised, but passed on without further query. A colored girl came to the door. To the inquiry whether her mistress was within, she answered in the affirmative. "Tell her I wish to see her," said Friend Hopper. The girl was evidently astonished at a visitor in Quaker costume, and of such grave demeanor; but she went and did the errand. A message was returned that her mistress was engaged and could not see any one. "Where is she?" he inquired. The girl replied that she was up-stairs. "I will go to her," said the importunate messenger.

The mistress of the house heard him, and leaning over the balustrade of the stairs, she screamed out, "What do you want with me, sir?"

In very loud tones he answered, "James Simpson, a minister of the Society of Friends, has appointed a meeting to be held this afternoon, in Penrose store,

Almond-street. It is intended for publicans, sinners, and harlots. I want thee to be there, and bring thy whole household with thee. Wilt thou come?"

She promised that she would; and he afterward saw her at the meeting melted into tears by the direct and affectionate preaching.

THEFT FROM NECESSITY.

One day, when the family were in the midst of washing, a man called at Isaac T. Hopper's house to buy soap fat, and was informed they had none to sell. A minute after he had passed out, the domestic came running in to say that he had stolen some of the children's clothes from the line. Friend Hopper followed him quickly, and called out, "Dost thou want to buy some soap-fat? Come back if thou dost."

When the man had returned to the kitchen, he said, "Now give up the clothes thou hast stolen."

The culprit was extremely confused, but denied that he had stolen anything.

"Give them up at once, without any more words. It will be much better for thee," said Friend Hopper, in his firm way.

Thus urged, the stranger drew from his bosom some small shirts and flannel petticoats. "My wife is very sick," said he. "She has a babe two weeks old, wrapped up in an old rag; and when I saw this comfortable clothing on the line, I was tempted to take it for the poor little creature. We have no fuel except a little tan. A herring is the last mouthful of food we have in the house; and when I came away, It was broiling on the hot tan."

His story excited pity; but fearing it might be made up for the occasion, Friend Hopper took him to a magistrate and said, "Please give me a commitment for this man. If he tells a true story, I will tear it up. I will go and see for myself."

When he arrived at the wretched abode, he found a scene of misery that pained him to the heart. The room was cold, and the wife was in bed, pale and suffering. Her babe had no clothing, except a coarse rag torn from the skirt of an old coat. Of course he destroyed the commitment immediately. His next step was to call upon the rich Quakers of his acquaintance, and obtain from them contributions of wood, flour, rice, bread, and warm garments. Employment was soon after procured for the man, and he was enabled to support his family comfortably. He never passed Friend Hopper in the street without making a low bow, and often took occasion to express his grateful acknowledgments.

PATRICK Mc KEEVER.

Patrick was a poor Irishman in Philadelphia. He and another man were arrested on a charge of burgla-

ry, convicted and sentenced to be hung. I am ignorant of the details of his crime, or why the sentence
was not carried into execution. There were probably
some palliating circumstances in his case ; for though
he was carried to the gallows, seated on his coffin,
he was spared for some reason, and his companion
was hung. He was afterward sentenced to ten
years imprisonment, and this was eventually short-
ened one year. During the last three years of his
term, Friend Hopper was one of the inspectors, and
frequently talked with him in a gentle, fatherly manner. The convict was a man of few words, and
hope seemed almost dead within him ; but though he
made no large promises, his heart was evidently
touched by the voice of kindness. As soon as he
was released, he went immediately to work at his
trade of tanning leather, and conducted himself in
the most exemplary manner. Being remarkable for
capability, and the amount of work he could accomplish, he soon had plenty of employment. He passed Friend Hopper's house every day, as he went to
his work, and often received from him words of
friendly encouragement.

Things were going on thus satisfactorily, when
his friend heard that constables were in pursuit of
him, on account of a robbery committed the night
before. He went straight to the mayor, and inquired

why orders had been given to arrest Patrick Mc-Keever.

"Because there has been a robbery committed in his neighborhood," replied the magistrate.

He inquired what proof there was that Patrick had been concerned in it.

"None at all," rejoined the mayor. "But he is an old convict, and that is enough to condemn him."

"It is *not* enough, by any means," answered Friend Hopper. "Thou hast no right to arrest any citizen without a shadow of proof against him. In this case, I advise thee by all means to proceed with humane caution. This man has severely atoned for the crime he did commit; and since he wishes to reform, his past history ought never to be mentioned against him. He has been perfectly honest, sober, and industrious, since he came out of prison. I think I know his state of mind; and I am willing to take the responsibility of saying that he is guiltless in this matter."

The mayor commended Friend Hopper's benevolence, but remained unconvinced. To all arguments he replied, "He is an old convict, and that is enough."

Patrick's kind friend watched for him as he passed to his daily labors, and told him that he would probably be arrested for the robbery that had been committed in his neighborhood. The poor fellow bowed down his head, the light vanished from his countenance, and hope seemed to have forsaken him utterly. "Well," said he, with a deep sigh, "I suppose I must make up my mind to spend the remainder of my days in prison."

"Thou wert not concerned in this robbery, wert thou?" inquired Friend Hopper, looking earnestly in his face.

"No, indeed I was not," he replied. "God be my witness, I want to lead an honest life, and be at peace with all men. But what good will *that* do me? Everybody will say, he has been in the State Prison, and that is enough."

His friend did not ask him twice; for he felt assured that he had spoken truly. He advised him to go directly to the mayor, deliver himself up, and declare his innocence. This wholesome advice was received with deep dejection. He had lost faith in his fellow-men; for they had been to him as enemies. "I know what will come of it," said he. "They will put me in prison whether there is any proof against me, or not. They won't let me out without somebody will be security for me; and who will be security for an old convict?"

"Keep up a good heart," replied Friend Hopper "Go to the mayor and speak as I have advised thee. If they talk of putting thee in prison, send for me."

Patrick acted in obedience to this advice, and was

treated just as he had expected. Though there was
not a shadow of proof against him, his being an old
convict was deemed sufficient reason for sending him
to jail.

Friend Hopper appeared in his behalf. "I am
ready to affirm that I believe this man to be inno
cent," said he. " It will be a very serious injury for
him to be taken from his business and detained in
prison until this can be proved. Moreover, the effect
upon his mind may be completely discouraging. I
will be security for his appearance when called for ;
and I know very well that he will not think of giving me the slip."

The gratitude of the poor fellow was overwhelm-
ing. He sobbed till his strong frame shook like a
leaf in the wind. The real culprits were soon after
discovered. For thirty years after and to the day of
his death, Patrick continued to lead a virtuous and
useful life ; for which he always thanked Friend
Hopper, as the instrument of Divine Providence.

THE UMBRELLA GIRL.

A young girl, the only daughter of a poor widow,
removed from the country to Philadelphia to earn
her living by covering umbrellas. She was very
handsome ; with glossy black hair, large beaming
eyes, and "lips like wet coral." She was just at
that susceptible age when youth is ripening into wo-

manhood, when the soul begins to be pervaded by
"that restless principle, which impels poor humans
to seek perfection in union."

At a hotel near the store for which she worked an
English traveller, called Lord Henry Stuart, had tak-
en lodgings. He was a strikingly handsome man,
and of princely carriage. As this distinguished stranger passed to and from his hotel, he encountered the
umbrella girl, and was attracted by her uncommon
beauty. He easily traced her to the store, where he
soon after went to purchase an umbrella. This was
followed up by presents of flowers, chats by the way-
side, and invitations to walk or ride; all of which
were gratefully accepted by the unsuspecting rustic;
for she was as ignorant of the dangers of a city as
were the squirrels of her native fields. He was
merely playing a game for temporary excitement.
She, with a head full of romance, and a heart melt-
ing under the influence of love, was unconsciously
endangering the happiness of her whole life.

Lord Henry invited her to visit the public gardens
on the Fourth of July. In the simplicity of her
heart, she believed all his flattering professions, and
considered herself his bride elect; she therefore accepted the invitation with innocent frankness. But
she had no dress fit to appear in on such a public occasion, with a gentleman of high rank, whom she
verily supposed to be her destined husband. While

these thoughts revolved in her mind, her eye was unfortunately attracted by a beautiful piece of silk, belonging to her employer. Could she not take it, without being seen, and pay for it secretly, when she had earned money enough? The temptation conquered her in a moment of weakness. She concealed the silk, and conveyed it to her lodgings. It was the first thing she had ever stolen, and her remorse was painful. She would have carried it back, but she dreaded discovery. She was not sure that her repentance would be met in a spirit of forgiveness.

On the eventful Fourth of July, she came out in her new dress. Lord Henry complimented her upon her elegant appearance, but she was not happy. On their way to the gardens, he talked to her in a manner which she did not comprehend. Perceiving this, he spoke more explicitly. The guileless young creature stopped, looked in his face with mournful reproach, and burst into tears. The nobleman took her hand kindly, and said, "My dear, are you an innocent girl?"

"I am, I am," she replied, with convulsive sobs. "Oh, what have I ever done, or said, that you should ask me such a question?"

The evident sincerity of her words stirred the deep fountains of his better nature. "If you are innocent," said he, "God forbid that I should make you otherwise. But you accepted my invitations

and presents so readily, that I supposed you understood me."

"What *could* I understand," said she, "except
that you intended to make me your wife?"

Though reared amid the proudest distinctions of
rank, he felt no inclination to smile. He blushed
and was silent. The heartless conventionalities of
the world stood rebuked in the presence of affectionate simplicity. He conveyed her to her humble
home, and bade her farewell, with a thankful consciousness that he had done no irretrievable injury to
her future prospects. The remembrance of her
would soon be to him as the recollection of last
year's butterflies. With her, the wound was deep.
In the solitude of her chamber she wept in bitter-
ness of heart over her ruined air-castles. And that
dress, which she had stolen to make an appearance
befitting his bride! Oh, what if she should be discovered? And would not the heart of her poor wi-
dowed mother break, if she should ever know that
her child was a thief?

Alas, her wretched forebodings proved too true.
The silk was traced to her; she was arrested on her
way to the store and dragged to prison. There she
refused all nourishment, and wept incessantly. On
the fourth day, the keeper called upon Isaac T.
Hopper, and informed him that there was a young
girl in prison, who appeared to be utterly friendless,

and determined to die by starvation. The kind-
hearted Friend immediately went to her assistance.
He found her lying on the floor of her cell, with her
face buried in her hands, sobbing as if her heart
would break. He tried to comfort her, but could
obtain no answer.

"Leave us alone," said he to the keeper. "Perhaps she will speak to me, if there is no one to hear."
When they were alone together, he put back the
hair from her temples, laid his hand kindly on her
beautiful head, and said in soothing tones, "My
child, consider me as thy father. Tell me all thou
hast done. If thou hast taken this silk, let me know
all about it. I will do for thee as I would for my
own daughter; and I doubt not that I can help thee
out of this difficulty."

After a long time spent in affectionate entreaty,
she leaned her young head on his friendly shoulder,
and sobbed out, "Oh, I wish I was dead. What
will my poor mother say when she knows of my disgrace?"

"Perhaps we can manage that she never shall
know it," replied he. Alluring her by this hope, he
gradually obtained from her the whole story of her
acquaintance with the nobleman. He bade her be
comforted, and take nourishment; for he would see
that the silk was paid for, and the prosecution withdrawn.

He went immediately to her employer, and told him the story. "This is her first offence," said he. "The girl is young, and she is the only child of a poor widow. Give her a chance to retrieve this one false step, and she may be restored to society, a useful and honored woman. I will see that thou art paid for the silk." The man readily agreed to withdraw the prosecution, and said he would have dealt otherwise by the girl, if he had known all the circumstances. "Thou shouldst have inquired into the merits of the case," replied Friend Hopper. "By this kind of thoughtlessness, many a young creature is driven into the downward path, who might easily have been saved."

The kind-hearted man next proceeded to the hotel, and with Quaker simplicity of speech inquired for Henry Stuart. The servant said his lordship had not yet risen. "Tell him my business is of importance," said Friend Hopper. The servant soon returned and conducted him to the chamber. The nobleman appeared surprised that a stranger, in the plain Quaker costume, should thus intrude upon his luxurious privacy. When he heard his errand, he blushed deeply, and frankly admitted the truth of the girl's statement. His benevolent visitor took the opportunity to "bear a testimony" against the selfishness and sin of profligacy. He did it in such a kind and fatherly manner, that the young man's heart was touched. He excused himself, by saying that he would not have tampered with the girl, if he had known her to be virtuous. "I have done many wrong things," said he, "but thank God, no betrayal of confiding innocence weighs on my conscience. I have always esteemed it the basest act of which man is capable." The imprisonment of the poor girl, and the forlorn situation in which she had been found, distressed him greatly. When Friend Hopper represented that the silk had been stolen for *his* sake, that the girl had thereby lost profitable employment, and was obliged to return to her distant home, to avoid the danger of exposure, he took out a fifty dollar note, and offered it to pay her expenses.

"Nay," said Isaac. "Thou art a very rich man, I presume. I see in thy hand a large roll of such notes. She is the daughter of a poor widow, and thou hast been the means of doing her great injury. Give me another."

Lord Henry handed him another fifty dollar note, and smiled as he said, "You understand your business well. But you have acted nobly, and I reverence you for it. If you ever visit England, come to see me. I will give you a cordial welcome, and treat you like a nobleman."

"Farewell, friend," replied the Quaker. "Though much to blame in this affair, thou too hast behaved nobly. Mayst thou be blessed in domestic life, and trifle no more with the feelings of poor girls; not even with those whom others have betrayed and deserted."

When the girl was arrested, she had sufficient presence of mind to assume a false name, and by that means, her true name had been kept out of the newspapers. "I did this," said she, "for my poor mother's sake." With the money given by Lord Stuart, the silk was paid for, and she was sent home to her mother well provided with clothing. Her name and place of residence forever remained a secret in the breast of her benefactor.

Years after these events transpired, a lady called at Friend Hopper's house, and asked to see him. When he entered the room, he found a handsomely dressed young matron, with a blooming boy of five or six years old. She rose quickly to meet him, and her voice choked as she said, "Friend Hopper, do you know me?" He replied that he did not. She fixed her tearful eyes earnestly upon him, and said, "You once helped me when in great distress." But the good missionary of humanity had helped too many in distress, to be able to recollect her without more precise information. With a tremulous voice, she bade her son go into the next room for a few minutes; then dropping on her knees, she hid her face in his lap, and sobbed out, "I am the girl who stole

the silk.   Oh, where should I now be, if it had not
been for you!"

When her emotion was somewhat calmed, she
told him that she had married a highly respectable
man, a senator of his native state.   Being on a visit
in Friend Hopper's vicinity, she had again and again
passed his dwelling, looking wistfully at the windows
to catch a sight of him; but when she attempted to
enter her courage failed.

"But I must return home to-morrow," said she,
"and I could not go away without once more seeing
and thanking him who saved me from ruin."   She
recalled her little boy, and said to him, "Look at
that gentleman, and remember him well; for he was
the best friend your mother ever had."   With an
earnest invitation to visit her happy home, and a fervent "God bless you!" she bade her benefactor farewell.

THE TWO YOUNG OFFENDERS.

In the neighborhood of Carlisle, Pennsylvania,
there lived a man whose temper was vindictive and
badly governed.   Having become deeply offended
with one of his neighbors, he induced his two sons
to swear falsely that he had committed an infamous
crime.   One of the lads was about fifteen years old,
and the other about seventeen.   The alleged offence was of so gross a nature, and was so at vari-

ance with the fair character of the person accused
that the witnesses were subjected to a very careful
and shrewd examination. They became embarrassed, and the flaws in their evidence were very obvious. They were indicted for conspiracy against an
innocent man; and being taken by surprise, they
were thrown into confusion, acknowledged thei.
guilt, and declined the offer of a trial. They were
sentenced to two years' imprisonment at hard labor
in the Penitentiary of Philadelphia.

Isaac T. Hopper, who was at that time one of the
inspectors, happened to be at the prison when they
arrived at dusk, hand-cuffed and chained together, in
custody of the sheriff. Their youth and desolate
appearance excited his compassion. "Keep up a
good heart, my poor lads," said he. "You can retrieve this one false step, if you will but make the
effort. It is still in your power to become respectable and useful men. I will help you all I can."

He gave particular directions that they should be
placed in a room by themselves, apart from the contagion of more hardened offenders. To prevent unprofitable conversation, they were constantly employed in the noisy occupation of heading nails.
From time to time, the humane inspector spoke
soothing and encouraging words to them, and commended their good behavior. When the Board of
Inspectors met, he proposed that the lads should be

recommended to the governor for pardon. Not succeeding in this effort, he wrote an article on the im-
propriety of confining juvenile offenders with old
hardened convicts. He published this in the daily
papers, and it produced considerable effect. When
the Board again met, Isaac T. Hopper and Thomas
Dobson were appointed to wait on the governor, to
obtain a pardon for the lads if possible. After considerable hesitation, the request was granted on con
dition that worthy men could be found, who would
take them as apprentices. Friend Hopper agreed to
find such persons; and he kept his word. One of
them was bound to a tanner, the other to a carpenter. But their excellent friend did not lose sight of
them. He reminded them that they were now going
among strangers, and their success and happiness
would mainly depend on their own conduct. He
begged of them, if they should ever get entangled
with unprofitable company, or become involved in
difficulty of any kind, to come to him, as they would
to a considerate father. He invited them to spend
all their leisure evenings at his house. For a long
time, it was their constant practice to take tea with
him every Sunday, and join the family in reading
the Bible and other serious books.

At the end of a year, they expressed a strong desire to visit their father. Some fears were entertained lest his influence over them should prove in-

jurious; and that being once freed from restraint, they would not willingly return to constant industry and regular habits. They, however, promised faithfully that they would, and Friend Hopper thought it might have a good effect upon them to know that they were trusted. He accordingly entered into bonds for them; thinking this additional claim on their gratitude would strengthen his influence over them, and help to confirm their good resolutions.

They returned punctually at the day and hour they had promised, and their exemplary conduct continued to give entire satisfaction to their employers. A short time after the oldest had fulfilled the term of his indenture, the tanner with whom he worked bought a farm, and sold his stock and tools to his former apprentice. Friend Hopper took him to the governor's house, dressed in his new suit of freedom clothes, and introduced him as one of the lads whom he had pardoned several years before; testifying that he had been a faithful apprentice, and much respected by his master. The governor was well pleased to see him, shook hands with him very cordially, and told him that he who was resolute enough to turn back from vicious ways, into the paths of virtue and usefulness, deserved even more respect than one who had never been tempted.

He afterward married a worthy young woman with a small property, which enabled him to build a neat two-story brick house. He always remained sober and industrious, and they lived in great comfort and respectability.

The younger brother likewise passed through his apprenticeship in a manner very satisfactory to his friends; and at twenty-one years of age, he also was introduced to the governor with testimonials of his good conduct. He was united to a very respectable young woman, but died a few years after his marriage.

Both these young men always cherished warm gratitude and strong attachment for Isaac T. Hopper. They both regularly attended the meetings of the Society of Friends, which had become pleasantly associated in their minds with the good influences they had received from their benefactor.

Friend Hopper was a strict disciplinarian while he was inspector, and it was extremely difficult for the prisoners to deceive him by any artful devices, or hypocritical pretences. But he was always in the habit of talking with them in friendly style, inquiring into their history and plans, sympathizing with their troubles and temptations, encouraging them to reform, and promising to assist them if they would try to help themselves. It was his custom to take a ramble in the country with his children every Saturday afternoon. All who were old enough to walk joined the troop. They always stopped at the prison, and were well pleased to deliver to the poor inmates, with their own small hands, such little comforts as their father had provided for the purpose. He was accustomed to say that there was not one among the convicts, however desperate they might be, with whom he should be afraid to trust himself alone at midnight with large sums of money in his pocket. An acquaintance once cautioned him against a prisoner, whose temper was extremely violent and revengeful, and who had been heard to swear that he would take the life of some of the keepers. Soon after this warning, Friend Hopper summoned the desperate fellow, and told him he was wanted to pile a quantity of lumber in the cellar. He went down with him to hold the light, and they remained more than an hour alone together, out of hearing of everybody. When he told this to the man who had cautioned him, he replied, "Well, I confess you have good courage. I would n't have done it for the price of the prison and all the ground it stands upon; for I do assure you he is a terrible fellow."

"I don't doubt he is," rejoined the courageous inspector; "but I knew he would n't kill *me*. I have always been a friend to him, and he is aware of it. What motive could he have for harming me?"

One of the prisoners, who had been convicted of man-slaughter, became furious, in consequence of being threatened with a whipping. When they attempted to bring him out of his dungeon to receive punishment, he seized a knife and a club, rushed back again, and swore he would kill the first person who came near him. Being a very strong man, and in a state of madness, no one dared to approach him. They tried to starve him into submission; but finding he was not to be subdued in that way, they sent for Friend Hopper, as they were accustomed to do in all such difficult emergencies. He went boldly into the cell, looked the desperado calmly in the face, and said, "It is foolish for thee to contend with the authorities. Thou wilt be compelled to yield at last. I will inquire into thy case. If thou hast been unjustly dealt by, I promise thee it shall be remedied." This kind and sensible remonstrance had the desired effect. From that time forward, he had great influence over the ferocious fellow, who was always willing to be guided by his advice, and finally became one of the most reasonable and orderly inmates of the prison.

I have heard Friend Hopper say that while he was inspector he aided and encouraged about fifty young convicts, as nearly as he could recollect; and all, except two, conducted in such a manner as to satisfy the respectable citizens whom he had induced to employ them. He was a shrewd observer of the countenances and manners of men, and doubtless

that was one reason why he was not often disap
pointed in those he trusted.

The humor which characterized his boyhood,
remained with him in maturer years, and often ef-
fervesced on the surface of his acquired gravity ; as
will appear in the following anecdotes.

Upon a certain occasion, a man called on him with
a due bill for twenty dollars against an estate he had
been employed to settle.   Friend Hopper put it away,
saying he would examine it and attend to it as soon
as he had leisure.   The man called again a short
time after, and stated that he had need of six dollars, and was willing to give a receipt for the whole
if that sum were advanced.   This proposition excited
suspicion, and the administrator decided in his own
mind that he would pay nothing till he had examined
the papers of the deceased.   Searching carefully
among these, he found a receipt for the money, men-
tioning the identical items, date, and circumstances
of the transaction ; stating that a due-bill had been
given and lost, and was to be restored by the credi-
tor when found.   When the man called again for
payment, Isaac said to him, in a quiet way, "Friend
Jones, I understand thou hast become pious lately."

He replied in a solemn tone, "Yes, thanks to
the Lord Jesus, I have found out the way of salvation."

"And thou hast been dipped I hear," continued the Quaker. "Dost thou know James Hunter?"

Mr. Jones answered in the affirmative.

"Well, he also was dipped some time ago," rejoined Friend Hopper; "but his neighbors say they did n't get the crown of his head under water. The devil crept into the unbaptized part, and has been busy within him ever since. I am afraid they did n't get *thee* quite under water. I think thou hadst better be dipped again."

As he spoke, he held up the receipt for twenty dollars. The countenance of the professedly pious man became scarlet, and he disappeared instantly.

A Dutchman once called upon Friend Hopper, and said, "A tief have stole mine goots. They tell me you can help me, may be." Upon inquiring the when and the where, Friend Hopper concluded that the articles had been stolen by a man whom he happened to know the police had taken up a few hours previous. But being disposed to amuse himself, he inquired very seriously, "What time of the moon was it, when thy goods were stolen? Having received information concerning that particular, he took a slate and began to cipher diligently. After a while, he looked up, and pronounced in a very oracular manner, "Thou wilt find thy goods."

"Shall I find mine goots?" exclaimed the delighted Dutchman; "and where is de tief?"

"Art thou quite sure about the age of the moon?" inquired the pretended magician. Being assured there was no mistake on that point, he ciphered again for a few minutes, and then answered, "Thou wilt find the thief in the hands of the police."

The Dutchman went away, evidently inspired with profound reverence. Having found his goods and the thief, according to prediction, he returned and asked for a private interview. "Tell me dat secret," said he, "and I will pay you a heap of money."

"What secret?" inquired Friend Hopper.

"Tell me how you know I will find mine goots, and where I will find de tief?" rejoined he.

"The plain truth is, I guessed it," was the reply; "because I had heard there was a thief at the police office, with such goods as thou described."

"But what for you ask about de moon?" inquired the Dutchman. "You make figures, and den you say, you will find your goots. You make figures again, den you tell me where is de tief. I go, and find mine goots and de tief, just as you say. Tell me how you do dat, and I will pay you a heap of money."

Though repeatedly assured that it was done only for a joke, he went away unsatisfied: and to the day of his death, he fully believed that the facetious Quaker was a conjuror.

When Friend Hopper hired one of two houses

where the back yards were not separated, he found himself considerably incommoded by the disorderly habits of his next neighbor. The dust and dirt daily swept into the yard were allowed to accumulate there in a heap, which the wind often scattered over the neater premises adjoining. The mistress of the house was said to be of an irritable temper, likely to take offence if asked to adopt a different system. He accordingly resolved upon a course, which he thought might cure the evil without provoking a dispute. One day, when he saw his neighbor in her kitchen, he called his own domestic to come out into the yard. Pointing to the heap of dirt, he exclaimed, loud enough to be heard in the next house, "Betsy, art thou not ashamed to sweep dust and litter into such a heap. See how it is blowing about our neighbor's yard! Art thou not ashamed of thyself?"

"I didn't sweep any dirt there," replied the girl. "They did it themselves."

"Pshaw! Pshaw! don't tell me that," rejoined he. "Our neighbor wouldn't do such an untidy thing. I wonder she hasn't complained of thee before now. Be more careful in future; for I should be very sorry to give her any occasion to say she couldn't keep the yard clean on our account."

The domestic read his meaning in the roguish expression of his eye, and she remained silent. The

lesson took effect. The heap of dirt was soon removed, and never appeared afterward.

Such a character as Isaac T. Hopper was of
course well known throughout the city where he
lived. Every school-boy had heard something of his
doings, and as he walked the street, everybody recognized him, from the chief justice to the chim-
ney-sweep. His personal appearance was calculated
to attract attention, independent of other circumstances. Joseph Bonaparte, who then resided at Borden-
town, was attracted toward him the first moment he
saw him, on account of a strong resemblance to his
brother Napoleon. They often met in the steam-
boat going down the Delaware, and on such occasions, the ex-king frequently pointed him out as the
most remarkable likeness of the emperor, that he
had ever met in Europe or America. He expressed
the opinion that with Napoleon's uniform on, he
might be mistaken for him, even by his own household ; and if he were to appear thus in Paris, nothing could be easier than for him to excite a revolution.

But the imperial throne, even if it had been directly offered to him, would have proved no temptation to a soul like his. In some respects, his character, as well as his person, strongly resembled Napoleon. But his powerful will was remarkably under
the control of conscience, and his energy was tem-

perèd by an unusual share of benevolence. If the
other elements of his character had not been balanced by these two qualities, he also might have been a
skilful diplomatist, and a successful leader of armies.
Fortunately for himself and others, he had a nobler
ambition than that of making widows and orphans
by wholesale slaughter. The preceding anecdotes
show how warmly he sympathized with the poor, the
oppressed, and the erring, without limitation of
country, creed, or complexion; and how diligently
he labored in their behalf. But from the great
amount of public service that he rendered, it must
not be inferred that he neglected private duties.
Perhaps no man was ever more devotedly attached
to wife and children than he was. His Sarah, as he
was wont to call her, was endowed with qualities
well calculated to retain a strong hold on the affections of a sensible and conscientious man. Her
kindly disposition, and the regular, simple habits ot
her life, were favorable to the preservation of that
beauty, which had won his boyish admiration. Her
wavy brown hair was softly shaded by the delicate
transparent muslin of her Quaker cap; her face had
a tender and benign expression; and her complexion
was so clear, that an old gentleman, who belonged
to the Society of Friends, and who was of course
not much addicted to poetic comparisons, used to say
he could never look at her without thinking of the

clear pink and white of a beautiful conch-shell. She
was scrupulously neat, and had something of that
chastened coquetry in dress, which is apt to charac-
terize the handsome women of her orderly sect.
Her drab-colored gown, not high in the neck, was
bordered by a plain narrow tucker of fine muslin, vi-
sible under her snow-white neckerchief. A white
under-sleeve came just below the elbow, where it
terminated in a very narrow band, nicely stitched,
and fastened with two small silver buttons, connected
by a chain. She was a very industrious woman, and
remarkably systematic in her household affairs;
thus she contrived to find time for everything, though
burdened with the care of a large and increasing
family. The apprentices always sat at table with
them, and she maintained a perfect equality between
them and her own children. She said it was her
wish to treat them precisely as she would like to
have *her* boys treated, if *they* should become apprentices. On Sunday evenings, which they called First
Day evenings, the whole family assembled to hear
Friend Hopper read portions of scripture, or writings
of the early Friends. On such occasions, the mother
often gave religious exhortations to the children and
apprentices, suited to the occurrences of the week,
and the temptations to which they were peculiarly
subject. During the last eight years of her life, she
was a recommended minister of the Society of

Friends, and often preached at their meetings. Her manners were affable, and her conversation peculiarly agreeable to young people. But she knew when silence was seemly, and always restrained her discourse within the limits of discretion. When any of her children talked more than was useful, she was accustomed to administer this concise caution : "My dear, it is a nice thing to say nothing, when thou hast nothing to say." Her husband was proud of her, and always manifested great deference for her opinion. She suffered much anxiety on account of the perils to which he was often exposed in his contests with slaveholders and kidnappers ; and for many years, the thought was familiar to her mind that she might one day see him brought home a corpse. While the yellow fever raged in Philadelphia, she had the same anxiety concerning his fearless devotion to the victims of that terrible disease, who were dying by hundreds around them. But she had a large and sympathizing heart, and she never sought to dissuade him from what he considered the path of duty. When one of his brothers was stricken with the fever, and the family with whom he resided were afraid to shelter him, she proposed to have him brought under their own roof, where he was carefully nursed till he died. She was more reluctant to listen to his urgent entreaties that she would retire into the country with the children, and remain with them beyond the reach of contagion; for her heart was divided between the husband of her youth and the nurslings of her bosom. But his anxiety concerning their children was so great, that she finally consented to pursue the course most conducive to his peace of mind; and he was left in the city with a colored domestic to superintend his household affairs. Through this terrible ordeal of pestilence he passed unscathed, though his ever ready sympathy brought him into frequent contact with the dying and the dead.

Besides this public calamity, which darkened the whole city for a time, Friend Hopper shared the common lot of humanity in the sad experiences of private life. Several of his children died at that attractive age, when the bud of infancy is blooming into childhood. Relatives and friends crossed the dark river to the unknown shore. On New Year's day, 1797, his mother departed from this world at fifty-six years old. In 1818, his father died at seventy-five years of age. His physical vigor was remarkable. When he had weathered seventy winters, he went to visit his eldest son, and being disappointed in meeting the stage to return, as he expected, he walked home, a distance of twenty-eight miles. At that advanced age, he could rest one hand on his cane and the other on a fence, and leap over as easily as a boy. He had long flowing black hair, which

fell in ringlets on his shoulders; and when he died,
it was merely sprinkled with gray. When his private accounts were examined after his decease, they
revealed the fact that he had secretly expended hundreds of dollars in paying the debts of poor people,
or redeeming their furniture when it was attached.

But though many dear ones dropped away from
his side, as Friend Isaac moved onward in his pilgrimage, many remained to sustain and cheer him.
Among his wife's brothers, his especial friend was
John Tatum, who lived in the vicinity of his native
village. This worthy man had great sympathy with
the colored people, and often sheltered the fugitives
whom his brother-in-law had rescued. He was remarkable for his love of peace; always preferring to
suffer wrong rather than dispute. The influence of
this pacific disposition upon others was strikingly illustrated in the case of two of his neighbors. They
were respectable people, in easy circumstances, and
the families found much pleasure in frequent intercourse with each other. But after a few years, one
of the men deemed that an intentional affront had
been offered him by the other. Instead of good-na-
tured frankness on the occasion, he behaved in a sul-
len manner, which provoked the other, and the result
was that eventually neither of them would speak
when they met. Their fields joined, and when they
were on friendly terms, the boundary was marked

by a fence, which they alternately repaired. But when there was feud between them, neither of them was willing to mend the other's fence. So each one built a fence for himself, leaving a very narrow strip of land between, which in process of time came to be generally known by the name of Devil's Lane, in allusion to the bad temper that produced it. A brook formed another portion of the boundary between their farms, and was useful to both of them. But after they became enemies, if a freshet occurred, each watched an opportunity to turn the water on the other's land, by which much damage was mutually done. They were so much occupied with injuring each other in every possible way, that they neglected their farms and grew poorer and poorer. One of them became intemperate; and everything about their premises began to wear an aspect of desolation and decay. At last, one of the farms was sold to pay a mortgage, and John Tatum, who was then about to be married, concluded to purchase it. Many people warned him of the trouble he would have with a quarrelsome and intemperate neighbor. But, after mature reflection, he concluded to trust to the influence of a peaceful and kind example, and accordingly purchased the farm.

Soon after he removed thither, he proposed to do away the Devil's Lane by building a new fence on the boundary, entirely at his own expense. His neighbor acceded to the proposition in a very surly manner, and for a considerable time seemed determined to find, or make some occasion for quarrel. But the young Quaker met all his provocations with forbearance, and never missed an opportunity to oblige him. Good finally overcame evil. The turbulent spirit, having nothing to excite it, gradually subsided into calmness. In process of time, he evinced a disposition to be kind and obliging also. Habits of temperance and industry returned, and during the last years of his life he was considered a remarkably good neighbor.

Friend Hopper's attachment to the religious society he had joined in early life was quite as strong, perhaps even stronger, than his love of kindred. The Yearly Meeting of Friends at Philadelphia was a season of great satisfaction, and he delighted to have his house full of guests, even to overflowing. On these occasions, he obeyed the impulses of his generous nature by seeking out the least wealthy and distinguished, who would be less likely than others to receive many invitations. In addition to these, who were often personal strangers to him, he had his own familiar and cherished friends. A day seldom passed without a visit from Nicholas Waln, who had great respect and affection for him and his wife, and delighted in their society. He cordially approved of their consistency in carrying out their consci-

entious convictions into the practices of daily life.
Some of Isaac's relatives and friends thought he devoted rather too much time and attention to philanthropic missions, but Nicholas Waln always stood by
him, a warm and faithful friend to the last. He was
a true gentleman, of courtly, pleasing manners, and
amusing conversation. Notwithstanding his weight
of character, he was so playful with the children,
that his visits were always hailed by them, as delightful opportunities for fun and frolic. He looked
beneath the surface of society, and had learned to
estimate men and things according to their real value,
not by a conventional standard. His wife did not
regard the pomps and vanities of the world with precisely the same degree of indifference that he did.
She thought it would be suitable to their wealth and
station to have a footman behind her carriage. This
wish being frequently expressed, her husband at last
promised to comply with it. Accordingly, the next
time the carriage was ordered, for the purpose of
making a stylish call, she was gratified to see a footman mounted. When she arrived at her place of
destination, the door of her carriage was opened, and
the steps let down in a very obsequious manner, by
the new servant; and great was her surprise and
confusion, to recognize in him her own husband!

Jacob Lindley, of Chester county, was another
frequent visitor at Friend Hopper's house; and many

were the lively conversations they had together. He
was a preacher in the Society of Friends, and missed
no opportunity, either in public or private, to protest
earnestly against the sin of slavery. He often cautioned Friends against laying too much stress on their
own peculiar forms, while they professed to abjure
forms. He said he himself had once received a les·
son on this subject, which did him much good. Once
when he was seated in meeting, an influential Friend
walked in, dressed in a coat with large metal buttons,
which he had borrowed in consequence of a drench-
ing rain! He seated himself opposite to Jacob
Lindley, who was so much disturbed by the glitter-
ing buttons, that "his meeting did him no good."
When the congregation rose to depart, he felt con-
strained to go up to the Friend who had so much
troubled him, and inquire why he had so grievously
departed from the simplicity enjoined upon members
of their Society. The good man looked down upon
his garments, and quietly replied, "I borrowed the
coat because my own was wet; and indeed, Jacob,
I did not notice what buttons were on it." Jacob
shook his hand warmly, and said, "Thou art a better Christian than I am, and I will learn of thee."

He often used to inculcate the same moral by relating another incident, which happened in old times,
when Quakers were accustomed to wear cocked hats
turned up at the sides. A Friend bought a hat of

this description, without observing that it was looped up with a button. As he sat in meeting with his hat on, as usual, he observed many eyes directed toward him, and some with a very sorrowful expression. He could not conjecture a reason for this, till he happened to take off his hat and lay it beside him. As soon as he noticed the button, he rose and said, "Friends, if religion consists in a button, I wouldn't give a button for it." Having delivered this short and pithy sermon, he seated himself, and resumed the offending hat with the utmost composure.

Once, when Jacob Lindley was dining with Friend Hopper, the conversation turned upon his religious experiences, and he related a circumstance to which he said he very seldom alluded, and never without feelings of solemnity and awe. Being seized with sudden and severe illness, his soul left the body for several hours, during which time he saw visions of heavenly glory, not to be described. When consciousness began to return, he felt grieved that he was obliged to come back to this state of being, and he was never after able to feel the same interest in terrestrial things, that he had felt before he obtained this glimpse of the spiritual world.

Arthur Howell was another intimate acquaintance of Friend Hopper. He was a currier in Philadelphia, a preacher in the Society of Friends, characterized by kindly feelings, and a very tender con-

science.   Upon one occasion, he purchased from the
captain of a vessel a quantity of oil, which he afterward sold at an advanced price.   Under these circumstances, he thought the captain had not received
so much as he ought to have ; and he gave him an
additional dollar on every barrel.   This man was remarkable for spiritual-mindedness and the gift of
prophecy.   It was no uncommon thing for him to
relate occurrences which were happening at the moment many miles distant, and to foretell the arrival
of people, or events, when there appeared to be no
external reasons on which to ground such expectations.

One Sunday morning, he was suddenly impelled
to proceed to Germantown in haste.   As he approached the village, he met a funeral procession.
He had no knowledge whatever of the deceased ;
but it was suddenly revealed to him that the occu-
pant of the coffin before him was a woman whose
life had been saddened by the suspicion of a crime,
which she never committed.   The impression became very strong on his mind that she wished him
to make certain statements at her funeral.   Accordingly, he followed the procession, and when they
arrived at the meeting-house, he entered and listened
to the prayer delivered by her pastor.   When the
customary services were finished, Arthur Howell
rose, and asked permission to speak.   "I did not

know the deceased, even by name," said he. "But
it is given me to say, that she suffered much and
unjustly. Her neighbors generally suspected her
of a crime, which she did not commit; and in a few
weeks from this time, it will be made clearly manifest to the world that she was innocent. A few
hours before her death, she talked on this subjec,
with the clergyman who attended upon her, and
who is now present; and it is given me to declare
the communication she made to him upon that occasion."

He then proceeded to relate the particulars of the
interview; to which the clergyman listened with
evident astonishment. When the communication
was finished, he said, "I don't know who this man
is, or how he has obtained information on this subject; but certain it is, he has repeated, word for
word, a conversation which I supposed was known
only to myself and the deceased."

The woman in question had gone out in the fields
one day, with her infant in her arms, and she returned without it. She said she had laid it down
on a heap of dry leaves, while she went to pick a
few flowers; and when she returned, the baby was
gone. The fields and woods were searched in vain
and neighbors began to whisper that she had committed infanticide. Then rumors arose that she was
dissatisfied with her marriage; that her heart re-

mained with a young man to whom she was previously engaged; and that her brain was affected by
this secret unhappiness. She was never publicly accused; partly because there was no evidence against
her, and partly because it was supposed that if she
did commit the crime, it must have been owing to
aberation of mind. But she became aware of the
whisperings against her, and the consciousness of
being an object of suspicion, combined with the
mysterious disappearance of her child, cast a heavy
cloud over her life, and made her appear more and
more unlike her former self. This she confided to
her clergyman, in the interview shortly preceding
her death; and she likewise told him that the young
man, to whom she had been engaged, had never for-
given her for not marrying him.

A few weeks after her decease, this young man
confessed that he had stolen the babe. He had followed the mother, unobserved by her, and had seen
her lay the sleeping infant on its bed of leaves. As
he gazed upon it, a mingled feeling of jealousy and
revenge took possession of his soul. In obedience
to a sudden impulse, he seized the babe, and carried
it off hastily. He subsequently conveyed it to a dis-
ant village, and placed it out to nurse, under an
assumed name and history. The child was found
alive and well, at the place he indicated. Thus the
mother's innocence was made clearly manifest to the

world, as the Quaker preacher had predicted at her
funeral.

I often heard Friend Hopper relate this anecdote,
and he always said that he could vouch for the
truth of it; and for several other similar things in
connection with the ministry of his friend Arthur.

A singular case of inward perception likewise occurred in the experience of his own mother. In her
Diary, which is still preserved in the family, she
describes a visit to some of her children in Philadelphia, and adds: "Soon after this, the Lord showed
me that I should lose a son. It was often told me,
though without sound of words. Nothing could be
more intelligible than this still, small voice. It
said, Thou wilt lose a son; and he is a pleasant
child."

Her son James resided with relatives in Philadelphia, and often went to bathe in the Delaware. On
one of these occasions, soon after his mother's visit,
a friend who went with him sank in the water, and
James lost his own life by efforts to save him. A
messenger was sent to inform his parents, who lived
at the distance of eight miles. While he staid in
the house, reluctant to do his mournful errand, the
mother was siezed with sudden dread, and heard
the inward voice saying, "James is drowned." She
said abruptly to the messenger, "Thou hast come
to tell me that my son James is drowned. Oh, how

did it happen?" He was much surprised, and asked why she thought so. She could give no explanation of it, except that it had been suddenly revealed to her mind.

I have heard and read many such stories of Quakers, which seem too well authenticated to admit of doubt. They themselves refer all such cases to "the inward light;" and that phrase, as they understand it, conveys a satisfactory explanation to their minds. I leave psychologists to settle the question as they can.

Those who are well acquainted with Quaker views, are aware that by "the inward light," they signify something higher and more comprehensive than conscience. They regard it as the voice of God in the soul, which will always guard man from evil, and guide him into truth, if reverently listened to, in stillness of the passions, and obedience of the will. These strong impressions on individual minds constitute their only call and consecration to the ministry, and have directed them in the application of moral principles to a variety of subjects, such as intemperance, war, and slavery. Men and women were impelled by the interior monitor to go about preaching on these topics, until their individual views became what are called "leading testimonies" in the Society. The abjuration of slavery was one of their earliest "testimonies." There was much preaching against it in their public meetings, and many committees were appointed to expostulate in private with those who held slaves. At an early period, it became an established rule of discipline for the Society to disown any member, who refused to manumit his bondmen.

Friend Hopper used to tell an interesting anecdote in connection with these committees. In the course of their visits, they concluded to pass by one of their members, who held only one slave, and he was very old. He was too infirm to earn his own living, and as he was very kindly treated, they supposed he would have no wish for freedom. But Isaac Jackson, one of the committee, a very benevolent and conscientious man, had a strong impression on his mind that duty required him not to omit this case. He accordingly went alone to the master, and stated how the subject appeared to him, in the inward light of his own soul. The Friend was not easily convinced. He brought forward many reasons for not emancipating his slave; and one of the strongest was that the man was too feeble to labor for his own support, and therefore freedom would be of no value to him. Isaac Jackson replied, "He labored for thee without wages, while he had strength, and it is thy duty to support him now. Whether he would value freedom or not, is a question he alone is competent to decide."

These friendly remonstrances produced such effect, that the master agreed to manumit his bondman, and give a written obligation that he should be comfortably supported during the remainder of his life, by him or his heirs. When the papers were prepared the slave was called into the parlor, and Isaac Jackson inquired, "Would'st thou like to be free?" He promptly answered that he should. The Friend suggested that he was now too feeble to labor much, and inquired how he would manage to obtain a living. The old man meekly replied, "Providence has been kind to me thus far; and I am willing to trust him the rest of my life."

Isaac Jackson then held up the papers and said, "Thou art a free man. Thy master has manumitted thee, and promised to maintain thee as long as thou mayest live."

This was so unexpected, that the aged bondman was completely overcome. For a few moments, he remained in profound silence; then, with a sudden impulse, he fell on his knees, and poured forth a short and fervent prayer of thanksgiving to his Heavenly Father, for prolonging his life till he had the happiness to feel himself a free man.

The master and his adviser were both surprised and affected by this eloquent outburst of grateful feeling. The poor old servant had seemed so comfortable and contented, that no one supposed freedom

was of great importance to him. But, as honest
Isaac Jackson observed, *he* alone was competent to
decide *that* question.

Quakers consider "the inward light" as a guide
not merely in cases involving moral principles, but
also in the regulation of external affairs; and in the
annals of their Society, are some remarkable instances of dangers avoided by the help of this internal
monitor.

Friend Hopper used to mention a case where a
strong impression had been made on his own mind,
without his being able to assign any adequate reason
for it. A young man, descended from a highly respectable Quaker family in New-Jersey, went to
South Carolina and entered into business. He married there, and as his wife did not belong to the Society of Friends, he was of course disowned. After
some years of commercial success, he failed, and
went to Philadelphia, where Friend Hopper became
acquainted with him, and formed an opinion not unfavorable. When he had been in that city some
time, he mentioned that his wife owned land in Carolina, which he was very desirous to cultivate, but
was prevented by conscientious scruples concerning
slave-labor. He said if he could induce some colored
people from Philadelphia to go there and work for
him as free laborers, it would be an advantage to
him, and a benefit to them. He urged Friend Hop-

per to exert his influence over them to convince
them that such precautions could be taken, as would
prevent any danger of their being reduced to slavery; saying that if he would consent to do so, he
doubtless could obtain as many laborers as he wanted. The plan appeared feasible, and Friend Hopper
was inclined to assist him in carrying it into execution. Soon after, two colored men called upon him,
and said they were ready to go, provided he thought
well of the project. Nothing had occurred to change
his opinion of the man, or to excite distrust concerning his agricultural scheme. But an impression came
upon his mind that the laborers had better not go;
an impression so strong, that he thought it right to
be influenced by it. He accordingly told them he
had thought well of the plan, but his views had
changed, and he advised them to remain where they
were. This greatly surprised the man who wished
to employ them, and he called to expostulate on the
subject; repeating his statement concerning the
great advantage they would derive from entering into his service.

"There is no use in arguing the matter," replied
Friend Hopper. "I have no cause whatever to sus-
pect thee of any dishonest or dishonorable intentions; but there is on my mind an impression of danger, so powerful that I cannot conscientiously have

any agency in inducing colored laborers to go with thee."

Not succeeding in his project, the bankrupt merchant went to New-Jersey for a time, to reside with his father, who was a worthy and influential member of the Society of Friends. An innocent, good natured old colored man, a fugitive from Virginia, had for some time been employed to work on the farm, and the family had become much attached to him. The son who had returned from Carolina was very friendly with this simple-hearted old servant, and easily gained his confidence. When he had learned his story, he offered to write to his master, and enable him to purchase his freedom for a sum which he could gradually repay by labor. The fugitive was exceedingly grateful, and put himself completely in his power by a full statement of all particulars. The false-hearted man did indeed write to the master; and the poor old slave was soon after arrested and carried to Philadelphia in irons. Friend Hopper was sent for, and went to see him in prison. With groans and sobs, the captive told how wickedly he had been deceived. "I thought he was a Quaker, and so I trusted him," said he. "But I saw my master's agent pay him fifty dollars for betraying me."

Friend Hopper assured him that the deceiver was not a Quaker; and that he did not believe any Quaker on the face of the earth would do such an unjust and cruel deed. He could devise no means to rescue the sufferer; and with an aching heart he was compelled to see him carried off into slavery, without being able to offer any other solace than an affectionate farewell.

The conduct of this base hypocrite proved that the warning presentiment against him had not been without foundation. Grieved and indignant at the wrong he had done to a helpless and unoffending fellow-creature, Friend Hopper wrote to him as follows: "Yesterday, I visited the poor old man in prison, whom thou hast so perfidiously betrayed. Gloomy and hopeless as his case is, I would prefer it to thine. Thou hast received fifty dollars as the reward of thy treachery; but what good can it do thee? Canst thou lay down thy head at night, without feeling the sharp goadings of a guilty conscience? Canst thou ask forgiveness of thy sins of our Heavenly Father, whom thou hast so grievously insulted by thy hypocrisy? Judas betrayed his master for thirty pieces of silver, and afterward hung himself. Thou hast betrayed thy brother for fifty; and if thy conscience is not seared, as with hot iron, thy compunction must be great. I feel no disposition to upbraid thee. I have no doubt thy own heart does that sufficiently; for our beneficent Creator will not suffer any to be at ease in their sins. Thy friend, I. T. H."

The worthy old Quaker in New-Jersey was not

aware of his son's villainous conduct until some time after. When the circumstances were made known to the family they were exceedingly mortified and afflicted.

Friend Hopper used to tell another story, which forms a beautiful contrast to the foregoing painful narrative. I repeat it, because it illustrates the tenderness of spirit, which has so peculiarly characterized the Society of Friends, and because I hope it may fall like dew on hearts parched by vindictive feelings. Charles Carey lived near Philadelphia, in a comfortable house with a few acres of pasture adjoining. A young horse, apparently healthy, though lean, was one day offered him in the market for fifty dollars. The cheapness tempted him to purchase; for he thought the clover of his pastures would soon put the animal in good condition, and enable him to sell him at an advanced price. He was too poor to command the required sum himself, but he borrowed it of a friend. The horse, being well fed and lightly worked, soon became a noble looking animal, and was taken to the city for sale. But scarcely had he entered the market, when a stranger stepped up and claimed him as his property, recently stolen. Charles Carey's son, who had charge of the animal, was taken before a magistrate. Isaac T. Hopper was sent for, and easily proved that the character of the young man and his father was above all suspicion.

But the stranger produced satisfactory evidence that he was the rightful owner of the horse, which was accordingly delivered up to him. When Charles Carey heard the unwelcome news, he quietly remarked, "It is hard for me to lose the money; but I am glad the man has recovered his property."

About a year afterward, having occasion to go to a tavern in Philadelphia, he saw a man in the bar-room, whom he at once recognized as the person who had sold him the horse. He walked up to him and inquired whether he remembered the transaction. Being answered in the affirmative, he said "I am the man who bought that horse. Didst thou know he was stolen?" With a stupified manner and a faltering voice, the stranger answered, "Yes."

"Come along with me, then," said Charles; "and I will put thee where. thou wilt not steal another horse very soon."

The thief resigned himself to his fate with a sort of hopeless indifference. But before they reached the magistrate's office, the voice within began to plead gently with the Quaker, and turned him from the sternness of his purpose. "I am a poor man," said he, "and thou hast greatly injured me. I cannot afford to lose fifty dollars; but to prosecute thee will not compensate me for the loss. Go thy way, and conduct thyself honestly in future."

The man seemed amazed. He stood for a moment, hesitating and confused; then walked slowly away. But after taking a few steps, he turned back and said, "Where can I find you, if I should ever be able to make restitution for the wrong I have done?"

Charles replied, "I trust thou dost not intend to jest with me, after all the trouble thou hast caused me?"

"No, indeed I do not," answered the stranger. "I hope to repay you, some time or other."

"Very well," rejoined the Friend, "if thou ever hast anything for me, thou canst leave it with Isaac T. Hopper, at the corner of Walnut and Dock-streets." Thus they parted, and never met again.

About a year after, Friend Hopper found a letter on his desk, addressed to Charles Carey. When it was delivered to him, he was surprised to find that it came from the man who had stolen the horse, and contained twenty dollars. A few months later, another letter containing the same sum, was left in the same way. Not long after, a third letter arrived, enclosing twenty dollars; the whole forming a sum sufficient to repay both principal and interest of the money which the kind-hearted Quaker had lost by his dishonesty.

This last letter stated that the writer had no thoughts of stealing the horse ten minutes before he did it. After he had sold him, he was so haunted by remorse and fear of detection, that life became a burthen to him, and he cared not what became of him. But when he was arrested, and so unexpectedly set at liberty, the crushing weight was taken from him. He felt inspired by fresh courage, and sustained by the hope of making some atonement for what he had done. He made strenuous efforts to improve his condition, and succeeded. He was then teaching school, was assessor of the township where he resided, and no one suspected that he had ever committed a dishonest action.

The good man, to whom this epistle was addressed, read it with moistened eyes, and felt that the reward of righteousness is peace.

For many years after Isaac T. Hopper joined the Society of Friends, a spirit of peace and of kindly communion prevailed among them. No sect has ever arisen which so nearly approached the character of primitive christianity, in all relations with each other and with their fellow men. But as soon as the early christians were relieved from persecution, they began to persecute each other; and so it was with the Quakers. Having become established and respected by the world, the humble and self-denying spirit which at the outset renounced and contended with the world gradually departed. Many of them were rich, and not unfrequently their fortunes were acquired by trading with slave-holders.

Such men were well satisfied to have the testimonies
of their spiritual forefathers against slavery read
over among themselves, at stated seasons; but they
felt little sympathy with those of their cotemporaries,
who considered it a duty to remonstrate publicly and
freely with all who were connected with the iniquitous system.

A strong and earnest preacher, by the name of
Elias Hicks, made himself more offensive than others
in this respect. He appears to have been a very
just and conscientious man, with great reverence for
God, and exceedingly little for human authority.
Everywhere, in public and in private, he lifted up his
voice against the sin of slavery. He would eat no
sugar that was made by slaves, and wear no gar-
ment which he supposed to have been produced by
unpaid labor. In a remarkable manner, he showed
this "ruling passion strong in death." A few hours
before he departed from this world, his friends, seeing him shiver, placed a comfortable over him. He
felt of it with his feeble hands, and made a strong
effort to push it away. When they again drew it up
over his shoulders, he manifested the same symptoms of abhorrence. One of them, who began to
conjecture the cause, inquired, "Dost thou dislike
it because it is made of cotton?" He was too far
gone to speak, but he moved his head in token of as-
sent. When they removed the article of slave pro-

duce, and substituted a woolen blanket, he remained
quiet, and passed away in peace.

He was accustomed to say, "It takes *live* fish to
swim *up* stream;" and unquestionably he and his
friend Isaac T. Hopper were both very much alive.
The quiet boldness of this man was altogether unman-
ageable.   In Virginia or Carolina, he preached more
earnestly and directly against slavery, than he did in
New-York or Pennsylvania, for the simple reason
that it seemed to be more needed there.   Upon one
of these occasions, a slaveholder who went to hear
him from curiosity, left the meeting in great wrath,
swearing he would blow out that fellow's brains if he
ventured near his plantation.   When the preacher
heard of this threat, he put on his hat and proceeded
straightway to the forbidden place.   In answer to his
inquiries, a slave informed him that his master was
then at dinner, but would see him in a short time.
He seated himself and waited patiently until the
planter entered the room.   With a calm and dignified manner, he thus addressed him :   "I understand
thou hast threatened to blow out the brains of Elias
Hicks, if he comes upon thy plantation.   I am Elias
Hicks."

The Virginian acknowledged that he did make
such a threat, and said he considered it perfectly justifiable to do such a deed, when a man came to
preach rebellion to his slaves.

"I came to preach the Gospel, which inculcates forgiveness of injuries upon slaves as well as upon other men," replied the Quaker. "But tell me, if thou canst, how this Gospel can be *truly* preached, without showing the slaves that they *are* injured, and thus making a man of thy sentiments feel as if they were encouraged in rebellion."

This led to a long argument, maintained in the most friendly spirit. At parting, the slaveholder shook hands with the preacher, and invited him to come again. His visits were renewed, and six months after, the Virginian emancipated all his slaves.

When preaching in the free states, he earnestly called upon all to abstain from slave-produce, and thus in a measure wash their own hands from participation in a system of abominable wickedness and cruelty. His zeal on this subject annoyed some of his brethren, but they could not make him amenable to discipline for it; for these views were in accordance with the earliest and strongest testimonies of the Society of Friends; moreover, it would have been discreditable to acknowledge *such* a ground of offence. But the secret dissatisfaction showed itself in a disposition to find fault with him. Charges were brought against his doctrines. He was accused of denying the authority of Scripture, and the divinity of Christ.

It was a departure from the original basis of the

Society to assume any standard whatsoever concerning creeds. It is true that the early Quakers wrote volumes of controversy against many of the prevailing opinions of their day; such as the doctrine of predestination, and of salvation depending upon faith, rather than upon works. All the customary external observances, such as holy days, baptism, and the Lord's Supper, they considered as belonging to a less spiritual age, and that the time had come for them to be done away. Concerning the Trinity, there appears to have been difference of opinion among them from the earliest time. When George Fox expressed a fear that William Penn had gone too far in defending "the true unity of God," Penn replied that he had never heard any one speak more plainly concerning the manhood of Christ, than George Fox himself. Penn was imprisoned in the Tower for "rejecting the mystery of the Trinity," in a book called "The Sandy Foundation Shaken." He afterward wrote "Innocency with her Open Face," regarded by some as a compromise, which procured his release. But though various popular doctrines naturally came in their way, and challenged discussion, while they were endeavoring to introduce a new order of things, the characteristic feature of their movement was attention to practical righteousness rather than theological tenets. They did not require their members to profess faith in any

creed. They had but one single bond of union;
and that was the belief that every man ought to be
guided in his actions, and in the interpretation of
Scripture, by the light within his own soul. Their
history shows that they mainly used this light to
guide them in the application of moral principles.
Upon the priesthood, in every form, they made un-
sparing warfare; believing that the gifts of the Spirit
ought never to be paid with money. They appointed
committees to visit the sick, the afflicted, and the
destitute, and to superintend marriages and funerals.
The farmer, the shoemaker, the physician, or the
merchant, followed his vocation diligently, and whenever the Spirit moved him to exhort his brethren, he
did so. The "First, and Fifth Day" of the week,
called by other denominations Sunday and Thurs-
day, were set apart by them for religious meetings.
Women were placed on an equality with men, by
being admitted to this free Gospel ministry, and appointed on committees with men, to regulate the
affairs of the Society. They abjured war under all
circumstances, and suffered great persecution rather
than pay military taxes. They early discouraged
the distillation or use of spirituous liquors, and disowned any of their members who distilled them from
grain. Protests against slavery were among their
most earnest testimonies, and it was early made a
rule of discipline that no member of the Society

should hold slaves. When the Quakers first arose, it was a custom in England, as it still is on the continent of Europe, to say *thou* to an inferior, or equal, and *you* to a superior. They saw in this custom an infringement of the great law of human brotherhood; and because they would "call no man master," they said *thou* to every person, without distinction of rank. To the conservatives of their day, this spiritual democracy seemed like deliberate contempt of authority; and as such, deserving of severe punishment. More strenuously than all other things, they denied the right of any set of men to prescribe a creed for others. The only authority they recognized was "the light within;" and for freedom to follow this, they were always ready to suffer or to die.

On all these subjects, there could be no doubt that Elias Hicks was a Quaker of the old genuine stamp. But he differed from many others in some of his theological views. He considered Christ as "the only Son of the most high God;" but he denied that "the *outward person,*" which suffered on Calvary was properly the Son of God. He attached less importance to miracles, than did many of his brethren. He said he had learned more of his own soul, and had clearer revelations of God and duty, while following his plough, than from all the books he had ever read. He reverenced the Bible as a

record of divine power and goodness, but did not
consider a knowledge of it essential to salvation;
for he supposed that a Hindoo or an African, who
never heard of the Scriptures, or of Christ, might
become truly a child of God, if he humbly and sincerely followed the divine light within, given to
every human soul, according to the measure of its
faithfulness.

Many of his brethren, whose views assimilated
more with orthodox opinions, accused him of having
departed from the principles of early Friends. But
his predecessors had been guided only by the light
within ; and he followed the same guide, without de-
ciding beforehand precisely how far it might lead
him. This principle, if sincerely adopted and consistently applied, would obviously lead to large and
liberal results, sufficient for the progressive growth
of all coming ages. It was so generally admitted to
be the one definite bond of union among early
Friends, that the right of Elias Hicks to utter his
own convictions, whether they were in accordance
with others or not, would probably never have been
questioned, if some influential members of the Society had not assumed more power than was delegated
to them ; thereby constituting themselves a kind of
ecclesiastical tribunal. It is the nature of such authority to seek enlargement of its boundaries, by en-
croaching more and more on individual freedom.

The friends of Elias Hicks did not adopt his views or the views of any other man as a standard of opinion. On the subject of the Trinity, for instance, there were various shadings of opinion among them. The probability seems to be that the influence of Unitarian sects, and of Orthodox sects had, in the course of years, gradually glided in among the Quakers, and more or less fashioned their theological opinions, though themselves were unconscious of it; as we all are of the surrounding air we are constantly inhaling.

But it was not the Unitarianism of Elias Hicks that his adherents fought for, or considered it necessary to adopt. They simply contended for his right to express his own convictions, and denied the authority of any man, or body of men, to judge his preaching by the assumed standard of any creed. Therefore, the real ground of the struggle seems to have been resistance to ecclesiastical power; though theological opinions unavoidably became intertwisted with it. It was a new form of the old battle, perpetually renewed ever since the world began, between authority and individual freedom.

The agitation, which had for some time been heaving under the surface, is said to have been brought into open manifestation by a sermon which Elias Hicks preached against the use of slave produce, in 1819. A bitter warfare followed. Those

who refused to denounce his opinions were accused
of being infidels and separatists; and they called
their accusers bigoted and intolerant. With regard
to disputed doctrines, both claimed to find sufficient
authority in the writings of early Friends; and each
side charged the other with mutilating and misrepre-
senting those writings. As usual in theological con-
troversies, the skein became more and more entangled, till there was no way left but to cut it in two.
In 1827 and 1828, a separation took place in the
Yearly Meetings of Philadelphia, New-York, and
several other places. Thenceforth, the members
were divided into two distinct sects. In some places
the friends of Elias Hicks were far the more numerous. In others, his opponents had a majority.
Each party claimed to be the genuine Society of
Friends, and denied the other's right to retain the
title. The opponents of Elias Hicks called themselves "Orthodox Friends," and named his adherents
"Hicksites." The latter repudiated the title, because they did not acknowledge him as their standard of belief, though they loved and reverenced his
character, and stood by him as the representative
of liberty of conscience. They called themselves
"Friends," and the others "the Orthodox."

The question which was the genuine Society of
Friends was more important than it would seem to a
mere looker on; for large pecuniary interests were

involved therein. It is well known that Quakers form a sort of commonwealth by themselves, within the civil commonwealth by which they are governed. They pay the public school-tax, and in addition build their own school-houses, and employ teachers of their own Society. They support their own poor, while they pay the same pauper tax as other citizens. They have burying grounds apart from others, because they have conscientious scruples concerning monuments and epitaphs. Of course, the question which of the two contending parties was the true Society of Friends involved the question who owned the meeting-houses, the burying grounds, and the school funds. The friends of Elias Hicks offered to divide the property, according to the relative numbers of each party ; but those called Orthodox refused to accept the proposition. Lawsuits were brought in various parts of the country. What a bitter state of animosity existed may be conjectured from the fact that the "Orthodox" in Philadelphia refused to allow "Hicksites" to bury their dead in the ground belonging to the undivided Society of Friends. On the occasion of funerals, they refused to deliver up the key ; and after their opponents had remonstrated in vain, they forced the lock.

I believe in almost every instance, where the "Hicksites" were a majority, and thus had a claim to the larger share of property, they offered to di-

vide in proportion to the relative numbers of the two
parties. After the separation in New-York, they renewed this offer, which had once been rejected; and
the "Orthodox" finally agreed to accept a stipulated
sum for their interest in the property. The Friends
called "Hicksites" numbered in the whole more than
seventy thousand.

Quakers in England generally took part against
Elias Hicks and his friends. Some, who were styled
"The Evangelical Party," went much beyond their
brethren in conformity with the prevailing denominations of Christians called Orthodox. Many of
them considered a knowledge of the letter of Scripture essential to salvation; and some even approved
of baptism by water; a singular departure from the
total abrogation of external rites, which characterized
Quakerism from the beginning. William and Mary
Howitt, the well known and highly popular English
writers, were born members of this religious Society.
In an article concerning the Hicksite controversy,
written for the London Christian Advocate, the former says: "My opinion is, that Friends will see
cause to repent the excision of that great portion of
their own body, on the plea of heretical opinions.
By sanctioning it, they are bound, if they act im-
partially and consistently, to expel others also for
heterodox opinions. This comes of violating the sacred liberty of conscience; of allowing ourselves to

LIFE OF ISAAC T. HOPPER. 285

be infected with the leaven of a blind zeal, instead
of the broad philanthropy of Christ. Is there no
better alternative? Yes. To adopt the principle of
William Penn; to allow freedom of opinion; and
while we permit the Evangelical party to hold *their*
favorite notions, so long as they consent to conform
to our system of public worship, to confess that we
have acted harshly to the Hicksites, and open our
arms to all who are sincere in their faith, and orderly
in their conduct."

As the adherents of Elias Hicks at that time
represented freedom of conscience, of course Isaac
T. Hopper belonged to that party, and advocated it
with characteristic zeal. In fact, he seems to have
been the Napoleon of the battle. It was not in his
nature intentionally to misrepresent any man; and
even when the controversy was raging most furiously, I believe there never was a time when he would
not willingly have acknowledged a mistake the moment he perceived it. But his temperament was
such, that wherever he deemed a principle of truth,
justice, or freedom was at stake, he could never quit
an adversary till he had demolished him completely,
and *convinced* him that he was demolished; though
he often felt great personal kindness toward the individual thus prostrated, and was always willing to
render him any friendly service. He used to say
that his resistance in this controversy was principally

roused by the disposition which he saw manifested
"to crush worthy, innocent Friends, for mere difference of opinion;" and no one, who knew him well,
could doubt that on this subject, as on others, he was
impelled by a sincere love of truth and justice. But
neither he nor any other person ever entered the
lists of theological controversy without paying dearly
for the encounter. Perpetual strife grieved and disturbed his own spirit, while his energy, perseverance,
and bluntness of speech, gained him many enemies.
Wherever this unfortunate sectarian schism was introduced, it divided families, and burst asunder the
bonds of friendship. For a long time, they seemed
to be a Society of Enemies, instead of a Society of
Friends. In this respect, no one suffered more acutely than Isaac T. Hopper. It was his nature to form
very strong friendships; and at this painful juncture, many whom he had long loved and trusted,
parted from him. Among them was his cousin Joseph Whitall, who had embraced Quakerism at the
same period of life, who had been the friend of his
boyhood, and the cherished companion of later years.
They had no personal altercation, but their intimacy
gradually cooled off, and they became as strangers.

He had encountered other difficulties also, at a
former period of his life, the shadows of which still
lay across his path. About twelve or fifteen years
after his marriage, his health began to fail. His

vigorous frame pined away to a mere shadow, and
he was supposed to be in a consumption. At the
same time, he found himself involved in pecuniary
difficulties, the burden of which weighed very heavily upon him, for many reasons. His strong sense of
justice made it painful for him to owe debts he could
not pay. He had an exceeding love of imparting to
others, and these pecuniary impediments tied down
his large soul with a thousand lilliputian cords. He
had an honest pride of independence, which chafed
under any obligation that could be avoided. His
strong attachment to the Society of Friends rendered
him sensitive to their opinion; and at that period
their rules were exceedingly strict concerning any of
their members, who contracted debts they were unable to pay. People are always ready to censure a
man who is unprosperous in worldly affairs; and if
his character is such as to render him prominent, he
is all the more likely to be handled harshly. Of
these trials Friend Hopper had a large share, and
they disturbed him exceedingly; but the consciousness of upright intentions kept him from sinking under the weight that pressed upon him.

He was always a very industrious man, and whatever he did was well done. But the fact was, the
claims upon his time and attention were too numerous to be met by any one mortal man. He had a
large family to support, and during many years his

house was a home for poor Quakers, and others, from far and near. He had much business to transact in the Society of Friends, of which he was then an influential and highly respected member. He was one of the founders and secretary of a society for the employment of the poor; overseer of the Benezet school for colored children; teacher, without recompense, in a free school for colored adults; inspector of the prison, without a salary; member of a fire-company; guardian of abused apprentices; the lawyer and protector of slaves and colored people, upon all occasions. When pestilence was raging, he was devoted to the sick. The poor were continually calling upon him to plead with importunate landlords and creditors. He was not unfrequently employed to settle estates involved in difficulties, which others were afraid to undertake. He had occasional applications to exert influence over the insane, for which he had peculiar tact. When he heard of a man beginning to form habits likely to prove injurious to himself or his family, he would go to him, whether his rank were high or low, and have private conversations with him. He would tell him some story, or suppose some case, and finally make him feel, "Thou art the man." He had a great gift in that way, and the exertion of it sometimes seasonably recalled those who were sliding into dangerous paths.

When one reflects upon the time that must have been bestowed on all these avocations, do his pecuniary embarrassments require any further explanation? A member of his own Society summed up the case very justly in few words. Hearing him censured by certain individuals, she replied, "The whole amount of it is this :—the Bible requires us to love our neighbor as well as ourselves ; and Friend Isaac has loved them better."

These straitened circumstances continued during the remainder of his residence in Philadelphia; and his family stood by him nobly through the trial. Household expenses were reduced within the smallest possible limits. His wife opened a tea-store, as an available means of increasing their income. The simple dignity of her manners, and her pleasing way of talking, attracted many ladies, even among the fashionable, who liked to chat with the handsome Quaker matron, while they were purchasing household stores. The elder daughters taught school, and took upon themselves double duty in the charge of a large family of younger children. How much they loved and honored their father, was indicated by their zealous efforts to assist and sustain him. I have heard him tell, with much emotion, how one of them slipped some of her earnings into his pocket, while he slept in his arm-chair. She was anxious to save him from the pain of being unable to meet necessary

expenses, and at the same time to keep him ignorant
of the source whence relief came.

His spirit of independence never bent under the
pressure of misfortune. He was willing to deprive
himself of everything, except the simplest necessaries
of life; but he struggled manfully against incurring
obligations. There was a Quaker fund for the gra-
tuitous education of children; but when he was
urged to avail himself of it, he declined, beoause
he thought such funds ought to be reserved for
those whose necessities were greater than his own.

The government added its exactions to other pecuniary annoyances; but it had no power to warp
the inflexibility of his principles. He had always
refused to pay the militia tax, because, in common
with all conscientious Quakers, he considered it
wrong to do anything for the support of war. It
seems no more than just that a sect, who pay a
double school-tax, and a double pauper-tax, and who
almost never occasion the state any expense by their
crimes, should be excused for believing themselves
bound to obey the injunction of Jesus, to return good
for evil; but politicians have decided that practical
Christianity is not always consistent with the duty
of citizens. Accordingly, when Friend Hopper refused to pay for guns and swords, to shoot and stab
his fellow men, they seized his goods to pay the tax.
The articles chosen were often of much greater value

than their demand, and were sacrificed by a hurried and careless sale. His wife had received a handsome outfit from her father, at the time of her marriage; but she was destined to see one article of furniture after another seized to pay the military fines, which were alike abhorrent to her heart and her conscience. Among these articles, was a looking glass, of an unusually large and clear plate, which was valuable as property, and dear to her as a bridal gift from her parents. She could not see it carried off by the officer, to meet the expenses of military reviews, without a sigh—perhaps a tear. But she was not a woman ever to imply a wish to have her husband compromise his principles.

Thus bearing up bravely against the pelting storms of life, he went on, hand in hand with his beloved Sarah. But at last, he was called to part with the steady friend and pleasant companion of his brightest and his darkest hours. She passed from him into the spiritual world on the eighteenth of the Sixth Month, (June,) 1822, in the forty-seventh year of her age. She suffered much from the wasting pains of severe dyspepsia; but religious hope and faith enabled her to endure all her trials with resignation, and to view the approach of death with cheerful serenity of soul. Toward the close of her life, the freshness of her complexion was injured by continual suffering; but though pale, she remained a handsome woman to the last. During her long illness, she received innumerable marks of respect and affection from friends and neighbors; for she was beloved by all who knew her. A short time before her death, she offered the following prayer for the dear ones she was so soon to leave; "O Lord, permit me to ask thy blessing for this family. Thy favor is better than all the world can give. For want of keeping close to thy counsel, my soul has often been pierced with sorrow. Pity my weakness. Look thou from heaven, and forgive. Enable me, I beseech thee, to renew my covenant, and so to live under the influence of thy Holy Spirit, as to keep it. Preserve me in the hour of temptation. Thou alone knowest how prone I am to err on the right side and on the left. Bless the children! O Lord, visit and re-visit their tender minds. Lead them in the paths of uprightness, for thy name's sake. I ask not riches nor honor for them; but an inheritance in thy ever-blessed truth." She left nine children, the youngest but six years old, to mourn the loss of a most tender careful and self-sacrificing mother.

While her bereaved husband was still under the shadow of this great grief, he was called to part with his son Isaac, who in little more than a year, followed his mother, at the early age of fifteen. He was a sedate gentle lad, and had always been a very pleasant child to his parents. His father cherished his memory with great tenderness, and seldom spoke of him without expressing his conviction that if he had lived he would have become a highly acceptable minister in the Society of Friends; a destiny which would have been more agreeable to his parental feelings, than having a son President of the United States.

Soon after this melancholy event, Friend Hopper went to Maryland, to visit two sisters who resided there. He was accompanied in this journey by his wife's brother, David Tatum. At an inn where they stopped for refreshment, the following characteristic incident occurred : A colored girl brought in a pitcher of water. "Art thou a slave ?" said Friend Hopper. When she answered in the affirmative, he started up and exclaimed, "It is against my principles to be waited upon by a slave." His more timid brother-in-law inquired, in a low tone of voice, whether he were aware that the mistress was within hearing. "To be sure I am," answered Isaac aloud. "What would be the use of saying it, if she were *not* within hearing ?" He then emptied the pitcher of water, and went out to the well to re-fill it for himself. Seeing the landlady stare at these proceedings, he explained to her that he thought it wrong to avail himself of unpaid labor. In reply, she complained of the ingratitude of slaves, and the hard condition of their masters. "It is very inconvenient to live so near a

free state," said she. "I had sixteen slaves; but
ten of them have run away, and I expect the rest
will soon go."

"I hope they will," said Isaac. "I am sure I
would run away, if I were a slave."

At first, she was disposed to be offended; but he
reasoned the matter with her, in a quiet and friendly
manner, and they parted on very civil terms. David
Tatum often used to tell this anecdote, after they
returned home; and he generally added, "I never
again will travel in a Southern state with brother
Isaac; for I am sure it would be at the risk of my
life."

Time soothes all afflictions; and those who have
dearly loved their first companion are sometimes
more likely than others to form a second connexion;
for the simple reason that they cannot learn to do
without the happiness to which they have been accustomed. There was an intimate friend of the family, a member of the same religious Society, named
Hannah Attmore. She was a gentle and quiet person, of an innocent and very pleasing countenance.
Her father, a worthy and tender spirited man, had
been an intimate friend of Isaac T. Hopper, and always sympathized with his efforts for the oppressed.
A strong attachment had likewise existed between
her and Friend Hopper's wife; and during her frequent visits to the house, it was her pleasure to vol-

unteer assistance in the numerous household cares. The fact that his Sarah had great esteem for her, was doubtless a strong attraction to the widower. His suit was favorably received, and they were married on the fourth of the second month, (February) 1824. She was considerably younger than her bridegroom ; but vigorous health and elastic spirits had preserved his youthful appearance, while her sober dress and grave deportment, made her seem older than she really was. She became the mother of four children, two of whom died in early childhood. Little Tho mas, who ended his brief career in three years and a half, was always remembered by his parents, and other members of the family, as a remarkably bright, precocious child, beautiful as an infant angel.

It has been already stated that the schism in the Society of Friends introduced much controversy concerning the theological opinions of its founders. There was consequently an increased demand for their writings, and the branch called "Hicksites" felt the need of a bookstore. Friend Hopper's business had never been congenial to his character, and of late years it had become less profitable. A large number of his wealthiest customers were "Orthodox;" and when he took part with Elias Hicks, they ceased to patronize him. He was perfectly aware that such would be the result; but whenever it was necessary to choose between his

principles and prosperity, he invariably followed what
he believed to be the truth. He was considered a
suitable person to superintend the proposed book-
store, and as the state of his financial affairs rendered a change desirable, he concluded to accede to the
proposition of his friends. For that purpose, he removed to the city of New-York in 1829.

In the autumn of the following year, some disputed claims, which his wife had on the estate of her
maternal grandfather in Ireland, made it necessary
for him to visit that country. Experience had pain-
fully convinced him that theological controversy
sometimes leads to personal animosity ; and that few
people were so open and direct in their mode of expressing hostility, as he himself was. Therefore,
before going abroad, he took the precaution to ask
letters from citizens of various classes and sects in
Philadelphia ; and he found no difficulty in obtaining
them from the most respectable and distinguished.
Matthew Carey, the well known philanthropist
wrote as follows : "As you are about to visit my
native country, and have applied to me for a testi-
monial concerning your character, I cheerfully comply with your request. I have been well acquainted
with you for about thirty-five years, and I can testify
that, during the whole of that time, you have been a
perfect pest to our Southern neighbors. A Southern
gentleman could scarcely visit this city, without

having his slave taken from him by your instrumentality ; so that they dread you, as they do the devil." After enjoying a mutual laugh over this epistle, another was written for the public, certifying that he had known Isaac T. Hopper for many years as "a useful and respectable citizen of the fairest character."

When Friend Hopper arrived in Ireland, he found many of the Quakers prejudiced against him, and many untrue stories in circulation, as he had expected. Sometimes, when he visited public places, he would overhear people saying to each other, in a low voice, "That's Isaac T. Hopper, who has given Friends so much trouble in America." A private letter from an "Orthodox" Quaker in Philadelphia was copied and circulated in all directions, greatly to his disadvantage. It represented him as a man of sanctified appearance, but wholly unworthy of credit ; that business of a pecuniary nature was a mere pretence to cover artful designs ; his real object being to spread heretical doctrines in Ireland, and thus sow dissension among Friends. In his journal of this visit to a foreign land, Friend Hopper says : "It is astonishing what strange ideas some of them have concerning me. They have been informed that I can find stolen goods, and am often applied to on such occasions. I think it would be no hard matter to make them believe me a wizard." This was probably a serious version of his pleasantry with the Dutchman about finding his goods by calculating the age of the moon.

Many of the Irish Friends had formed from hearsay the most extravagant misconceptions concerning the Friends called "Hicksites." They supposed them to be outright infidels, and that the grossest immoralities were tolerated among them; that they pointed loaded pistols at the "Orthodox" brethren, and drove them out of their own meeting-houses by main force. One of them expressed great surprise when Friend Hopper informed him that they were in the constant habit of reading the Scriptures in their families, and maintained among themselves the same discipline that had always been used in the Society. Sometimes when he attended Quaker meetings during the early portion of his visit, the ministers preached at him, by cautioning young people to beware of the adversary, who was now going about like a cunning serpent, in which form he was far more dangerous, than when he assumed the appearance of a roaring lion. But after a while, this tendency was rebuked by other preachers, who inculcated forbearance in judging others; reminding their hearers that the spirit of the Gospel always breathed peace and good will toward men. As for Isaac himself, he behaved with characteristic openness. When a stranger, in Quaker costume, introduced himself, and invited him to go home and dine with him, he replied, "I am represented by some people as a very bad man; and I do not wish to impose myself upon the hospitality of strangers, without letting them know who I am."

The stranger assured him that he knew very well who he was, and cared not a straw what opinions they accused him of; that he was going to have a company of Friends at dinner, who wished to converse with him. He went accordingly, and was received with true Irish hospitality and kindness.

Upon another occasion, a Quaker lady, who did not know he was a "Hicksite," observed to him, "I suppose the Society of Friends are very much thinned in America, since so many have gone off from them." He replied, "It is always best to be candid. I belong to the party called Hicksites, deists, and schismatics; and I suppose they are the ones to whom thou hast alluded as having gone off from the Society. I should like to talk with thee concerning the separation in America; for we have been greatly misrepresented. But I came to this country solely on business, and I have no wish to say or do anything that can unsettle the mind, or wound the feelings of any Friend. She seemed very much surprised, and for a minute or two covered her face with her hands. But when the company broke up, some hours after, she followed him into the entry, and cor-

dially invited him to visit her. "What! canst thou
tolerate the company of a heretic?" he exclaimed.
She replied with a smile, "Yes, such a one as thou
art."

In fact, wherever he had a chance to make himself known, prejudices melted away under the influence of his frank and kindly manners. Some people
of other sects, as well of his own, took an interest in
him for the very reasons that caused distrust and
dislike in others; viz: because they had heard of
him as the champion of perfect liberty of conscience,
who considered it unnecessary to bind men by any
creed whatsoever. Among these, he mentions in his
journal, Professor Stokes of Dublin, who relinquished a salary of two thousand eight hundred pounds a
year, because he could not conscientiously subscribe
to the doctrine of the Trinity. It was proposed to
dismiss him from the college altogether; but he demanded a hearing before the trustees and students.
This privilege could not be denied, without infring-
ing the laws of the institution; and deeming that
such a discussion might prove injurious, they concluded to retain him, on a salary of eight hundred
pounds. Friend Hopper describes him thus: "He
is an intelligent and liberal-minded man, and has a
faculty of exposing the errors and absurdities of the
Athanasian Creed to much purpose. He was of a
good spirit, and I was much gratified with his com-

pany. He insisted upon accompanying me home in
the evening, and though I remonstrated against it,
on account of his advanced age, he attended me to
the door of my lodgings."

During this visit to Ireland, Friend Hopper was
treated with great hospitality and respect by many
who were wealthy, and many who were not wealthy; by members of the Society of Friends, and of
various other religious sects. He formed a high
estimate of the Irish character, and to the day of his
death, always spoke with warm affection of the
friends he found there. In his journal, he often
alludes with pleasure to the children he met with, in
families where he visited; for he was always extremely partial to the young. Speaking of a visit to
a gentleman in the environs of Dublin, by the name
of Wilson, he says: "I rose early in the morning,
and the eldest daughter, about ten or eleven years
old, very politely invited me to walk with her. We
rambled about in the pastures, and through beautiful
groves of oak, beech and holly. The little creature
tried her very best to amuse me. She told me about
the birds and the hares, and other inhabitants of the
woods. She inquired whether I did not want very
much to see my wife and children; and exclaimed,
"How I should like to see you meet them! It would
give you so much pleasure!" He speaks of a little
girl in another family, who seemed very much at-

tracted toward him, and finally whispered to her
father, "I want to go and speak to that Friend." She
was introduced accordingly, and they had much
pleasant chat together.

In one of the families where he visited, they told
him an instructive story concerning a Quaker who
resided in Dublin, by the name of Joseph Torrey.
One day when he was passing through the streets,
he saw a man leading a horse, which was evidently
much diseased. His compassionate heart was pained
by the sight, and he asked the man where he was
going. He replied, "The horse has the staggers,
and I am going to sell him to the carrion-butchers."

"Wilt thou sell him to me for a crown!" inquired
Joseph. The man readily assented, and the poor
animal was led to the stable of his new friend, where
he was most kindly tended. Suitable remedies and
careful treatment soon restored him to health and
beauty. One day, when Friend Torrey was riding
him in Phœnix Park, a gentleman looked very earnestly at the horse, and at last inquired whether his
owner would be willing to sell him. "Perhaps I
would," replied Joseph, "if I could get a very good
master for him."

"He so strongly resembles a favorite horse I once
had, that I should think he was the same, if I didn't
know he was dead," rejoined the stranger.

"Did he die in thy stable?" inquired Joseph.

The gentleman replied, "No. He had the staggers very badly, and I sent him to the carrion-butchers."

"I should be sorry to sell an animal to any man, who would send him to the carrion-butchers because he was diseased," answered Joseph. "If thou wert ill, how wouldst thou like to have thy throat cut, instead of being kindly nursed?"

With some surprise, the gentleman inquired whether he intended to compare him to a horse. "No," replied Joseph; "but animals have feelings, as well as human beings; and when they are afflicted with disease, they ought to be carefully attended. If I consent to sell thee this horse, I shall exact a promise that thou wilt have him kindly nursed when he is sick, and not send him to have his throat cut."

The gentleman readily promised all that was required, and said he should consider himself very fortunate to obtain a horse that so much resembled his old favorite. When he called the next day, to complete the bargain, he inquired whether forty guineas would be a satisfactory price. The conscientious Quaker answered, "I have good reason to believe the horse was once thine; and I am willing to restore him to thee on the conditions I have mentioned. I have saved him from the carrion-butchers, but I will charge thee merely what I have expended for his food and medicine. Let it be a lesson to thee to treat animals kindly, when they are diseased. Never again send to the butchers a faithful servant, that cannot plead for himself, and may, with proper attention, again become useful to thee."

How little Friend Hopper was inclined to minister to aristocratic prejudices, may be inferred from the following anecdote. One day, while he was visiting a wealthy family in Dublin, a note was handed to him, inviting him to dine the next day. When he read it aloud, his host remarked, "Those people are very respectable, but not of the first circles. They belong to our church, but not exactly to our set. Their father was a mechanic."

"Well I am a mechanic myself," said Isaac. "Perhaps if thou hadst known that fact, thou wouldst not have invited *me* ?"

"Is it possible," exclaimed his host, "that a man of your information and appearance can be a mechanic !"

"I followed the business of a tailor for many years," rejoined his guest. "Look at my hands ! Dost thou not see marks of the shears ? Some of the mayors of Philadelphia have been tailors. When I lived there, I often walked the streets with the Chief Justice. It never occurred to me that it was any honor, and I don't think it did to him."

Upon one occasion, Friend Hopper went into the Court of Chancery in Dublin, and kept his hat on,

according to Quaker custom.   While he was listening to the pleading, he noticed that a person who sat
near the Chancellor fixed his eyes upon him with a
very stern expression.   This attracted the attention
of lawyers and spectators, who also began to look at
him.   Presently an officer tapped him on the shoulder, and said, "Your hat, sir !"

"What's the matter with my hat ?" he inquired.

"Take it off ?" rejoined the officer.   "You are in
his Majesty Court of Chancery."

"That is an honor I reserve for his Majesty's Master," he replied.   "Perhaps it is my shoes thou
meanest ?"

The officer seemed embarrassed, but said no
more ; and when the Friend had stayed as long as he
felt inclined, he quietly withdrew.

One day, when he was walking with a lawyer in
Dublin, they passed the Lord Lieutenant's castle.
He expressed a wish to see the Council Chamber,
but was informed that it was not open to strangers.
"I have a mind to go and try," said he to his com-
panion.   "Wilt thou go with me ?"

"No indeed," he replied; "and I would advise
you not to go."

He marched in, however, with his broad beaver
on, and found the Lord Lieutenant surrounded by a
number of gentleman.   "I am an American," said
he.   "I have heard a great deal about the Lord

Lieutenant's castle, and if it will give no offence, I should like very much to see it."

His lordship seemed surprised by this unceremonious introduction, but he smiled, and said to a servant, "Show this American whatever he wishes to see."

He was conducted into various apartments, where he saw pictures, statues, ancient armor, antique coins, and many other curious articles. At parting, the master of the mansion was extremely polite, and gave him much interesting information on a variety of topics. When he rejoined his companion, who had agreed to wait for him at some appointed place, he was met with the inquiry, "Well, what luck?"

"O, the best luck in the world," he replied. "I was treated with great politeness."

"Well certainly, Mr. Hopper, you are an extraordinary man," responded the lawyer. "I wouldn't have ventured to try such an experiment."

At the expiration of four months, having completed the business which rendered his presence in Ireland necessary, he made a short visit to England, on his way home. There also his hat was objected to on several occasions. While in Bristol, he asked permission to look at the interior of the Cathedral. He had been walking about some little time, when a rough-looking man said to him, in a very surly tone, "Take off your hat, sir!"

He replied very courteously, "I have asked permission to enter here to gratify my curiosity as a stranger. I hope it is no offence."

"Take off your hat!" rejoined the rude man. "If you don't, I'll take it off for you."

Friend Hopper leaned on his cane, looked him full in the face, and answered very coolly, "If thou dost, I hope thou wilt send it to my lodgings; for I shall have need of it this afternoon. I lodge at No. 35, Lower Crescent, Clifton." The place designated was about a mile from the Cathedral. The man stared at him, as if puzzled to decide whether he were talking to an insane person, or not. When the imperturbable Quaker had seen all he cared to see, he deliberately walked away.

At Westminster Abbey he paid the customary fee of two shillings sixpence for admission. The door-keeper followed him, saying, "You must uncover yourself, sir."

"Uncover myself!" exclaimed the Friend, with an affectation of ignorant simplicity. "What dost thou mean? Must I take off my coat?"

"Your coat!" responded the man, smiling. "No indeed. I mean your hat."

"And what should I take off my hat for?" he inquired.

"Because you are in a church, sir," answered the door-keeper.

"I see no church here," rejoined the Quaker. "Perhaps thou meanest the house where the church assembles. I suppose thou art aware that it is the *people*, not the *building*, that constitutes a church?"

The idea seemed new to the man, but he merely repeated, "You must take off your hat, sir."

But the Friend again inquired, "What for? On account of these images? Thou knowest Scripture commands us not to worship graven images."

The man persisted in saying that no person could be permitted to pass through the church without uncovering his head. "Well friend," rejoined Isaac, "I have some conscientious scruples on that subject; so give me back my money, and I will go out."

The reverential habits of the door-keeper were not quite strong enough to compel him to that sacrifice; and he walked away, without saying anything more on the subject.

When Friend Hopper visited the House of Lords, he asked the sergeant-at-arms if he might sit upon the throne. He replied, "No, sir. No one but his majesty sits there."

"Wherein does his majesty differ from other men?" inquired he. "If his head were cut off, wouldn't he die?"

"Certainly he would," replied the officer.

"So would an American," rejoined Friend Hopper. As he spoke, he stepped up to the gilded rail-

ing that surrounded the throne, and tried to open
the gate. The officer told him it was locked.
"Well won't the same key that locked it unlock it ?"
inquired he. "Is this the key hanging here?"

Being informed that it was, he took it down and
unlocked the gate. He removed the satin covering
from the throne, carefully dusted the railing with his
handkerchief, before he hung the satin over it, and
then seated himself in the royal chair. "Well,"
said he, "do I look anything like his majesty?"

The man seemed embarrassed, but smiled as he
answered, "Why, sir, you certainly fill the throne
very respectably."

There were several noblemen in the room, who
seemed to be extremely amused by these unusual
proceedings.

At a place called Jordans, about twenty-two miles
from London, he visited the grave of William Penn.

In his journal, he says : "The ground is surrounded by a neat hedge, and is kept in good order. I
picked some grass and moss from the graves of William Penn, Thomas Ellwood, and Isaac Pennington ;
and some ivy and holly from the hedge ; which I intend to take with me to America, as a memorial of
my visit. I entered the meeting-house, and sat on
the benches which had been occupied by George
Fox, William Penn, and George Whitehead, in years
long since passed away. It brought those old

Friends so distinctly before the view of my mind, that my heart was ready to exclaim, 'Surely this is no other than the house of God, and this is the gate of heaven.' I cannot describe my feelings. The manly and majestic features of George Fox, and the mournful yet benevolent countenance of Isaac Pennington, seemed to rise before me. But this is human weakness. Those men bore the burthen and heat of their own day; they faithfully used the talents committed to their trust; and I doubt not they are now reaping the reward given to faithful servants. It is permitted us to love their memories, but not to idolize them. They could deliver neither son or daughter by their righteousness; but only their own souls."

"In the great city of London everything tended to satisfy me that the state of our religious Society is generally very low. A light was once kindled there, that illuminated distant lands. As I walked the streets, I remembered the labors, the sufferings, and the final triumph of those illustrious sons of the morning, George Fox, George Whitehead, William Penn, and a host of others; men who loved not their lives in comparison with the holy cause of truth and righteousness, in which they were called to labor. These worthies have been succeeded by a generation, who seem disposed to garnish the sepulchres of their fathers, and live upon the fruit of their labors,

without submitting to the power of that Cross, which
made them what they were. There appears to me
to be much formality and dryness among them;
though there are a few who mourn, almost without
hope, over the desolation that has been made by the
world, the flesh, and the devil."

There were many poor emigrants on board the
merchant ship, in which Friend Hopper returned
home. He soon established friendly communication
with them, and entered with sympathy into all their
troubles. He made frequent visits to the steerage
during the long voyage, and always had something
comforting and cheering to say to the poor souls.
There was a clergyman on board, who also wished
to benefit them, but he approached them in an official way, to which they did not so readily respond.
One day, when he invited the emigrants to join him
in prayer, an old Irish woman replied, "I'd rather
play a game o'cards, than hear you prache and
pray." She pointed to Friend Hopper, and added,
" *He* comes and stays among us, and always spakes
a word o' comfort, and does us some good. But *you*
come and prache and pray, and then you are gone.
One look from that Quaker gintleman is worth all
the praching and praying that be in you."

The vessel encountered a dense fog, and ran on a
sand bank as they approached the Jersey shore. A
tremendous sea was rolling, and dashed against the

ship with such force, that she seemed every moment in danger of being shattered into fragments. If there had been a violent gale of wind, all must have been inevitably lost. The passengers were generally in a state of extreme terror. Screams and groans were heard in every direction. But Friend Hopper's mind was preserved in a state of great equanimity. He entreated the people to be quiet, and try to keep possession of their faculties, that they might be ready to do whatever was best, in case of emergency. Seeing him so calm, they gathered closely round him, as if they thought he had some power to save them. There was a naval officer on board, whose frenzied state of feeling vented itself in blasphemous language. Friend Hopper, who was always disturbed by irreverent use of the name of Deity, was peculiarly shocked by it under these solemn circumstances. He walked up to the officer, put his hand on his shoulder, and looking him in the face, said, "From what I have heard of thy military exploits, I supposed thou wert a brave man; but here thou art pouring forth blasphemies, to keep up the appearance of courage, while thy pale face and quivering lips show that thou art in mortal fear. I am ashamed of thee. If thou hast no reverence for Deity thyself, thou shouldst show some regard for the feelings of those who have." The officer ceased swearing, and treated his adviser with marked res pect. A friendship was formed between them, which continued as long as the captain lived.

The clergyman on board afterward said to Friend Hopper, "If any other person had talked to him in that manner, he would have knocked him down."

In about two hours, the vessel floated off the sand-bar and went safely into the harbor of New-York. At the custom-house, the clergyman was in some perplexity about a large quantity of books he had brought with him, on which it was proposed to charge high duties. "Perhaps I can get them through for thee," said Friend Hopper. "I will try." He went up to the officer, and said, "Isn't it a rule of the custom-house not to charge a man for the tools of his trade?" He replied that it was. "Then thou art bound to let this priest's books pass free," rejoined the Friend. "Preaching is the trade he gets his living by; and these books are the tools he must use." The clergyman being aware of Quaker views with regard to a paid ministry, seemed doubtful whether to be pleased or not, with *such* a mode of helping him out of difficulty. However, he took the joke as good naturedly as it was offered, and the books passed free, on the assurance that they were all for his own library.

Friend Hopper's bookstore in New-York was a place of great resort for members of his own sect His animated style of conversation, his thousand

and one anecdotes of runaway slaves, his descriptions of keen encounters with the "Orthodox," in the process of separation, attracted many listeners. His intelligence and well-known conscientiousness commanded respect, and he was held in high estimation by his own branch of the Society, though the opposite party naturally entertained a less favorable opinion of the "Hicksite" champion. Such a character as he was must necessarily always be a man of mark, with warm friends and bitter enemies.

His resemblance to Bonaparte attracted attention in New-York, as it had done in Philadelphia. Not long after he removed to that city, there was a dramatic representation at the Park Theatre, in which Placide personated the French Emperor. While this play was attracting public attention, the manager happened to meet Friend Hopper in the street. As soon as he saw him, he exclaimed, "Here is Napoleon himself come back again!" He remarked to some of his acquaintance that he would gladly give that Quaker gentleman one hundred dollars a night, if he would consent to appear on the stage in the costume of Bonaparte.

About this period northern hostility to slavery took a new form, more bold and uncompromising than the old Abolition Societies. It demanded the immediate and unconditional emancipation of every slave, in a voice which has not yet been silenced,

and never will be, while the oppressive system continues to disgrace our country. Of course, Friend
Hopper could not otherwise than sympathize with
any movement for the abolition of slavery, based on
pacific principles. Pictures and pamphlets, published
by the Anti-Slavery Society were offered for sale in
nis book-store. During the popular excitement on this
subject, in 1834, he was told that his store was about
to be attacked by an infuriated rabble, and he had
better remove all such publications from the window. "Dost thou think I am such a coward as to
forsake my principles, or conceal them, at the bidding of a mob?" said he. Presently, another messenger came to announce that the mob were already
in progress, at the distance of a few streets. He
was earnestly advised at least to put up the shut-
ters, that their attention might not be attracted by
the pictures. "I shall do no such thing," he replied.
The excited throng soon came pouring down the
street, with loud and discordant yells. Friend Hopper walked out and stood on the steps. The mob
stopped in front of his store. He looked calmly and
firmly at them, and they looked irresolutely at him,
like a wild animal spell-bound by the fixed gaze of a
human eye. After a brief pause, they renewed their
yells, and some of their leaders called out, "Go on,
to Rose-street!" They obeyed these orders, and in
the absence of Lewis Tappan, a well-known aboli-

tionist, they burst open his house, and destroyed his furniture.

In 1835, Judge Chinn, of Mississippi, visited New-York, and brought with him a slave, said to have cost the large sum of fifteen hundred dollars. A few days after their arrival in the city, the slave eloped, and a reward of five hundred dollars was offered for his apprehension. Friend Hopper knew nothing about him; but some mischievous person wrote a note to Judge Chinn, stating that the fugitive was concealed at his store, in Pearl-street. A warrant was procured and put into the hands of a constable frequently employed in that base business. At that season of the year, many Southerners were in the city to purchase goods. A number of them accompanied the judge to Pearl-street, and distributed themselves at short distances, in order to arrest the slave, in case he attempted to escape. They preferred to search the store in the absence of Friend Hopper, and watched nearly an hour for a favorable opportunity. Meanwhile, he was entirely unconscious of their proceedings; and having occasion to call at a house a few doors below, he left the store for a short time in charge of one of his sons. As soon as he was gone, four or five men rushed in. Not finding the object of their pursuit, they jumped out of a back window, and began to search some buildings in the rear. When people complained of such unceremonious intrusion upon their premises, the constable excused himself by saying they were trying to apprehend a felon. Friend Hopper's son called out that it was a slave, not a felon, they were in search of; for he heard them say so. This made the constable very angry; for, like most slave-catchers, he was eager for the reward, but rather ashamed of the services by which he sought to obtain it. He swore roundly, and one of his party gave the young man a blow on his face.

Friend Hopper, being sent for, returned immediately; and for some time after, he observed a respectable looking person occasionally peeping into the store, and skulking out of sight as soon as he thought himself observed. At last, he went to the door, and said, "My friend, if thou hast business with me, come in and let me know what it is; but don't be prying about my premises in that way." He walked off, and joined a group of people, who seemed to be much excited. Friend Hopper followed, and found they were the men who had been recently searching his store. He said to their leader, "Art thou the impertinent fellow who has been intruding upon my premises, in my absence?" The constable replied that he had a warrant, and was determined to execute it. Though a stranger to his countenance, Friend Hopper was well aware that he was noted for hunting slaves, and being unable to disguise his abhorrence of the odious business, he said, "Judas betrayed his master for thirty pieces of silver; and for a like sum, I suppose thou wouldst seize thy brother by the throat, and send him into interminable bondage. If thy conscience were as susceptible of conviction as his was, thou wouldst do as he did; and thus rid the community of an intolerable nuisance."

One of the Southerners repeated the word "Brother!" in a very sneering tone.

"Yes," rejoined Friend Hopper, "I said brother."

He returned to his store, but was soon summoned into the street again, by a complaint that the constable and his troop of slaveholders were very roughly handling a colored man, saying he had no business to keep in their vicinity. When Friend Hopper interfered, to prevent further abuse, several of the Southerners pointed bowie-knives and pistols at him. He told the constable it was his duty, as a police-officer, to arrest those men for carrying deadly weapons and making such a turmoil in the street; and he threatened to complain of him if he did not do it. He complied very reluctantly, and of course the culprits escaped before they reached the police-office.

A few days after, as young Mr. Hopper was walking up Chatham-street, on his way home in the evening, some unknown person came behind him, knocked him down, and beat him in a most savage man-

ner, so that he was unable to leave his room for
many days. No doubt was entertained that this
brutal attack was by one of the company who were
on the search for Judge Chinn's slave.

It was afterward rumored that the fugitive had arrived safely in Canada. I never heard that he returned to the happy condition of slavery; though his
master predicted that he would do so, and said he
never would have been so foolish as to leave it, if it
had not been for the false representations of abolitionists.

In 1836, the hatred which Southerners bore to
Friend Hopper's name was manifested in a cruel and
altogether unprovoked outrage on his son, which
caused the young man a great deal of suffering, and
well nigh cost him his life. John Hopper, Esq., now
a lawyer in the city of New-York, had occasion to
go to the South on business. He remained in
Charleston about two months, during which time he
was treated with courtesy in his business relations,
and received many kind attentions in the intercourse
of social life. One little incident that occurred during his visit illustrates the tenacious attachment of
Friends to their own mode of worship. When he
left home, his father had exhorted him to attend
Friends' meeting while he was in Charleston. He
told him that a meeting had been established there
many years ago, but he supposed there were not

half a dozen members remaining, and probably they
had no ministry; for the original settlers had died,
or left Carolina on account of their testimony against
slavery. But as Quakers believe that silent worship
is often more blessed to the soul, than the most
eloquent preaching, he had a strong desire that his
son should attend the meeting constantly, even if he
found but two or three to unite with him. The
young man promised that he would do so. Accordingly, when he arrived in Charleston, he inquired for the meeting-house, and was informed that
it was well nigh deserted. On the first day of the
week, he went to the place designated, and found a
venerable, kind-looking Friend seated under the
preachers' gallery. In obedience to a signal from
him, he took a seat by his side, and they remained
there in silence nearly two hours. Then the old man
turned and shook hands with him, as an indication
that the meeting was concluded, according to the
custom of the Society of Friends. When he found
that he was talking to the son of Isaac T. Hopper,
and that he had promised to attend meeting there,
during his stay in Charleston, he was so much affected, that his eyes filled with tears. "Oh, I shall
be glad of thy company," said he; "for most of the
time, this winter, I am here all alone. My old
friends and companions have all died, or moved
away. I come here twice on First days, and once

on Fifth day, and sit all, all alone, till I feel it right
to leave the house and go home."

This lonely old worshipper once had an intimate
friend, who for a long time was his only companion
in the silent meeting.   At the close, they shook
hands and walked off together, enjoying a kindly
chat on their way home.   Unfortunately, some difficulty afterward occurred between them, which com
pletely estranged them from each other.   Both still
clung to their old place of worship.   They took
their accustomed seats, and remained silent for a
couple of hours; but they parted without shaking
hands, or speaking a single word.   This alienation
almost broke the old man's heart.   After awhile, he
lost even this shadow of companionship, and there
remained only "the voice within," and echoes of
memory from the empty benches.

While Mr. Hopper remained in Charleston, he
went to the Quaker meeting-house every Sunday,
and rarely found any one there except the perse-
vering old Friend, who often invited him to go home
with him.   He seemed to take great satisfaction in
talking with him about his father, and listening to
what he had heard him say concerning the Society
of Friends.   When the farewell hour came, he was
much affected; for he felt it not likely they would
ever meet again; and the conversation of the young
stranger had formed a link between him and the

Quakerism he loved so well. The old man continued to sit alone under the preacher's gallery till the house took fire and was burned to the ground. He died soon after that event, at a very advanced age.

Another incident, which occurred during Mr. Hopper's stay in Charleston, seemed exceedingly trivial at the time, but came very near producing fatal consequences. One day, when a clergyman whom he visited was showing him his library, he mentioned that his father had quite an antiquarian taste for old documents connected with the Society of Friends. At parting, the clergyman gave him several pamphlets for his father, and among them happened to be a tract published by Friends in Philadelphia, describing the colony at Sierra Leone, and giving an account of the slave trade on the coast of Africa. He put the pamphlets in his trunk, and started for Savannah, where he arrived on the twenty-eighth of January. At the City Hotel, he unfortunately encountered a marshal of the city of New-York, who was much employed in catching runaway slaves, and of course sympathized with slaveholders. He pointed the young stranger out, as a son of Isaac T. Hopper, the notorious abolitionist. This information kindled a flame immediately, and they began to discuss plans of vengeance. The traveller, not dreaming of danger, retired to his room soon after

supper. In a few minutes, his door was forced open
by a gang of intoxicated men, escorted by the New-
York marshal. They assailed him with a volley of
blasphemous language, struck him, kicked him, and
spit in his face. They broke open and rifled his
trunk, and searched his pockets for abolition documents. When they found the harmless little Quaker
tract about the colony at Sierra Leone, they screamed with exultation. They shouted, "Here is what
we wanted! Here is proof of abolitionism!" Some
of them rushed out and told the mob, who crowded
the bar-room and entries, that they had found a trunk
full of abolition tracts. Others seized Mr. Hopper
violently, telling him to say his last prayers, and go
with them. The proprietor of the City Hotel was
very naturally alarmed for the safety of the building.
He was in a great passion, and conjured them to
carry their victim down forthwith; saying he could
do nothing with the mob below, who were getting
very impatient waiting for him. Turning to Mr.
Hopper, he said, "Young man, you are in a very
unfortunate situation. You ought never to have left
your home. But it is your own doing; and you de-
serve your fate." When appealed to for protection,
he exclaimed, "Good God! you must not appeal to
me. This is a damned delicate business. I shall
not be able to protect my own property. But I will
go for the mayor."

One of the bar-keeper's confidential friends sent
him a slip of paper, on which was written, "His
only mode of escape is by the window;" and the
bar-keeper, who had previously shown himself de-
cidedly unfriendly, urged him again and again to
profit by this advice. He occupied the third story,
and the street below his window was thronged with
an infuriated mob, thirsting and clamoring for his
blood. In view of these facts, it seems not very un-
charitable to suppose that the advice was given to
make sure of his death, apparently by his own act,
and thus save the city of Savannah from the disgrace of the deed. Of the two terrible alternatives,
he preferred going down-stairs into the midst of the
angry mob, who were getting more and more mad-
dened by liquor, having taken forcible possession of
the bar. He considered his fate inevitable, and had
made up his mind to die. But at the foot of the
stairs, he was met by the mayor and several aldermen, whose timely arrival saved his life. After asking some questions, and receiving the assurance that
he came to Savannah solely on commercial business,
the magistrates accompanied Mr. Hopper to his
room, and briefly examined his books and papers.
The mayor then went down and addressed the mob,
assuring them that he should be kept in custody during the night; that strict investigation should be
made, and if there was the slightest evidence of his

being an abolitionist, he should not be suffered to go
at large.   The mayor and a large body of civil officers accompanied the prisoner to the guard-house,
and a number of citizens volunteered their services,
to strengthen the escort; but all their efforts scarcely sufficed to keep him from the grasp of the infuriated multitude.   He was placed in a noisome cell, to
await his trial, and the customary guard was increased for his protection.   Portions of the mob continued
howling round the prison all night, and the mayor
was sent for several times to prevent their bursting
in.   A gallows was erected, with a barrel of feathers
and a tub of tar in readiness under it, that they might
amuse themselves with their victim before they murdered him.

Next morning, at five o'clock, the prisoner was
brought before the mayor for further examination.
Many of the mob followed him to the door of the
office to await the issue.   The evidence was satisfactory that he belonged to no anti-slavery society,
and that his business in Savannah had no connection
whatever with that subject.   As for the pamphlet
about Sierra Leone, the mayor said he considered
that evidence in his favor; because it was written in
support of colonization.   Before the examination
closed, there came a driving rain, which dispersed
the mob lying in wait round the building.   Aided by
this lucky storm their destined victim passed out

without being observed. At parting, the mayor
said to him, "Young man, you may consider it a
miracle that you have escaped with your life."

He took refuge on board the ship Angelique,
bound for New-York, and was received with much
kindness and sympathy by Captain Nichols, the
commander. There was likewise a sailor on board,
who happened to be one of the many that owed a
debt of gratitude to Friend Hopper; and he swore
he would shoot anybody that attempted to harm his
son. In a short time, a messenger came from the
mayor to announce that the populace had discovered
where Mr. Hopper was secreted, and would probably
attack the vessel. In this emergency, the captain
behaved nobly toward his hunted fellow-citizen. He
requested him to lie down flat in the bottom of a
boat, which he himself entered and conducted to a
brig bound for Providence. The captain was a
New-England man, but having been long engaged in
Southern trade, his principles on the subject of
slavery were adapted to his interest. He gave the
persecuted young traveller a most ungracious reception, and said if he thought he was an abolitionist he
would send him directly back to Savannah. However, the representations of Captain Nichols induced
him to consent that he should be put on board.
They had a tedious passage of thirty-five days,
during which there was a long and violent storm,

that seemed likely to wreck the vessel. The mob
had robbed Mr. Hopper of his money and clothing.
He had no comfortable garments to shield him from
the severe cold, and his hands and feet were frozen.
At last, he arrived at Providence, and went on board
the steamer Benjamin Franklin, bound for New-
York. There he had the good fortune to meet with
a colored waiter, whose father had been redeemed
from slavery by Friend Hopper's exertions. He was
assiduously devoted to the son of his benefactor, and
did everything in his power to alleviate his distressed
condition.

When the traveller arrived at his home, he was so
haggard and worn down with danger and fatigue,
that his family scarcely recognized him. His father
was much excited and deeply affected, when he
heard what perils he had gone through merely on
account of his name. He soon after addressed the
following letter to the mayor of Savannah:

NEW-YORK, 4th month, 18th, 1836.

"FRIEND,

My object in addressing thee is to express
my heartfelt gratitude for thy exertions in saving
the life of my son, which I have cause to believe
was in imminent peril, from the violence of unreasonable men, while in your city a few weeks ago. I am
informed that very soon after his arrival in Savan-

nah, the fact became known to a marshal of this
city, who was then there, and who, by his misrepresentations, excited the rabble to a determination to
perpetrate the most inhuman outrage upon him, and
in all probability to take his life; and that preparations were made, which, if carried into effect, would
doubtless have produced that result.

Tar and feathers, as a mode of punishment, I am
inclined to think is rather of modern invention; and
I am doubtful whether they will be more efficient
than whipping, cutting off ears, the rack, the halter
and the stake.   Superstition and intolerance have
long ago called in all these to their aid, in suppress-
ing reformation in religion; but they were unable to
accomplish the end designed; and if I am not greatly
mistaken, they would prove entirely insufficient to
stop the progress of emancipation.

If it is the determination of the people of Savannah to deliver up to a lawless and blood-thirsty mob
every person coming among them whose sentiments
are opposed to slavery, I apprehend there are very
few at the North who would not be obnoxious to
their hostility.   For I believe they all view slavery
as an evil that must be abolished at no very distant
day.   Would it not be well for the people of the
South to reflect upon the tendency of their conduct?
Where such aggressions upon humanity are committed, the slaves will naturally inquire into the

cause ; and when they are informed that it is in consequence of their oppressed and degraded condition,
and that the persons thus persecuted are charged
with being their friends, they cannot feel indifferent.
One such scene as was witnessed in the case of my
son would tend more to excite a spirit of insurrection and insubordination among them, than ten thousand 'incendiary pamphlets,' not one word of which
any of them could read.   My son went to Savannah
solely on his own private business, without any intention of interfering with the slaves, or with the
subject of slavery in any way.   But even supposing
the charge to have been true, do not your laws
award sufficient punishment ?   How could you stand
silently by, and witness proceedings that would put
to blush the Arab, or the untutored inhabitant of the
wilderness in our own country ?   The negroes, whom
you affect to despise so much, would set an example
of benevolence and humanity, when on their own
soil, if a stranger came among them, which you cannot be prepared to imitate, till you have made great
improvements in civilization.

The people of Savannah profess Christianity ;
but what avails profession, where latitude is given to
the vilest and most depraved passions of the human
heart ?   Suppose the mob had murdered my son ; a
young man who went among you in the ordinary
course of his business, and who, even according to

your understanding of the term, had done no evil; a
young man of fair reputation, with numerous near
relatives and friends to mourn over the barbarous
deed; would you have been guiltless? I think the
just witness in your consciences would answer
No.

I have long deplored the evils of slavery, and
my sympathy has often been much excited for the
master, as well as the slave. I am aware of the
difficulties attending the system, and I should rejoice
if I could aid in devising some mode of relief, that
would satisfy the claims of justice and humanity,
and at the same time be acceptable to the inhabitants of the South.

It is certainly cause of deep regret that the
Southern people suffer their angry passions to become so highly excited on this subject, which, of all
others, ought to be calmly considered. For it remains a truth that 'the wrath of man worketh not
the righteousness of God,' neither can it open his
eyes to see in what his best interest consists. O,
that your ears may be open to the voice of wisdom
before it is too late! The language of an eminent
statesman, who was a slaveholder, often occurs to
me: 'I tremble for my country when I reflect that
God is just, and that his justice will not sleep forever.' Surely we have high authority for believing
that 'For the crying of the poor, and the sighing of

the needy, God will arise.' I hope I shall not be suspected of entertaining hostile or unkind feelings toward the people of the South, when I say that I believe slavery must and will be abolished. As sure as God is merciful and good, it is an evil that cannot endure forever.

An inspired apostle says, that our gracious Creator 'hath made of one blood all nations of men;' and our Saviour gave this commandment: 'As ye would that men should do to you, do ye also to them likewise.' If we believe these declarations, and I hope none doubt their authority, I should think reasoning unnecessary to convince us that to oppress and enslave our fellow men cannot be pleasing to Him, who is just and equal in all his ways.

My concern for the welfare of my fellow men is not confined to color, or circumscribed by geographical lines. I can never see human suffering without feeling compassion, and I would always gladly alleviate it, if I had it in my power. I remember that we are all, without distinction of color or locality, children of the same Universal Parent, who delights to see the human family dwell together in peace and harmony. I am strongly inclined to the opinion that the proceedings of that portion of the inhabitants of the North who are called abolitionists, would not produce so much agitation and excitement at the South, if the people there felt entirely satisfied that

slavery was justifiable in the sight of infinite purity
and justice. An eminent minister of the Gospel,
about the middle of the seventeenth century, often
urged upon the attention of people this emphatic injunction : 'Mind the light !' 'All things that are reproved are made manifest by the light ; for whatsoever doth make manifest is light.' Now, if this light,
or spirit of truth, 'a manifestation of which is given
to every man to profit withal,' should be found testifying in your consciences against injustice and oppression, regard its admonitions ! It will let none
remain at ease in their sins. It will justify for well
doing ; but to those who rebel against it, and disregard its reproofs, it will become the 'worm that di-
eth not, and the fire that is not quenched.'

I am aware that complaints are often made, because obstacles are thrown in the way of Southerners reclaiming their fugitive slaves. But bring the
matter home to yourselves. Suppose a white man
resided among you, who, for a series of years, had
conducted with sobriety, industry, and probity, and
had given frequent evidence of the kindness of his
heart, by a disposition to oblige whenever opportunity offered ; suppose he had a wife and children de-
pendent upon him, and supported them comfortably
and respectably ; could you see that man dragged
from his bed, and from the bosom of his family, in
the dead time of night, manacled, and hurried away

into a distant part of the country, where his family
could never see him again, and where they knew he
must linger out a miserable existence, more intolerable than death, amid the horrors of slavery? I ask
whether you could witness all this, without the most
poignant grief? This is no picture of the fancy.
It is a sober reality. The only difference is, the
men thus treated are black. But in my view, this
does not diminish the horrors of such cruel' deeds.
Can it be expected then, that the citizens of this
state, or indeed of any other, would witness all this,
without instituting the severest scrutiny into the le-
gality of the proceedings? More especially, when
it is known that the persons employed in this nefari-
ous business of hunting up fugitive slaves are men
destitute of principle, whose hearts are callous as
flint, and who would send a free man into bondage
with as little compunction as they would a slave, if
they could do it with impunity.

Of latter time, we hear much said about a dis-
solution of the Union. Far better, in my view, that
this should take place, if it can be effected without
violence, than to remain as we are; when a peacea-
ble citizen cannot enter your territory on his own
lawful business, without the risk of being murdered
by a ruthless mob.

With reverent thankfulness to Him, who numbers the hairs of our heads, without whose notice not

even a sparrow falls to the ground, and to whose providence I consider myself indebted for the redemption of my beloved son from the hands of barbarians, permit me again to say that I feel sincerely grateful to thee and others, who kindly lent aid, though late, in rescuing him from the violence of unreasonable and wicked men, who sought his life without a cause. I may never have it in my power to do either of you personally a kindness; but some other member of the great family of mankind may need assistance in a way that I can relieve him. If this should be the case, I hope I shall not fail to embrace the opportunity.

With fervent desires that the beneficent Creator and Father of the Universe may open the eyes of all to see that 'the fast which he hath chosen is to loose the bands of wickedness, to undo the heavy burdens and to let the oppressed go free, and that ye break every yoke.'

I am thy sincere friend,

ISAAC T. HOPPER."

Soon after the circumstances above related, the mayor of New-York revoked the warrant of the marshal, who had been so conspicuous in the outrage. This step was taken in consequence of his own admissions concerning his conduct.

In 1837, a little incident occurred, which may be interesting to those who are curious concerning phre-

nology. At a small social party in New-York, a discussion arose on that subject; and, as usual, some
were disposed to believe and others to ridicule. At
last the disputants proposed to test the question by
careful experiment. Friend Hopper was one of the
party, and they asked him to have his head examined
by the well-known O. S. Fowler. Having a good
natured willingness to gratify their curiosity, he consented. It was agreed that he should not speak during the operation, lest the tones of his voice might
serve as an index of his character. It was further
stipulated that no person in the room should give
any indication by which the phrenologist might be
enabled to judge whether he was supposed to be
speaking correctly or not. The next day, Mr. Fowler was introduced blindfolded into a room, where
Isaac T. Hopper was seated with the party of the
preceding evening. Having passed his hands over
the strongly developed head, he made the following
statement, which was taken down by a rapid writer,
as the words fell from his lips.

"The first and strongest manifestation of this
character is efficiency. Not one man in a thousand
is capable of accomplishing so much. The strong
points are very strong; the weak points are weak;
so that he is an eccentric and peculiar character.

The pole-star of his character is moral courage.

He has very little reverence, and stands in no awe of the powers that be. He pays no regard to forms or ceremonies, or established customs, in church or state. He renders no homage to great names, such as D.D.; L.L.D.; or Excellency. He treats his fellow men with kindness and affection, but not with sufficient respect and courtesy.

He is emphatically republican in feeling and character. He makes himself free and familiar with every one. He often lets himself down too much. This constitutes a radical defect in his character.

He will assert and maintain human rights and liberty at every hazard. In this cause, he will stake anything, or suffer anything. This constitutes the leading feature of his character. Every other element is blended into this.

I should consider him a very cautious man in fact, though in appearance he is very imprudent; especially in remarks on moral subjects.

He is too apt to denounce those whom he considers in error; to apply opprobrious epithets and censure in the strongest terms, and the boldest manner.

I have seldom, if ever, met with a larger organ of conscientiousness.

Nothing so much delights him as to advocate and propagate moral principles; no matter how unpopular the principles may be.

He has very little credulity.

He is one of the closest observers of men and things anywhere to be found. He sees, as it were by intuition everything that passes around him, and understands just when and where to take men and things; just how and where to say things with effect; and in all he says, he speaks directly to the point.

He says and does a great many severe and cutting things. If anybody else said and did such things, they would at once get into hot water; but he says and does them in such a manner, that even his enemies, and those against whom his censures are aimed, cannot be offended with him. He is always on the verge of difficulty, but never *in* difficulty.

He is hated mainly by those not personally acquainted with him. A personal interview, even with his greatest enemies, generally removes enmity; because of the smoothness and easiness of his manners.

He has at command a great amount of well-digested information on almost every subject, and makes admirable use of his knowledge. He has a great many facts, and always brings them in their right place. His general memory of particulars, incidents, places, and words, is really wonderful. But he has a weak memory concerning names, dates, numbers, and colors. He never recognizes persons by their dress, or by the color of anything pertaining to them.

He tells a story admirably, and acts it out to the life. He makes a great deal of fun, and keeps others in a roar of laughter, while he is sober himself. For his fun, he is as much indebted to the manner as to the matter. He makes his jokes mainly by happy comparisons, striking illustrations, and the imitative power with which he expresses them.

He possesses a great amount of native talent, but it is so admirably distributed, that he appears to have more than he actually possesses.

His attachment to his friends is remarkably strong and ardent. But he will associate with none except those whose moral characters are unimpeachable.

He expects and anticipates a great deal; enters largely into things; takes hold of every measure with spirit; and is always overwhelmed with business. Move where he will, he cannot be otherwise than a distinguished man."

That this description was remarkably accurate in most particulars will be obvious to those who have read the preceding anecdotes. It is not true, however, that he was enthusiastic in character, or that he had the appearance of being so. He was far too

practical and self-possessed, to have the reputation
of being "half crazy," even among those who are
prone to regard everything as insane that is out of
the common course.   Neither do I think he was
accustomed to "let himself down too much;" for according to my radical ideas, a man *cannot* "let himself down," who "associates only with those whose
moral characters are unimpeachable."   It is true
that he was pleasant and playful in conversation
with all classes of people; but he was remarkably
free from any tinge of vulgarity.   It is true, also,
that he was totally and entirely unconscious of any
such thing as distinctions of rank.   I have been
acquainted with many theoretical democrats, and
with not a few who tried to be democratic, from
kind feelings and principles of justice; but Friend
Hopper and Francis Jackson of Boston are the only
two men I ever met, who were born democrats; who
could not help it, if they tried; and who would not
know *how* to try; so completely did they, by nature,
ignore all artificial distinctions.   Of course, I do not
use the word democrat in its limited party sense,
but to express their perfect unconsciousness that any
man was considered to be above them, or any man
beneath them.   If Friend Hopper encountered his
wood-sawyer, after a considerable absence, he would
shake hands warmly, and give him a cordial welcome.   If the English Prince had called upon him,

he would have met with the same friendly reception, and would probably have been accosted something after this fashion : "How art thou, friend Albert? They tell me thou art amiable and kindly disposed toward the people; and I am glad to see thee." Those who observe the parting advice given by Isaac's mother, when he went to serve his apprenticeship in Philadelphia, will easily infer that this peculiarity was hereditary. Some men, who rise above their original position, either in character or fortune, endeavor to conceal their early history. Others obtrude it upon all occasions, in order to magnify themselves by a contrast between what they have been and what they are. But he did neither the one nor the other. The subject did not occupy his thoughts. He spoke of having been a tailor, whenever it came naturally in his way, but never for the sake of doing so. His having been born in a hen-house was a mere external accident in his eyes ; and in the same light he regarded the fact that Victoria was born in a palace. What was the spiritual condition of the two at any given age, was the only thing that seemed to him of real importance.

His steadfastness in maintaining moral principles, "however unpopular those principles might be," was severely tried in the autumn of 1838. At a late hour in the night, two colored men came to his house;

and one introduced the other as a stranger in the city, who had need of a lodging. Friend Hopper of course conjectured that he might be a fugitive slave; and this conjecture was confirmed the next morning. The stranger was a mulatto, about twenty-two years old, and called himself Thomas Hughes. According to his own account, he was the son of a wealthy planter in Virginia, who sold his mother with himself and his twin sister when they were eleven months old. His mother and sister were subsequently sold, but he could never ascertain where they were sent. When he was about thirteen, he was purchased by the son of his first master. Being hardly dealt with by this relative, he one day remonstrated with him for treating his own brother with so much severity. This was, of course, deemed a great piece of insolence in a bondman, and he was punished by being sold to a speculator, carried off hand-cuffed, with his feet tied under the horse's belly, and finally shipped for Louisiana with a coffle of five hundred slaves. He was bought by a gambler, who took him to Louisville, Kentucky. When he had lived there three years, his master, having lost large sums of money, told him he should be obliged to sell him. Thomas had meanwhile ascertained that his father had removed to Kentucky, and was still a very wealthy man. He obtained permission to go and see him, with the hope that he

would purchase him and set him free. Accordingly,
he called upon him, and told him that he was Thomas, the son of his slave Rachel, who had always
assured him that he was his father. The rich
planter did not deny poor Rachel's assertion, but in
answer to her son's inquiries, he plainly manifested
that he neither knew nor cared who had bought her,
or to what part of the country she had been sent.
Thomas represented his own miserable condition, in
being sold from one to another, and subject to the
will of whoever happened to be his owner. He in-
treated his father to purchase him, with a view to
manumission ; but himself and his proposition were
both treated with supreme contempt. Thus rejected
by his father, and unable to discover any traces of
his mother, he returned disheartened to Louisville,
and was soon after sent to New-Orleans to be sold.
Mr. John P. Darg, a speculator in slaves, bought
him ; and he soon after married a girl named Mary,
who belonged to his new master. Mr. Darg went to
New-York, to visit some relatives, and took Thomas
with him. It was only a few days after their arrival
in the city, that the slave left him, and went to Isaac
T. Hopper to ask a lodging. When he acknowledged that he was a fugitive, intending to take
refuge in Canada, it was deemed imprudent for him
to remain under the roof of a person so widely
known as an abolitionist ; but a very benevolent and

intelligent Quaker lady, near eighty years old, named Margaret Shoemaker, gladly gave him shelter.

When Friend Hopper went to his place of business, after parting with the colored stranger, he saw an advertisement in a newspaper called the Sun, offering one thousand dollars reward for the apprehension and return of a mulatto man, who had stolen seven or eight thousand dollars from a house in Varick-street. A proportionate reward was offered for the recovery of any part of the money. Though no names were mentioned, he had reason to conjecture that Thomas Hughes might be the mulatto in question. He accordingly sought him out, read the advertisement to him, and inquired whether he had stolen anything from his master. He denied having committed any theft, and said the pretence that he had done so was a mere trick, often resorted to by slaveholders, when they wanted to catch a runaway slave. That this remark was true, Friend Hopper knew very well by his own experience; he therefore concluded it was likely that Thomas was not guilty. He expressed this conviction in conversation on the subject with Barney Corse, a benevolent member of the Society of Friends, who was kindly disposed toward the colored people. In compliance with Friend Hopper's request, that gentleman waited upon the editor of the Sun, accompanied by a lawyer, and was assured that a large amount of money real-

ly had been stolen from Mr. Darg, and that if he
could recover it, he was willing to give a pledge for
the manumission of the slave, beside paying the promised reward to whoever would enable him to get
possession of the money. Barney Corse called upon Mr. Darg, who promptly confirmed the statement made by the editor in his name. The Friend
then promised that he, and others who were interested for the slave, would do their utmost to obtain
tidings of the money, and see it safely restored, on
those conditions ; but he expressly stipulated that
he could not do it otherwise, because he had conscientious scruples, which would prevent him, in all
cases, from helping to return a fugitive slave to his
master.

It is to be observed that the promise of manumission was given as the highest bribe that could be
offered to induce the slave to refund the money he
had taken; for though in argument slaveholders
generally maintain that their slaves have no desire
for freedom, they are never known to *act* upon that
supposition. In this case, the offer served a double
purpose ; for it stimulated the benevolent zeal of
Friend Hopper and Barney Corse, and induced the
fugitive to confess what he had done. He still denied
that he had any intention of stealing, but declared
that he took the money merely to obtain power over
his master, hoping that the promise to restore it

would secure his manumission. It is impossible to tell whether he spoke truth or not; for poor Thomas had been educated in a bad school of morals. Sold by his father, abused by his brother, and for years compelled to do the bidding of gamblers and slave-speculators, how could he be expected to have very clear perceptions of right and wrong? The circumstances of the case, however, seem to render it rather probable that he really was impelled by the motive which he assigned for his conduct. Mr. Darg declared that he had previously considered him an honest and faithful servant; that he was in the habit of trusting him with the key of his trunk, and frequently sent him to it for money. The bank-bills he had purloined were placed in the hands of two colored men in New-York, because, as he said, he could not return them himself, but must necessarily employ somebody to do it for him, in the intended process of negotiating for his freedom.

Friend Hopper, his son-in-law James S. Gibbons, and Barney Corse, were very earnest to recover the money, for the best of reasons. In the first place, they greatly desired to secure the manumission of the slave. In the second place, the honesty of their characters led them to wish that the master should recover what was his own. In both instances, they wished to restore stolen property to the rightful owner; to Thomas Hughes the free use of his own faculties and limbs, which had been stolen from him, and to Mr. Darg the money that had been purloined from him. It is not likely that the Southerner would have ever regained any portion of the amount stolen, had it not been for their exertions. But, by careful and judicious management, they soon recovered nearly six thousand dollars, which was immediately placed in one of the principal banks of the city, with a full statement of the circumstances of the case to the cashier. Over one thousand more was heard of as having been deposited with a colored man in Albany. Friend Hopper proposed that Barney Corse should go in pursuit of it, accompanied by the colored man who sent it there. He agreed to do so; but he deemed it prudent to have a previous interview with Mr. Darg, to obtain his written promise to manumit Thomas, to pay the necessary expenses of the journey, and to exonerate from criminal prosecution any person or persons connected with the robbery, provided that assurance proved necessary in order to get possession of the money. All this being satisfactorily accomplished, he went to Albany and brought back the sum said to have been deposited there. Ten or fourteen hundred dollars were still wanting to complete the amount, which Mr. Darg said he had lost; but they had hopes of obtaining that also, by confronting various individuals, who had become involved with this complicated affair. Meanwhile, Barney Corse and James S. Gibbons called upon Mr. Darg to inform him of the amount recovered and safely deposited in the bank, and to pay him the sum brought from Albany. Instead of giving the deed of manumission, which had been his own voluntary offer at the outset, and which he knew had been the impelling motive to exertion, Mr. Darg had two police-officers in an adjoining room to arrest Barney Corse for having stolen money in his possession. He was of course astonished at such an ungrateful return for his services, but at once expressed his readiness to go before any magistrate that might be named.

It would not be easy to give an adequate idea of the storm of persecution that followed. Popular prejudice against abolitionists was then raging with uncommon fury; and police-officers and editors availed themselves of it to the utmost to excite hostility against individuals, who had been actuated by a kind motive, and who had proceeded with perfect openness throughout the whole affair. The newspapers of the city were pro-slavery, almost without exception. The idea of sending abolitionists to the State Prison was a glorious prospect, over which they exulted mightily. They represented that Thomas had been enticed from his master by these pretended philanthropists, who had advised him to steal the money, as a cunning mode of obtaining manu-

mission. As for the accused, all they asked was a
speedy and thorough investigation of their conduct.
The case was however postponed from week to
week, and offers were made meanwhile to compromise the matter, if Barney Corse would pay the balance of the lost money. He had wealthy connex-
ions, and perhaps the prosecutors hoped to extort
money from them, to avoid the disgrace of a trial.
But Barney Corse was far from wishing to avoid a
trial.

At this juncture of affairs, Friend Hopper took a
step, which raised a great clamor among his enemies, and puzzled some of his friends at the time,
because they did not understand his motives. He
sued Mr. Darg for the promised reward of one thousand dollars. He had several reasons for this proceeding. In the first place, the newspapers continually pointed him out as a man over whose head a criminal prosecution was pending; while he had at the
same time had good reason to believe that his accusers
would never venture to meet him before a court of
justice; and a proper regard for his own character
made him resolved to obtain a legal investigation of
his conduct by some process. In the second place
Mr. Darg had subjected Barney Corse to a great
deal of trouble and expense; and Friend Hopper
thought it no more than fair that expenses caused by
his own treachery should be paid from his own pock-

et. In the third place, David Ruggles, a worthy colored man, no way implicated in the transaction, had been arrested, and was likely to be involved in expense. In the fourth place, the police officers, who advised the arrest of Barney Corse, made themselves very conspicuous in the persecution. He believed they had been actuated by a desire to obtain the reward for themselves; and as they had no just claim to it, he determined to defeat them in this attempt. He therefore sued for the reward himself, though he never intended to use a dollar of it. This was manifested at the time, by a declaration in the newspapers, that if he recovered the reward, he would give all over the expenses to some benevolent society. It was frequently intimated to him that there should be no further proceedings against him, if he would withdraw this suit; but he constantly replied that a trial was what he wanted. Finding all overtures rejected, a complaint was laid before the Grand Jury; and such was the state of popular prejudice, that twelve out of nineteen of that body concurred in finding a bill against men of excellent moral character, without any real evidence to sustain the charge. Barney Corse had never taken measures to prevent the arrest of Thomas Hughes. He simply declined to render any assistance. He believed that he was under no legal obligation to do otherwise; and he knew for a certainty that he was under no moral obligation ; because conscience would not allow him to aid in returning a runaway slave to his master.   Nevertheless, he and Isaac T. Hopper, and James S. Gibbons, were indicted for "feloniously receiving, harboring, aiding and maintaining said Thomas, in order that he might escape from arrest, and avoid conviction and punishment."   Friend Hopper was advised that he might avail himself of some technical defects in the indictment ; but he declined doing it ; always insisting that a public investigation was what he wanted.

The trial was carried on in the same spirit that characterized the previous proceedings.   A colored man, known to have had dishonest possession of a portion of the lost money, was admitted to testify, on two successive trials, against Barney Corse, who had always sustained a fair character.   The District Attorney talked to the jury of "the necessity of appeasing the South."   As if convicting an honest and kind-hearted Quaker of being accomplice in a felony could do anything toward settling the questions that divided North and South on the subject of slavery ! One of the jury declared that he never would acquit an abolitionist.   Mr. Darg testified of himself during the trial, that he never intended to manumit Thomas, and had made the promise merely as a means of obtaining his money.   The newspapers spoke as if the guilt of the accused was not to be doubted, and informed the jury that the public expected them to convict these men.

In fact, the storm lowered so darkly, that some friends of the persecuted individuals began to feel uneasy. But Friend Hopper's mind was perfectly undisturbed. Highly respectable lawyers offered to conduct the cause for him; but he gratefully declined, saying he preferred to manage it for himself. He informed the court that he presumed they understood the law, and he was quite sure that he understood the facts; therefore, he saw no need of a lawyer between them. The Court of Sessions was held every month, and he appeared before it at almost every term, to demand a trial. At last, in January 1840, when the hearing had been delayed fifteen months, he gave notice that unless he was tried during that term, he should appear on the last day of it, and request that a *nolle prosequi* should be ordered. The trial not coming on, he appeared accordingly, and made a very animated speech, in which he dwelt with deserved severity on the evils of the police system, and on the efforts of a corrupt press to pervert the public mind. He said he did not make these remarks to excite sympathy. He was not there to ask for mercy, but to demand justice. "And I would have you all to understand distinctly," continued the brave old man, "that I have no wish to evade the charge against me for being an

abolitionist. I *am* an abolitionist. In that, I am
charged truly. I have been an abolitionist from my
early years, and I always expect to remain so. For
this, I am prosecuted and persecuted. I most sincerely believe that slavery is the greatest sin the
Lord Almighty ever suffered to exist upon this earth.
As sure as God is good and just, he will put an end
to it; and all opposition will be in vain. As regards
myself, I can only say, that having lived three-score
and nearly ten years, with a character that placed
me above suspicion in such matters as have been
urged against me, I cannot now forego the principles
which have always influenced my conduct in relation
to slavery. Neither force on the one hand, nor persuasion on the other, will ever alter my course of
action."

One of the New-York papers, commenting on
this speech, at the time, states that "the old gentleman was listened to very attentively. He was composed, dignified, and clear in his manner, and evidently had much effect on the court and a large
number of spectators. He certainly needed no counsel to aid him."

The court ordered a *nolle prosequi* to be entered,
and the defendants were all discharged. The suit
for the reward proceeded no further. David Ruggles
had been early discharged, and the whole case had
been completely before the public in pamphlet form;

therefore the principal objects for urging it no longer existed.

Though the friends of human freedom made reasonable allowance for a man brought up under such demoralizing influences as Thomas Hughes had been, they of course felt less confidence in him, than they would have done had he sought to obtain liberty by some more commendable process. Being aware of this, he returned to his master, not long after he acknowledged the theft. At one time, it was proposed to send him back to the South; but he swore that he would cut his throat rather than return into slavery. The best lawyers declared their opinion that he was legally entitled to freedom, in consequence of his master's written promise to manumit him if the money were restored; consequently some difficulties would have attended any attempt to coerce him. He was tried on an indictment for grand larceny, convicted, and sentenced to the State Prison for two years; the shortest term allowed for the offence charged against him. Through the whole course of the affair, he proved himself to be a very irresolute and unreliable character. At one time, he said that his master was a notorious gambler; then he denied that he ever said so; then he affirmed that his first statement was true, though he had been frightened into contradicting it. When his time was out at Sing Sing, he expressed to Friend

Hopper and others his determination to remain at
the North; but after an interview with Mr. Darg, he
consented to return to the South with him.   Although he was thus wavering in character, he could
never be persuaded to say that any abolitionist advised him to take his master's money.   He always
declared that no white man knew anything about
it, until after he had placed it out of his own hands;
and that the friends who were willing to aid him in
procuring his manumission had always expressed
their regret that he had committed such a wrong
action.   He deserved praise for his consistency on
this point; for he had the offer of being exempted
from prosecution himself, and used as a witness,
if he would say they advised him to steal the money.

When Thomas Hughes consented to return to the
South with Mr. Darg, it was with the full understanding that he went as a free man, consenting to
be his servant.   This he expressed during his last
interview with Friend Hopper, in Mr. Darg's presence.   But the newspapers represented that he had
voluntarily gone back into slavery; and such was
their exultation over his supposed choice, that a person unacquainted with the history of our republic
might have inferred that the heroes of the revolution
fought and died mainly for the purpose of convincing
their posterity of the superior advantages of slavery

over freedom. However, it was not long before
Thomas returned to New-York, and told the following story: "A short time before my release from
prison, Mr. Darg brought my wife to see me, and
told me we should both be free and enjoy each other's
society as long as we lived, if I would go with him.
He said I should suffer here at the North; for the
abolitionists would do nothing for me. I went with
him solely with the hope of living with Mary. I
thought if he attempted to hold me as a slave, we
would both run away, the first opportunity. He told
me we should meet Mary in Washington; but when
we arrived in Baltimore, he shut me up in jail, and
told me Mary was sold, and carried off South. I
cannot describe how I felt. I never expect to see
her again. He asked me if I consented to come
with him on Mary's account, or on his own account.
I thought it would make it better for me to say on
his account; and I said so. I hope the Lord will
forgive me for telling a falsehood. When I had
been in jail some time, he called to see me, and said
that as I did not come with him on account of my
wife, he would not sell me; that I should be free,
and he would try to buy Mary for me."

Thomas said he was informed that certain people
in New-York wrote to Mr. Darg, advising him not to
sell him, because the abolitionists predicted that he
would do so; and he thought that was the reason

why he was not sold. If this supposition was correct,
it is a great pity that his master was not induced by
some better motive to avoid an evil action. Thomas
uniformly spoke of Mrs. Darg with respect and
gratitude. He said, " She was always very kind to
me and Mary. I know she did not want to have
me sold, or to have Mary sold; for I believe she
loved her. I feel very sorry that I could not live
with her and be free; but I had rather live in the
State Prison all my life than to be a slave."

I never heard what became of Thomas. Friend
Shoemaker used to tell me, years afterward, how she
secreted him, and rejoiced in the deed. I heard the
good lady, when more than ninety years old, just before
her death, talk the matter over; and her kindly, intelligent countenance smiled all over, as she recounted how she had contrived to dodge the police, and
avoid being a witness in the case. The Fugitive
Slave Law would be of no avail to tyrants, if all the
women at the North had as much moral courage, and
were as benevolent and quick-witted as she was.

Those who were most active in persecuting Friend
Hopper and Barney Corse convinced the public, by
their subsequent disreputable career, that they were
not men whose word could be relied upon.

Dr. R. W. Moore, of Philadelphia, in a letter to
Friend Hopper concerning this troublesome case,
says: "I am aware thou hast passed through many

trials in the prosecution of this matter. Condemned by the world, censured by some of thy friends, and discouraged by the weak, thou hast had much to bear. But thou hast been able to foil thy enemies, and to pass through the flames without the smell of fire on thy garments. Thy christian firmness is an example to us all. It reminds one of those ancient Quakers, who, knowing themselves in the right, suffered wrongs rather than compromise their principles. For the sake of mankind, I am sorry there are not more such characters among us. They would do more to exalt our principles, than a host of the professors of the present day."

A year or two later, another incident occurred, which excited similar exultation among New-York editors, that a human being had been so wise as to prefer slavery to freedom; and there was about as much cause for such exultation as there had been in the case of Thomas Hughes.

Mrs. Burke of New-Orleans went to New-York to visit a relative by the name of Morgan. She brought a slave to attend upon her, and took great care to prevent her becoming acquainted with the colored people. I don't know how city editors would account for this extreme caution, consistently with their ideas of the blessedness of slavery. They might argue that there was danger free colored people would be so attracted by her charming pictures

of bondage, that they would emigrate to the South
in larger numbers than would supply the slave-mar-
kets, and thus occasion some depression in an honorable branch of trade in this republic. However
they might please to explain it, the simple fact was,
Mrs. Burke did not allow her slave to go into the
street. Of course, she must have had some other
motive than the idea that *freedom* could be attractive to her. The colored people became aware of the
careful constraint imposed upon the woman, and
they informed the abolitionists. Thinking it right
that slaves should be made aware of their legal
claim to freedom, when brought or sent into the free
states, with knowledge and consent of their masters, they applied to Judge Oakley for a writ of *habeas corpus*, by virtue of which the girl was brought
before him. While she was in waiting, Friend Hopper heard of the circumstance, and immediately proceeded to the court-room. There he found Mr.
Morgan and one of his southern friends talking busily with the slave. The woman appeared frightened
and undecided, as is often the case, under such circumstances. Those who wished her to return to the
South plied her with fair promises. They represented abolitionists as a set of kidnappers, who seized
colored strangers under friendly pretences, and nobody could tell what became of them afterward. It
was urged that her condition would be most misera-

ble with the "free niggers" of the North, even if the
abolitionists did not sell her, or spirit her away to
some unknown region.

On the other hand, the colored people, who had
assembled about the court-room, were very eager to
escue her from slavery. She did not understand
heir motives, or those of the abolitionists; for they
had been diligently misrepresented to her. "What
do they want to do it *for?*" she asked, with a per-
plexed air. "What will they do with me?" She
was afraid there was some selfish motive concealed.
She dared not trust the professions of strangers,
whose characters had been so unfavorably represented. Friend Hopper found her in this confused state
of mind. The Southerner was very willing to speak
for her. He gave assurance that she did not want
her freedom; that she desired to return to the
South; and that she had been in no respect distrain-
ed of her liberty in the city of New-York.

"Thou art a very respectable looking man," said
Friend Hopper; "but I have known slaveholders, of
even more genteel appearance than thou art, tell
gross falsehoods where a slave was in question. I
tell thee plainly, that I have no confidence in slaveholders, in any such case. I have had too much
acquaintance with them. I know their game too
well."

The Southerner said something about its being

both mean and wrong to come between master and servant.

"Such may be thy opinion," replied Friend Hopper; "but my views of duty differ from thine in this matter." Then turning to the woman, he said, "By the laws here, thou art free. No man has a right to make thee a slave again. Thou mayest stay at the North, or go back to New-Orleans, just as thou choosest."

The Southerner here interposed to say, "Mind what that old gentleman says. You can go back to New-Orleans, to your husband, if you prefer to go."

"But let me tell thee," said Friend Hopper to the woman, "that if thou stayest here, thou wilt be free; but if they carry thee back, they may sell thee away from thy husband Dost thou wish to be free?"

The tears gushed from her eyes in full flood, and she replied earnestly, "I do want to be free. To be *sure* I do want to be free; but then I want to go to my husband."

Mr. Morgan and his Southern friend grew excited. With an angry glance at the old gentleman, the latter exclaimed, "I only wish we had you in New-Orleans! We'd hang you up in twenty-four hours."

"Then you are a set of savages," replied Friend Hopper.

" *You* are a set of thieves," retorted he.

"Well, savages may be thieves also," rejoined the abolitionist, with a significant smile.

"You are no gentleman," responded the other, in an irritated tone.

"I don't profess to be a gentleman," answered the impassive Quaker. "But I am an honest old man; and perhaps that will do as well."

This remark occasioned a general smile. Indeed it was pleasant to observe, throughout this scene in the court-room, that popular sympathy was altogether on the side of freedom. It was a strange blind instinct on the part of the people, considering how diligently they had been instructed otherwise by pulpit and press; but so it was.

When the slave was summoned into the judge's room, Friend Hopper followed; being extremely desirous to have her understand her position clearly. He found Mr. Morgan and his Southern friend in close and earnest conversation with her. When he attempted to approach her, he was unceremoniously shoved aside, with the remark, "Don't push me away!"

"I did not push thee," said Friend Hopper; "and see that thou dost not push *me!*" He then inquired of the woman if he had rightly understood that her husband was free. She replied in the affirmative. "Then let me tell thee," said the kind-hearted old gentleman, "that we will send for him, and obtain employment for him here, if it is thy choice to remain."

Again she wept, and repeated, "I do want to be free." But she was evidently bewildered and distrustful, and did not know how to understand the opposite professions that were made to her.

On representation of the claimant's friends, Judge Oakley adjourned the case till the next morning; telling the woman she was at liberty to go with whom she pleased. The colored people had assembled in considerable numbers, and were a good deal excited. Experience led them to suppose that she would either be cajoled into consenting to return to slavery, or else secretly packed off to New-Orleans, if she were left in Southern hands. They accordingly made haste to hustle her away. But their well-intended zeal terrified the poor bewildered creature, and she escaped from them, and went back to her mistress.

The pro-slavery papers chuckled, as they always do, when some poor ignorant victim is deceived by false representation, alarmed by an excitement that she does not comprehend, afraid that strangers are not telling her the truth, or that they have not the power to protect her; and in continual terror of future punishment, if she should attempt to take her freedom, and yet be unable to maintain it. Great is the triumph of republicans, when, under such trying circumstances, *one* poor bewildered wretch goes back to slavery; but of the *hundreds,* who every month take their freedom, through fire and flood, and all manner of deadly perils, they are as silent as the grave.

In the spring of 1841, I went to New-York to edit the Anti-Slavery Standard, and took up my abode with the family of Isaac T. Hopper. The zealous theological controversy among Friends naturally subsided after the separation between the opposing parties had become an old and settled fact. Consequently the demand for Quaker books diminished more and more. The Anti-Slavery Society, at that time, needed a Treasurer and Book-Agent; and Friend Hopper was proposed as a suitable person for that office. As only a small portion of his time was occupied with the sale of books he had on hand, he concluded to accept the proposition. He was then nearly seventy years old; but he appeared at least twenty years younger, in person and manners. His firm, elastic step seemed like a vigorous man of fifty. He would spring from the Bowery cars, while they were in motion, with as much agility as a lad of fourteen. His hair was not even sprinkled with gray. It looked so black and glossy, that a young lady, who was introduced to him, said she thought he wore a wig unnaturally dark for his age. It was a favorite joke of his to make strangers believe he wore a wig; and they were not easily satisfied that he spoke in jest, until they examined his head.

The roguery of his boyhood had subsided into a love of little mischievous tricks; and the playful tone of humor, that rippled through his conversation, frequently reminded me of the Cheeryble Brothers so admirably described by Dickens. If some on rang at the door, and inquired for Mr. Hopper, he always answered, "There is no such. person lives here." If the stranger urged that he had been directed by a man who said he knew Mr. Hopper, he would persevere in saying, "There must be some mistake. No such person lives here." At last, when the disappointed visitor turned to go away, he would call out, "Perhaps thou means Isaac T. Hopper? That is *my* name."

Being called upon to give a receipt to a Catholic priest for some money deposited in his hands, he simply wrote "Received of John Smith." When the priest had read it, he handed it back and said, "I am disbursing other people's money, and shall be obliged to show this receipt; therefore, I should like to have you write my name, the Reverend John Smith." "I have conscientious scruples about using titles," replied Friend Hopper. "However, I will try to oblige thee." He took another slip of paper, and wrote, "Received of John Smith, who *calls* himself the Reverend." The priest smiled, and accepted the compromise; being well aware that the pleasantry originated in no personal or sectarian prejudice.

He always had something facetious to say to the people with whom he traded. The oyster-men, the coal-men, and the women at the fruit-stalls in his neighborhood, all knew him as a pleasant old gentleman, always ready for a joke. One day, when he was buying some peaches, he said to the woman, "A serious accident happened at our house last night. I killed two robbers." "Dear me!" she exclaimed. "Were they young men, or old convicts? Had they ever been in Sing Sing?" "I don't know about that," replied he. "I should think they might have been by the noise they made. But I despatched them before they had stolen much. The walls are quite bloody." "Has a Coroner's inquest been called?" inquired the woman. When he answered, "No," she lifted her hands in astonishment, and exclaimed, "Well now, I do declare! If anybody else had done it, there would have been a great fuss made about it; but you are a privileged man, Mr. Hopper." When he was about to walk away, he turned round and said, "I did not mention to thee that the robbers I killed were two mosquitoes." The woman had a good laugh, and he came home as pleased as a boy, to think how completely his serious manner had deceived her.

One day he went to a hosiery store, and said to the man, "I bought a pair of stockings here yesterday. They looked very nice; but when I got home, I found two large holes in them; and I have come for another pair. The man summoned his wife, and informed her of what the gentleman had said.

"Bless me! Is it possible, sir?" she exclaimed.

"Yes," replied Friend Hopper, I found they had holes as large as my hand."

"It is very strange," rejoined she; "for I am sure they were new. But if you have brought them back, of course we will change them."

"O," said he, "upon examination, I concluded that the big holes were made to put the feet in; and I liked the stockings so well, that I have come to buy another pair."

At another time, he entered a crockery shop, where a young girl was tending. He made up a very sorrowful face, and in whining tones, told her that he was in trouble and needed help. She asked him to wait till the gentleman came; but he continued to beseech that she would take compassion on him. The girl began to be frightened by his importunity, and looked anxiously toward the door. At last, the man of the shop came in; and Friend Hopper said, "This young woman thinks she cannot help me out of my trouble; but I think she can. The fact is, we are going to have company, and so many of our tumblers are broken, that I came to ask if she would sell me a few."

One day, when he was walking quickly up the Bowery, his foot slipped on a piece of orange-peel, and he fell prostrate on the sidewalk. He started up instantly, and turning to a young man behind him, he said, "Couldst thou have done that any better?"

He very often mingled with affairs in the street, as he passed along. One day, when he saw a man beating his horse brutally, he stepped up to him and said, very seriously, "Dost thou know that some people think men change into animals when they die?"

The stranger's attention was arrested by such an unexpected question, and he answered that he never was acquainted with anybody who had that belief.

"But some people do believe it," rejoined Friend Hopper; "and they also believe that animals may become men. Now I am thinking if thou shouldst ever be a horse, and that horse should ever be a man, with such a temper as thine, the chance is thou wilt get some cruel beatings." Having thus changed the current of his angry mood, he proceeded to expostulate with him in a friendly way; and the poor beast was reprieved, for that time, at least.

He could imitate the Irish brogue very perfectly; and it was a standing jest with him to make every Irish stranger believe he was a countryman. During

his visit to Ireland, he had become so well acquainted with various localities, that I believe he never in
any instance failed to deceive them, when he said,
"Och! and sure I came from old Ireland meself."
After amusing himself in this way for a while, he
would tell them, "It is true I did come from Ireland;
but, to confess the truth, I went there first."

Once, when he saw two Irishmen fighting, he
seized one of them by the arm, and said, "I'm from
ould Ireland. If thou *must* fight, I'm the man for
thee. Thou hadst better let that poor fellow alone.
I'm a dale stouter than he is; and sure it would be
braver to fight me." The man thus accosted looked
at him with surprise, for an instant, then burst out
laughing, threw his coat across his arm, and walked
off.

Another time, when he found two Irishmen quarrelling, he stepped up and inquired what was the
matter. "He's got my prayer-book," exclaimed one
of them; "and I'll give him a bating for it; by St.
Patrick, I will." "Let me give thee a piece of advice," said Friend Hopper. "It's a very hot day,
and bating is warm work. I'm thinking thou had'st
better put it off till the cool o' the morning." The
men, of course, became cooler before they had done
listening to this playful remonstrance.

Once, when he was travelling in the stage, they
passed a number of Irishmen with cart-loads of

stones, to mend the road. Friend Hopper suggested to the driver that he had better ask them to remove a very large stone, which lay directly in the way and seemed dangerous. "It will be of no use if I do," replied the driver. "They'll only curse me, and tell me to go round the old road, over the hill; for the fact is, this road is not fairly opened to the public yet." Friend Hopper jumped out, and asked if they would turn that big stone aside. "And sure ye've no business here at all," they replied. "Ye may·jist go round by the ould road." "Och!" said Friend Hopper, "and is this the way I'm trated by my coontryman? I'm from Ireland meself; and sure I did'nt expect to be trated so by my coontry men in a strange coontry."

"And are ye from ould Ireland?" inquired they.

"Indade I am," he replied.

"And what part may ye be from?" said they.

"From Mount Mellick, Queen's County," rejoined he; and he began to talk familiarly about the priest and the doctor there, till he got the laborers into a real good humor, and they removed the stone with the utmost alacrity. The passengers in the stage listened to this conversation, and supposed that he was in reality an Irish Quaker. When he returned to them and explained the joke, they had a hearty laugh over his powers of mimicry.

His tricks with children were innumerable. They

would often be lying in wait for him in the street;
and if he passed without noticing them, they would
sometimes pull at the skirts of his coat, to obtain the
customary attention. Occasionally, he would observe a little troop staring at him, attracted by the
singularity of his costume. Then, he would stop,
face about, stretch out his leg, and say, "Come now,
boys! Come, and take a good look!" It was his
delight to steal up behind them, and tickle their
necks, while he made a loud squealing noise. The
children, supposing some animal had set upon them,
would jump as if they had been shot. And how he
would laugh! When he met a boy with dirty face
or hands, he would stop him, and inquire if he ever
studied chemistry. The boy, with a wondering
stare, would answer, "No." "Well then, I will
teach thee how to perform a curious chemical experiment," said Friend Hopper. "Go home, take a
piece of soap, put it in water, and rub it briskly on
thy hands and face. Thou hast no idea what a
beautiful froth it will make, and how much whiter
thy skin will be. That's a chemical experiment. I
advise thee to try it."

The character of his wife was extremely modest
and reserved; and he took mischievous pleasure in
telling strangers the story of their courtship in a way
that made her blush. "Dost thou know what Hannah answered, when I asked if she would marry

me?" said he. "I will tell thee how it was. I was walking home with her one evening, soon after the death of her mother, and I mentioned to her that as she was alone now, I supposed she intended to make some change in her mode of living. When she said yes, I told her I had been thinking it would be very pleasant to have her come and live with me. 'That would suit me exactly,' said she. This prompt reply made me suppose she might not have understood my meaning; and I explained that I wanted to have her become a member of my family; but she replied again, 'There is nothing I should like better.'"

The real fact was, the quiet and timid Hannah Attmore was not dreaming of such a thing as a proposal of marriage. She supposed he spoke of receiving her as a boarder in his family. When she at last perceived his meaning, she slipped her arm out of his very quickly, and was too much confused to utter a word. But it amused him to represent that she seized the opportunity the moment it was offered.

There was one of the anti-slavery agents who did everything in a dashing, wholesale style, and was very apt to give peremptory orders. One day he wrote a letter on business, to which the following postscript was appended: "Give the hands at your office a tremendous blowing up. They need it."

Friend Hopper briefly replied: "According to thy orders, I have given the hands at our office a tremendous blowing up. They want to know what it is for. Please inform me by return of mail."

When the Prison Association of New-York petitioned to be incorporated, he went to Albany on business therewith connected. He was then a stranger at the seat of government, though they afterward came to know him well. When he was seated in the senate-chamber, a man came to him and told him to take off. his hat. He replied, "I had rather not. I am accustomed to keep it on."

"But it is contrary to the rules," rejoined the officer. "I am ordered to turn out any man who refuses to uncover his head."

The Quaker quietly responded, "Very well, friend, obey thy orders."

"Then, will you please to walk out, sir?" said the officer.

"No," replied Friend Hopper. "Didst thou not tell me thou wert ordered to turn me out?" Dost thou suppose I am going to do thy duty for thee?"

The officer looked embarrassed, and said, half smiling, "But how am I to get you out?"

"Carry me out, to be sure," rejoined Friend Hopper. "I see no other way."

The officer went and whispered to the Speaker,

who glanced at the noble-looking old gentleman, and advised that he should be let alone.

Sometimes his jests conveyed cutting sarcasms. One day, when he was riding in an omnibus, he opened a port-monnaie lined with red. A man with very flaming visage, who was somewhat intoxicated, and therefore very much inclined to be talkative, said, "Ah, that is a very gay pocket-book for a Quaker to carry."

"Yes, it is very red," replied Friend Hopper; "but is not so red as thy nose." The passengers all smiled, and the man seized the first opportunity to make his escape.

A poor woman once entered an omnibus, which was nearly full, and stood waiting for some one to make room. A proud-looking lady sat near Friend Hopper, and he asked her to move a little, to accommodate the new comer. But she looked very glum, and remained motionless. After examining her countenance for an instant, he said, "If thy face often looks so, I should n't like to have thee for a neighbor." The passengers exchanged smiles at this rebuke, and the lady frowned still more deeply.

One of the jury in the Darg case was "a son of Abraham," rather conspicuous for his prejudice against colored people. Some time after the proceedings were dropped, Friend Hopper happened to meet him, and entered into conversation on the subject. The Jew was very bitter against "that rascally thief, Tom Hughes." "It does not become *thee* to be so very severe," said Friend Hopper; "for thy ancestors were slaves in Egypt, and went off with the gold and silver jewels they borrowed of their masters."

One day he met several of the Society of Friends, whom he had not seen for some time. Among them was an Orthodox Friend, who was rather stiff in his manners. The others shook hands with Isaac; but when he approached "the Orthodox," he merely held out his finger.

"Why dost thou offer me thy finger?" said he.

"I don't allow people of certain principles to get very deep hold of *me*," was the cold reply.

"Thou needest have no uneasiness on that score," rejoined Friend Hopper; "for there never was anything deep in thee to get hold of.'

The sense of justice, so conspicuous in boyhood, always remained a distinguishing trait in his character. Once, after riding half a mile, he perceived that he had got into the wrong omnibus. When he jumped out, the driver called for pay; but he answered, "I don't owe thee anything. I've been carried the wrong way." This troubled him afterward, when he considered that he had used the carriage and horses, and that the mistake was his own fault. He kept on the look-out for the driver, but did not happen to see him again, until several weeks afterward. He called to him to stop, and paid the sixpence.

"Why, you refused to pay me, when I asked you," said the driver.

"I know I did," he replied; "but I repented of it afterward. I was in a hurry then, and I did not reflect that the mistake was my fault, not thine; and that I ought to pay for riding half a mile with thy horses, though they did carry me the wrong way." The man laughed, and said he didn't often. meet with such conscientious passengers.

The tenacity of the old gentleman's memory was truly remarkable. He often repeated letters, which he had written or received twenty years before on some memorable occasion; and if opportunity occurred to compare them with the originals, it would be found that he had scarcely varied a word. He always maintained that he could distinctly remember some things, which happened before he was two years old. One day, when his parents were absent, and Polly was busy about her work, he sat bolstered up in his cradle, when a sudden gust of wind blew a large piece of paper through the entry. To his uneducated senses, it seemed to be a living creature, and he screamed violently. It was several hours before he recovered from his extreme terror. When his parents returned, he tried to make them understand how a strange thing had come into the house, and run, and jumped, and made a noise. But his lisping language was so very imperfect, that they were unable to conjecture what had so frightened him. For a long time after, he would break out into sudden screams, whenever the remembrance came over him. At seventy-five years old, he told me he remembered exactly how the paper then appeared to him, and what sensations of terror it excited in his infant breast.

He had a large old-fashioned cow-bell, which was always rung to summon the family to their meals. He resisted having one of more modern construction, because he said that pleasantly reminded him of the time when he was a boy, and used to drive the cows to pasture. Sometimes, he rang it much longer than was necessary to summon the household. On such occasions, I often observed him smiling while he stood shaking the bell; and he would say, "I am thinking how Polly looked, when the cow kicked her over; milk-pail and all. I can see it just as if it happened yesterday. O, what fun it was!"

He often spoke of the first slave whose escape he managed, in the days of his apprenticeship. He was wont to exclaim, "How well I remember the anxious, imploring look that poor fellow gave me, when I told him I would be his friend! It rises up

before me now.   If I were a painter, I could show it
to thee."

But clearly above all other things, did he remember every look and tone of his beloved Sarah; even
in the days when they trudged to school together,
hand in hand.   The recollection of this first love,
closely intertwined with his first religious impressions, was the only flowery spot of romance in the
old gentleman's very practical character.   When he
was seventy years of age, he showed me a piece of
writing she had copied for him, when she was a girl
of fourteen.   It was preserved in the self-same en-
velope, in which she sent it, and pinned with the
same pin, long since blackened by age.   I said, " Be
careful not to lose that pin."

"Lose it !" he exclaimed.   "No money could
tempt me to part with it.   I loved the very ground
she trod upon."

He was never weary of eulogizing her comely
looks, beautiful manners, sound principles, and sensible conversation.   The worthy companion of his
later life never seemed troubled by such remarks.
She not only "listened to a sister's praises with un-
wounded ear," but often added a heartfelt tribute to
the virtues of her departed friend.

It is very common for old people to grow careless
about their personal appearance, and their style of

conversation; but Friend Hopper was remarkably
free from such faults. He was exceedingly pure in
his mind, and in his personal habits. He never alluded to any subject that was unclean, never made
any indelicate remark, or used any unseemly expression. There was never the slightest occasion for
young people to feel uneasy concerning what he
might say. However lively his mood might be, his
fun was always sure to be restrained by the nicest
sense of natural propriety. He shaved, and took a
cold plunge-bath every day. Not a particle of mud
or dust was allowed to remain upon his garments.
He always insisted on blacking his own shoes; for
it was one of his principles not to be waited upon,
while he was well enough to wait upon himself.
They were always as polished as japan; and every
Saturday night, his silver buckles were made as
bright as a new dollar, in readiness to go to meeting
the next day. His dress was precisely like that worn
by William Penn. At the time I knew him, I believe he was the only Quaker in the country, who
had not departed from that model in the slightest
degree. It was in fact the dress of all English gentlemen, in King Charles's time; and the only peculiarity of William Penn was, that he wore it without
embroidery or ornament of any kind, for the purpose
of protesting against the extravagance of the fash-

ionable world. Therefore, the *spirit* of his intention
and that of other early Friends, would be preserved
by wearing dress cut according to the prevailing
mode, but of plain materials, and entirely unornamented. However, Friend Hopper was attached to
the ancient costume from early association, and he
could not quite banish the idea that any change in it
would be a degree of conformity to the fashions of
the world. The long stockings, and small clothes
buckled at the knee, were well adapted to his finely
formed limbs; and certainly he and his lady-like
Hannah, in their quaint garb of the olden time,
formed a very agreeable picture.

He had no peculiarities with regard to eating or
drinking. He always followed the old-fashioned
substantial mode of living, to which he had been accustomed in youth, and of which moderation in all
things was the rule. For luxuries he had no taste.
He thought very little about his food; but when it
was before him, he ate with the vigorous appetite
natural to strong health and very active habits.
When his health failed for a time in Philadelphia,
and he seemed wasting away to a shadow, his physician recommended tobacco. He found great benefit
from it, and in consequence of the habit then formed
he became an inveterate smoker, and continued so
till he was past seventy years old.

Being out of health for a short time, at that period, the doctor told him he thought smoking was not
good for his complaint. He accordingly discontinued
the practice, and formed a resolution not to renew
it. When he recovered, it cost him a good deal of
physical annoyance to conquer the long-settled habit;
but he had sufficient strength of mind to persevere
in the difficult task, and he never again used tobacco
in any form. Speaking of this to his son Edward,
he said, "The fact is, whoever cures himself of any
selfish indulgence, becomes a better man. It may
seem strange that I should set out to improve at my
age; but better late than never."

He was eminently domestic in his character.
Perhaps no man ever lived, who better enjoyed
staying at home. He loved to invite his grand-
children, and write them pleasant little notes about
the squirrel-pie, or some other rarity, which he had
in preparation for them. He seldom went out of his
own family circle, except on urgent business, or to
attend to some call of humanity. He was always
very attentive in waiting upon his wife to meeting,
or elsewhere, and spent a large portion of his evenings in reading to her from the newspapers, or some
book of Travels, or the writings of early Friends.
No man in the country had such a complete Quaker
library. He contrived to pick up every rare old

volume connected with the history of his sect. He had a wonderful fondness and reverence for many of those books. They seemed to stand to him in the place of old religious friends, who had parted from his side in the journey of life. There, at least, he found Quakerism that had not degenerated; that breathed the same spirit as of yore.

I presume that his religious opinions resembled those of Elias Hicks. But I judged so mainly from incidental remarks; for he regarded doctrines as of small importance, and considered theology an unprofitable topic of conversation. Practical righteousness, manifested in the daily affairs of life, was in his view the sum and substance of religion. The doctrine of the Atonement never commended itself to his reason, and his sense of justice was disturbed by the idea of the innocent suffering for the guilty. He moreover thought it had a pernicious tendency for men to rely on an abstract article of faith, to save them from their sins. With the stern and gloomy sects, who are peculiarly attracted by the character of Deity as delineated in the Old Testament, he had no sympathy. The Infinite One was ever present to his mind, as a loving Father to all his children, whether they happened to call him by the name of Brama, Jehovah, God, or Allah.

He was strongly attached to the forms of Quakerism, as well as to the principles. It troubled him, when some of his children changed their mode of dress, and ceased to say *thee* and *thou*. He groaned when one of his daughters appeared before him with a black velvet bonnet, though it was exceedingly simple in construction, and unornamented by feather or ribbon. She was prepared for this reception, and tried to reconcile him to the innovation by representing that a white or drab-colored silk bonnet showed every stain, and was therefore very uneconomical for a person of active habits. "Thy good mother was a very energetic woman," he replied; "but she found no difficulty in keeping her white bonnet as nice as a new pin." His daughter urged that it required a great deal of trouble to keep it so; and that she did not think dress was worth so much trouble. But his groan was only softened into a sigh. The fashion of the bonnet his Sarah had worn, in that beloved old meeting-house at Woodbury, was consecrated in his memory; and to his mind, the outward type also stood for an inward principle. I used to tell him that I found something truly grand in the original motive for saying *thee* and *thou*; but it seemed to me that it had degenerated into a mere hereditary habit, since the custom of applying *you* exclusively to superiors had vanished from the English language. He admitted the force of this argument; but he deprecated a departure from their old forms, because he considered it useful, especially to the young, to carry the cross of being marked and set apart from the world. But though he was thus strict in what he required of those who had been educated as Quakers, he placed no barrier between himself and people of other sects. He loved a righteous man, and sympathized with an unfortunate one, without reference to his denomination. In fact, many of his warmest and dearest friends were not members of his own religious society.

Early in life he formed an unfavorable opinion of the effect of capital punishment. His uncle Tatum considered it a useful moral lesson to take all his apprentices to hear the tragedy of George Barnwell, and to witness public executions. On one of these occasions, he saw five men hung at once. His habits of shrewd observation soon led him to conclude that such spectacles generally had a very hardening and bad influence on those who witnessed them, or heard them much talked about. In riper years, his mind was deeply interested in the subject, and he read and reflected upon it a great deal. The result of his investigations was a settled conviction that executions did not tend to diminish crime, but rather to increase it, by their demoralizing effect on the community. He regarded them with abhorrence, as a barbarous custom, entirely out of place in a civilized country and a Christian age.

Concerning the rights of women, he scarcely needed any new light from modern theories; for, as a Quaker, he had been early accustomed to practical equality between men and women in all the affairs of the Society. He had always been in the habit of listening to them as preachers, and of meeting them on committees with men, for education, for the care of the poor, for missions to the Indians, and for financial regulations. Therefore, it never occurred to him that there was anything unseemly in a woman's using any gift with which God had endowed her, or transacting any business, which she had the ability to do well.

After his removal to New-York, incidents now and then occurred, which formed pleasant links with his previous life in Philadelphia. Sometimes slaves, whom he had rescued many years before, or convicts, whom he had encouraged to lead a better life, called to see him and express their gratitude. Sometimes their children came to bless him. There was one old colored woman, who never could meet him without embracing him. Although these demonstrations were not always convenient, and did not partake of the quiet character of Quaker discipline, he would never say anything to repress the overflowings of her warm old heart. As one of his sons passed through Bond-street, he saw an old colored man rubbing his knees, and making the most lively gesticulations of delight. Being asked what was the matter, he pointed across the street, and exclaimed, "O, if I was only sure that was Friend Hopper of Philadelphia! If I was only *sure!*" When told that he was not mistaken, he rushed up to the old gentleman, threw his arms about his neck, and hugged him.

When I told him of Julia Pell, a colored Methodist preacher, whose fervid untutored eloquence had produced an exciting effect on my mind, he invited her to come and take tea with him. In the course of conversation, he discovered that she was the daughter of Zeke, the slave who outwitted his purchaser; as described in the preceding narratives. It was quite an interesting event in her life to meet with the man who had written her father's manumission papers, while she was in her infancy. When the parting hour came, she said she felt moved to pray; and dropping on her knees, she poured forth a brief but very earnest prayer, at the close of which she said: "O Lord, I beseech thee to shower down blessings on that good old man, whom thou hast raised up to do such a blessed work for my down-trodden people."

Friend Hopper's fund of anecdotes, especially with regard to colored people, was almost inexhaustible.

He related them with so much animation, that he was constantly called upon to repeat them, both at public meetings and in private conversation; and they never failed to excite lively interest. Every stranger, who was introduced to him, tried to draw him out; and it was an easy matter; for he loved to oblige people, and it is always pleasant for an old soldier to fight his battles over again. In this readiness to recount his own exploits, there was nothing that seemed like silly or obtrusive vanity. It often reminded me of the following just remark in the Westminster Review, applied to Jeremy Bentham "The very egotism in which he occasionally indulged was a manifestation of a *want* of self-thought. This unpopular failing is, after all, one of the characteristics of a natural and simple mind. It requires much *thought* about one's self to *avoid* speaking of one's self."

It has been already mentioned that Friend Hopper passed through a fiery trial in his own religious society, during the progress of the schism produced by the preaching of Elias Hicks. Fourteen years had elapsed since the separation. The "Hicksite" branch had become an established and respectable sect. In cities, many of them were largely engaged in Southern trade. I have heard it stated that millions of money were thus invested. They retained sympathy with the theological opinions of Elias

Hicks, but his rousing remonstrances against slavery
would have been generally very unwelcome to their
ears.   They cherished the names of Anthony Benezet, John Woolman, and a host of other departed
worthies, whose labors in behalf of the colored people reflected honor on their Society.   But where was
the need of being so active in the cause, as Isaac T.
Hopper was, and always had been?   "The way did
not open" for *them* to be so active; and why should
his.zeal rebuke *their* listlessness?   Was it friendly,
was it respectful in him, to do more than his religious Society thought it necessary to do?   It is astonishing how troublesome a living soul proves to be,
when they try to shut it up within the narrow limits
of a drowsy sect!

   I had a friend in Boston, whose wealthy and aristocratic parents brought him up according to the
most approved model of genteel religion.   He learned the story of the Good Samaritan, and was early
accustomed to hear eulogies pronounced on the holy
Jesus, who loved the poor, and associated with the
despised.   When the boy became a man he joined
the Anti-Slavery Society, and openly avowed that
he regarded Africans as brethren of the great human
family.   His relatives were grieved to see him pur-
suing such an injudicious and disrespectable course.
Whereupon, a witty reformer remarked, "They took
most commendable pains to present Jesus and the

Good Samaritan as models of character, but they were surprised to find that he had taken them at their word."

The case was somewhat similar with Isaac T. Hopper. He had imbibed anti-slavery principles in full flood at the fountain of Quakerism. Their best and greatest men were conspicuous as advocates of those principles. Children were taught to revere those men, and their testimonies were laid up in honorable preservation, to be quoted with solemn formality on safe occasions. Friend Hopper acted as if these professions were in good earnest; and thereby he disturbed his sect, as my Boston friend troubled his family, when he made practical use of their religious teaching.

That many of the modern Quakers should be blinded by bales of cotton, heaped up between their souls and the divine light, is not remarkable; for cotton is an impervious material. But it is a strange anomaly in their history that any one among them should have considered himself guided by the Spirit to undertake the especial mission of discouraging sympathy with the enslaved. A minister belonging to that branch of the Society called "Hicksites," who usually preached in Rose-street Meeting, New-York, had imbibed very strong prejudices against all modern reforms; and he manifested his aversion with a degree of excitement, in language, tone, and gesture, very unusual in that quiet sect. Those who labored in the cause of temperance, anti-slavery, or non-resistance, he was wont to stigmatize as "hireling lecturers," "hireling book-agents," and "emissaries of Satan." Soon after Thomas Hughes consented to return to the South, in consequence of the fair professions of Mr. Darg, this preacher chimed in with the exulting tones of the pro-slavery press, by alluding to it in one of his public discourses as fol lows. After speaking of the tendency of affliction to produce humility, he went on to say, "As a slave, who had suffered the effects of his criminal conduct, and been thus led to calm reflection, recently chose to go back with this master into slavery, and endure all the evils of that condition, notwithstanding his former experience of them, rather than stay with those hypocritical workers of popular righteousness who had interfered in his behalf. For my own part, I commend his choice. I had a thousand times rather be a slave, and spend my days with slave-holders, than to dwell in companionship with abolitionists."

The state of things among Quakers in the city of New-York may be inferred from the fact that this minister was exceedingly popular, and his style of preaching cordially approved by a majority of them. One of the editors of the Anti-Slavery Standard, at that time, wrote a severe, though by no means abu-

sive article on the subject, headed "Rare Specimen
of a Quaker Preacher." This gave great offence,
and Isaac T. Hopper was very much blamed for it.
He, and his son-in-law James S. Gibbons, and his
friend Charles Marriott, then belonged to the Executive Committee of the Anti Slavery Society ; and
it was assumed to be their duty to have prevented
the publication of the sarcastic article.   Charles
Marriot was absent from the city when it was published, and Friend Hopper did not see it till after it
was in print.   When they urged these facts, and
stated, moreover, that they had no right to dictate
to the editor what he should say, or what he should
not say, they were told that they ought to exculpate
themselves by a public expression of their disappro-
bation.   But as they did not believe the editorial article contained any mis-statement of facts, they could
not conscientiously say any thing that would satisfy
the friends of the preacher.   It would be tedious to
relate the difficulties that followed.   There were
visits from overseers, and prolonged sessions of committees ; a great deal of talking *with* the accused,
and still more talking *about* them.   A strong disposition was manifested to make capital against them
out of the Darg Case.   Robert H. Morris, who was
presiding Judge while that case was pending, and
afterward Mayor of New-York, had long known
Friend Hopper, and held him in much respect.   When

he was told that some sought to cast imputations on his character, he was greatly surprised, and offered to give favorable testimony in any form that might be desired. J. R. Whiting, the District Attorney, expressed the same readiness; and private misrepresentations were silenced by a published certificate from them, testifying that throughout the affair Friend Hopper had merely "exhibited a desire to procure the money for the master, and the manumission of the slave."

The principal argument brought by Friends, against their members uniting with Anti-Slavery Societies, was that they were thus led to mix indiscriminately with people of other denominations, and brought into contact with hireling clergymen. There seemed some inconsistency in this objection, coming from the mouths of men who belonged to Rail Road Corporations, and Bank Stock Companies, and who mingled constantly with slaveholders in Southern trade; for the early testimonies of the Society were quite as explicit against slavery, as against a paid ministry. However, those of their members who were abolitionists were willing to obviate this objection, if possible. They accordingly formed an association among themselves, "for the relief of those held in slavery, and the improvement of the free people of color." But when this benevolent association asked for the use of Rose-street Meeting-house,

their request was not only refused, but condemned
as disorderly. Affairs were certainly in a very sin
gular position. Both branches of the Society of
Friends were entirely inert on the subject of slavery.
Both expressed pity for the slave, but both agreed
that "the way did not open" for them to *do* any
thing. If individual members were thus driven to
unite in action with other sects upon a subject which
seemed to them very important, they were called
disorganizers. When they tried to conciliate by
forming an association composed of Quakers only,
they were told that "as the Society of Friends saw
no way to move forward in this concern, such associations appeared to reflect upon *them ;*" implying
that they failed in discharging their duty as a religious body. What could an earnest, direct character, like Isaac T. Hopper, do in the midst of a sect
thus situated? He proceeded as he always did.
He walked straight forward in what seemed to him
the path of duty, and snapped all the lilliputian
cords with which they tried to bind him.

Being unable to obtain any apology from their offending members, the Society proceeded to administer its discipline. A complaint was laid before the
Monthly Meeting of New-York, in which Isaac T.
Hopper, James S. Gibbons, and Charles Marriott,
were accused of "being concerned in the publication
and support of a paper calculated to excite discord

and disunity among Friends." Friend Hopper published a statement, characterised by his usual boldness, and disturbed his mind very little about the result of their proceedings. April, 1842, he wrote
thus, to his daughter, Sarah H. Palmer, of Philadelphia : "During my late indisposition, I was induced
to enter into a close examination of my own heart ;
and I could not find that I stood condemned there
for the part I have taken in the anti-slavery cause,
which has brought upon me so much censure from
those 'who know not God, nor his son Jesus Christ.
They profess that they know God, but in works they
deny him.' I have not yet given up our Society as
lost. I still live in the faith that it will see better
days. I often remember the testimony borne by
that devoted and dignified servant of the Lord, Mary Ridgeway ; which was to this import : 'The
Lord, in his infinite wisdom and mercy, has gathered
this Society to be a people, and has placed his name
among them ; and He has given them noble testimonies to hold up to the nations ; but if they prove un-
faithful, those testimonies will be given unto others,
who may be compared to the stones of the street ;
and *they* will wear the crowns that were intended for
this people, who will be cast out, as salt that has
lost its savor.' We may plume ourselves upon being the *children* of Abraham, but in the days of solemn inquisition. which surely will come, it will only

add to our condemnation, because we have not done the *works* of Abraham."

"The Yearly Meeting will soon be upon us, when we shall have a final ·decision in our cases. I feel perfectly resigned to the result, be it what it may. Indeed, I have sometimes thought I should be happi er *out* of the Society than *in* it. I should feel more at liberty to 'cry aloud and spare not, to lift up my voice like a trumpet, and show the people their transgressions, and the house of Jacob their sins.' I believe no greater benefit could be conferred on the Society. There are yet many in it who see and deplore its departure from primitive uprightness, but who are afraid to come out as they ought against the evils that prevail in it."

An aged and very worthy Friend in Philadelphia, named Robert Moore, who deeply sympathized with the wrongs of colored people, wrote to Friend Hopper as follows: "From 1822 to 1827, we had many interesting conversations in thy little front room, respecting the distracted state of our Society, and the efforts made to sustain our much beloved brother Elias Hicks, against those who were anxious for his downfall and excommunication. This great excitement grew hotter till the separation in 1827; we not being able to endure any longer the intolerance of the party in power. Well, it appears that the persecuted have now, in their turn, become persecutors; and those who went through the fire aforetime are devoted to pass through it again. But, my dear friend, I hope thou and all who are doomed to suffer for conscience sake, will stand firm, and not deviate one inch from what you believe to be your duty. They may cast you out of the synagogue, which I fear has become so corrupt that a seat among them has ceased to be an honor, or in any way desirable; but you will pass through the furnace unscathed. Not a hair of your heads will be singed."

The ecclesiastical proceedings in this case were kept pending more than a year, I think; being carried from the Monthly Meeting to the Quarterly, and thence to the Yearly Meeting. Thirty-six Friends were appointed a committee in the Yearly Meeting. They had six sessions, and finally reported that, after patient deliberation, they found eighteen of their number in favor of confirming the decision of the Quarterly Meeting; fifteen for reversing it; and three who declined giving any judgment in the case. Upon this report, the Yearly Meeting confirmed the decision of the inferior tribunals; and Isaac T. Hopper, James S. Gibbons, and Charles Marriott were excommunicated; in Quaker phrase, disowned.

I thus expressed myself at the time; and the lapse of ten years has not changed my view of the case: Excommunication for *such* causes will cut off from the Society their truest, purest, and tenderest spirits

There is Isaac T. Hopper, whose life has been one long chapter of benevolence, an unblotted record of fair integrity. A man so exclusive in his religious attachments that the principles of his Society are to his mind identical with Christianity, and its minutest forms sacred from innovation. A man whose name is first mentioned wherever Quakerism is praised, or benevolence to the slave approved.

There is Charles Marriott, likewise widely known, and of high standing in the Society; mild as a lamb, and tender-hearted as a child; one to whom conflict with others is peculiarly painful, but who nevertheless, when principles are at stake, can say, with the bold-hearted Luther, "God help me! I cannot otherwise."

There is James S. Gibbons, a young man, and therefore less known; but wherever known, prized for his extreme kindness of heart, his steadfast honesty of purpose, his undisguised sincerity, and his unflinching adherence to his own convictions of duty. A Society has need to be very rich in moral excellence, that can afford to throw away three such members.

Protests and disclaimers against the disownment of these worthy men came from several parts of the country, signed by Friends of high character; and many private letters were addressed to them, expressive of sympathy and approbation. Friend Hopper was always grateful for such marks of respect and friendship; but his own conscience would have sustained him without such aid. He had long felt a deep sadness whenever he was reminded of the *spiritual* separation between him and the religious Society, whose preachers had exerted such salutary influence on his youthful character; but the *external* separation was of no consequence. He attended meeting constantly, as he had ever done, and took his seat on the bench under the preachers' gallery, facing the audience, where he had always been accustomed to sit, when he was an honored member of the Society. Charles Marriott, who was by temperament a much meeker man, said to him one day, "The overseers have called upon me, to represent the propriety of my taking another seat, under existing circumstances. I expect they will call upon thee, to give the same advice."

"I expect they *won't*," was Isaac's laconic reply; and they never did.

His daughter, Abby H. Gibbons, soon after resigned membership in the Monthly Meeting of New-York for herself and her children; and his sons Josiah and John did the same. The grounds stated were that "the meeting had manifestly departed from the original principles and testimonies of the Society of Friends; that the plainest principles of civil and religious freedom had been violated in the whole proceedings in relation to their father; and

that the overseers had prepared an official document
calculated to produce false impressions with regard
to him; accusing him of 'grossly reproachful conduct' in the well known Darg Case; whereas there
was abundant evidence before the public that his
proceedings in that case were influenced by the purest and most disinterested motives."

The Philadelphia Ledger, after stating that the
Society of Friends in New-York had disowned some
of their prominent members for being connected,
directly or indirectly, with an Abolition Journal,
added the following remark: "This seems rather
singular; for we had supposed that Friends were
favorably inclined toward the abolition of slavery.
But many of their members are highly respectable
merchants, extensively engaged in Southern trade.
We are informed that they are determined to dis-
countenance all pragmatic interference with the legal
and constitutional rights of their brethren at the
South. The Quakers have always been distinguished for minding their own business, and per-
mitting others to attend to theirs. They would be
the last people to meddle with the rights of *property.*"

The Boston Times quoted the paragraph from
the Philadelphia Ledger, with the additional remark,
"There is no logician like money."

Whether Friends in New-York felt flattered by

these eulogiums, I know not; but they appear to
have been well deserved.

In 1842 and the year following, Friend Hopper
travelled more than usual. In August '42, he visited his native place, after an absence of twenty years.
He and his wife were accompanied from Philadelphia by his son Edward and his daughter Sarah H.
Palmer. Of course, the haunts of his boyhood had
undergone many changes. Panther's Bridge had
disappeared, and Rabbit Swamp and Turkey Cause
way no longer looked like the same places. He
visited his father's house, then occupied by strangers, and found the ruins of his great-grandfather's
dwelling. Down by the pleasant old creek, shaded
with large walnut trees and cedars, stood the tombs
of many of his relatives; and at Woodbury were
the graves of his father and mother, and the parents
of his wife. Every spot had something interesting
to say of the past. His eyes brightened, and his
tongue became voluble with a thousand memories.
Had I been present to listen to him then, I should
doubtless have been enabled to add considerably to
my stock of early anecdotes. He seemed to have
rought away from this visit a peculiarly vivid recol-
ection of "poor crazy Joe Gibson." This demented
being was sometimes easily controlled, and willing
to be useful; at other times, he was perfectly furious
and ungovernable. Few people knew how to man-

age him; but Isaac's parents acquired great influence over him by their uniform system of forbearance and tenderness; their own good sense and benevolence having suggested the ideas which regulate the treat ment of insanity at the present period. The day spent in Woodbury and its vicinity was a bright spot in Friend Hopper's life, to which he always reverted with a kind of saddened pleasure. The heat of the season had been tempered by floating clouds, and when they returned to Philadelphia, there was a faint rainbow in the east. He looked lovingly upon it, and said, "These clouds seem to have followed us all day, on purpose to make everything more pleasant."

In the course of the same month he accepted an invitation to attend the Anti-Slavery Convention at Norristown, Pennsylvania. His appearance there was quite an event. Many friends of the cause, who were strangers to him, were curious to obtain a sight of him, and to hear him address the meeting. Charles C. Burleigh, in an eloquent letter to the Convention, says: "I am glad to hear that Isaac T. Hopper is to be present. That tried old veteran, with his eye undimmed, his natural strength unabated, his resolute look, and calm determined manner, before which the blustering kidnapper, and the self-important oppressor have so often quailed! With the scars of a hundred battles, and the wreaths of an hundred victories in this glorious warfare. With his example of half a century's active service in this holy cause, and his still faithful adherence to it, through evil as well as good report, and in the face of opposition as bitter as sectarian bigotry can stir up. Persecution cannot bow the head, which seventy winters could not blanch, nor the terrors of ex-communication chill the heart, in which age could not freeze the kindly flow of warm philanthropy."

I think it was not long after this excursion that his sister Sarah came from Maryland to visit him. She was a pleasant, sensible matron, much respected by all who knew her. I noted down at the time several anecdotes of childhood and youth, which bubbled up in the course of conversations between her and her brother. In her character the hereditary trait of benevolence was manifested in a form somewhat different from his. She had no children of her own, but she brought up, on her husband's farm, nineteen poor boys and girls, and gave most of them a trade. Nearly all of them turned out well.

In the winters of 1842 and '43, Friend Hopper complied with urgent invitations to visit the Anti-Slavery Fair, in Boston; and seldom has a warmer welcome been given to any man. As soon as he appeared in Amory Hall, he was always surrounded by a circle of lively girls attracted by his frank manners, his thousand little pleasantries, and his keen enjoyment of young society. A friend of mine used to say that when she saw them clustering round him, in furs and feathered bonnets, listening to his words so attentively, she often thought it would make as fine a picture as William Penn explaining his treaty to the Indians.

Ellis Gray Loring in a letter to me, says: "We greatly enjoyed Friend Hopper's visit. You cannot conceive how everybody was delighted with him; particularly all our gay young set; James Russell Lowell, William W. Story, and the like. The old gentleman seemed very happy; receiving from all hands evidence of the true respect in which he is held." Mrs. Loring, writing to his son John, says: "We have had a most delightful visit from your father. Our respect, wonder, and love for him increased daily. I am sure he must have received some pleasure, he bestowed so much. We feel his friendship to be a great acquisition."

Samuel J. May wrote to me: "I cannot tell you how much I was charmed by my interview with Friend Hopper. To me, it was worth more than all the Fair beside. Give my most affectionate respects to him. He very kindly invited me to make his house my home when I next come to New-York; and I am impatient for the time to arrive, that I may accept his invitation."

Edmund Quincy, writing to Friend Hopper's

daughter, Mrs. Gibbons, says: "You cannot think
how glad we were to see the dear old man. He
spent a night with me, to my great contentment, and
that of my wife; and to the no small edification of
our little boy, to whom breeches and buckles were a
great curiosity. My Irish gardener looked at them
with reverence; having probably seen nothing so
aristocratic, since he left the old country. I love
those relics of past time. The Quakers were not so
much out, when they censured their members for
turning *sans culottes*. Think of Isaac T. Hopper in
a pair of pantaloons strapped under his feet! There
is heresy in the very idea. But, costume apart, we
were as glad to see Father Hopper, as if he had
been our real father in the flesh. I hope he had a
right good time. If he had not, I am sure it was
not for want of being made much of. I trust his
visits to Boston will grow into one of our domestic
institutions."

In the old gentleman's account of his visit to the
Fair, he says: "I was struck with the extreme propriety with which everything was conducted, and
with the universal harmony and good-will that prevailed among the numerous friends of the cause, who
had collected from all parts of the old Commonwealth, on this interesting occasion. Many of the
most distinguished citizens were purchasers, and appeared highly gratified, though not connected with

the anti-slavery cause. Lord Morpeth, late Lord
Lieutenant of Ireland, attended frequently, made
some presents to the Fair, and purchased several articles. I would call him by his christian name, if I
knew it; for it is plain enough that he was not baptized, 'Lord'. His manners were extremely friendly
and agreeable, and he expressed himself highly
pleased with the exhibition. I had an interesting
conversation with him on the subject of slavery;
particularly in relation to the Amistad captives, and
the case of the Creole."

"I had an opportunity to make a valuable addition
to my collection of the works of ancient Friends.
On the book-table, I found that rare old volume,
'The Way Cast Up,' written by George Keith,
while in unity with the Society. I took it home
with me to my chamber; and as I glanced over it,
my mind was moved to a painful retrospect of the
Society of Friends in its original state, when its
members were at liberty to follow the light, as manifested to them in the silence and secrecy of their
own souls. I seemed to see them entering places
appointed for worship by various professors, and
there testifying against idolatry, superstition, and a
mercenary priesthood. I saw them entering the
courts, calling upon judges and lawyers to do justice. I saw them receive contumely and abuse, as a
reward for these acts of dedication. My imagina-

tion followed them to loathsome dungeons, where many of them died a lingering death. I saw the blood trickling from the lacerated backs of innocent men and women. I saw William Robinson, Marmaduke Stevenson, Mary Dyer, and William Leddra, pass through the streets of Boston, pinioned, and with halters about their necks, on the way to execution; yet rejoicing that they were found worthy to suffer, even unto death, for their fidelity to Christ; sustained through those last bitter moments by an approving conscience and the favor of God.

"I now see the inhabitants of that same city surpassed by none on the globe, for liberality, candor, and benevolence. I see them taking the lead of very many of the descendants of the martyrs referred to, in many things, and at an immeasurable distance. I compared the state of the Society of Friends in the olden time with what it now is. In some sections of the country, they, in their turn, have become persecutors. Not with dungeons, halter, and fire; for those modes of punishment have gone by; but by ejecting their members from religious fellowship, and defaming their characters for doing that which they conscientiously believe is required at their hands; casting out their names as evil-doers for honestly endeavoring to support one of the most dignified testimonies ever given to the Society of Friends to hold up before a sinful world

These reflections pained me deeply ; for all the convictions of my soul, and all my early religious recollections, bind me fast to the principles of Friends ;
and I cannot but mourn to see how the world has
shorn them of their strength. I spent nearly a
sleepless night, and was baptized with my tears."

"In the morning, my mind was in some degree re-
assured with the hope that there are yet left, throughout the land, 'seven thousand in Israel, all the knees
which have not bowed unto Baal, and every mouth
which has not kissed him;' and that among these
shall yet 'arise judges, as at the first, and counsel-
lors, and lawgivers, as in the beginning.' My soul
longeth for the coming of that day, more than for
the increase of corn, and wine, and oil."

In the Spring of 1843, Friend Hopper visited
Rhode Island, and Bucks County, in Pennsylvania,
to address the people in behalf of the enslaved. He
was accompanied by Lucinda Wilmarth, a very intelligent and kind-hearted young person, who sometimes spoke on the same subject. After she returned
to her home in Massachusetts, she wrote as follows,
to the venerable companion of her mission ; "Dear
Father Hopper, I see by the papers that Samuel
Johnson has gone home. I well remember our call
upon him, on the second Sunday morning of our so-
journ in that land of roses. I also remember his radiant and peaceful countenance, which told of a life

well spent, and of calm and hopeful anticipations of the future. I love to dwell upon my visit to Pennsylvania. I never saw happier or more lovely homes. Never visited dwellings where those little household divinities, goodness, order, and cheerfulness, held more universal sway I was enabled to view men and things from an entirely new point of view. I had previously seen nothing of Quakerism, except in a narrow orthodox form, with which I had no sympathy. I was much pleased with the apparent freedom and philanthropy of the Friends I met there. I know not whether it was their peculiar *ism*, that made them so comparatively free and liberal. Perhaps I unconsciously assigned to their Quakerism what merely belonged to their manhood. But the fact is, they came nearer to realizing the ideal of Quakerism, associated in my mind with Fox and Penn, than any people I have ever seen.

"I stopped at Providence on my way home. As soon as I entered Isaac Hale's door, little Alice began to skip with joy, as she did that day when we returned so unexpectedly to dine; but the next moment, she looked down the stair-case, and exclaimed in a most anxious tone, 'Why *did'nt* Grandfather Hopper come? What *did* you come alone for? What *shall* I do?' On my arrival home, the first noisy greetings of my little brothers and sisters had scarcely subsided, before they began to inquire,

'Why did'nt your *other* father come, too?' They
complained that you had not written a single ''Tale
of Oppression' for the Standard since you were here.
But a week after, my little sister came running with
an open newspaper in her hand, exclaiming, 'Father
Hopper has made another story!' She has named
her doll for your little granddaughter, Lucy Gibbons, because you used to talk about her; and every
day she reads the book you gave her.''

Friend Hopper found great satisfaction in the pe-
rusal of the above letter, not only on account of his
great regard for the writer, but because many of the
Friends in Bucks County were the delight of his
heart. He was always telling me that if I wanted
to see the best farms, the best Quakers, and the
most comfortable homes in the world, I must go to
Bucks County. In his descriptions, it was a blooming land of peace and plenty, approaching as near
to an earthly paradise, as could be reasonably expected.

At the commencement of 1845, the American
Anti-Slavery Society made some changes in their
office at New-York, by which the duties of editor
and treasurer, were performed by the same person;
consequently Friend Hopper's services were no
longer needed. When he retired from the office
he had held during four years, the Society unani-

mously voted him thanks for the fidelity with which he had discharged the duties entrusted to him.

At that time, several intelligent and benevolent gentlemen in the city of New-York were much interested in the condition of criminals discharged from prisons, without money, without friends, and with a character so blasted, that it was exceedingly difficult to procure employment. However sincerely desirous such persons might be to lead a better life, it seemed almost impossible for them to carry their good resolutions into practice. The inconsiderate harshness of society forced them back into dishonest courses, even when it was contrary to their own inclinations. That this was a fruitful source of crime, and consequently a great increase of expense to the state, no one could doubt who candidly examined the subject. To meet the wants of this class of sufferers, it was proposed to form a Prison Association, whose business it should be to inquire into individual cases, and extend such sympathy and assistance as circumstances required. This subject had occupied Friend Hopper's mind almost as early as the wrongs of the slave. He attended the meetings, and felt a lively interest in the discussions, in which he often took part. The editor of the New-York Evening Mirror, alluding to one of these occasions, says: "When Mr. Hopper rose to offer some remarks, we thought the burst of applause which greeted the quaint old man, (in the very costume of Franklin) was a spontaneous homage to goodness; and we thanked God and took courage for poor human nature."

His well-known benevolence, his peculiar tact in managing wayward characters, his undoubted integrity, and his long experience in such matters, naturally suggested the idea that he was more suitable than any other person to be Agent of the Association. It was a situation extremely well-adapted to his character, and if his limited circumstances would have permitted, he would have been right glad to have discharged its duties gratuitously. He named three hundred dollars a year, as sufficient addition to his income, and the duties were performed with as much diligence and zeal, as if the recompence had been thousands. Although he was then seventy-four years old, his hand-writing was firm and even, and very legible. He kept a Diary of every day's transactions, and a Register of all the discharged convicts who applied for assistance; with a monthly record of such information as could be obtained of their character and condition, from time to time. The neat and accurate manner in which these books were kept was really surprising in so old a man. The amount of walking he did, to attend to the business of the Association, was likewise remarkable. Not one in ten thousand, who had lived so many years, could have endured so much fatigue.

In his labors in behalf of this class of unfortunate people he was essentially aided by Abby H. Gibbons, who resided nearer to him than his other daughters, and who had the same affectionate zeal to sustain him, that she had manifested by secretly slipping a portion of her earnings into his pocket, in the days of her girlhood. She was as vigilant and active in behalf of the women discharged from prison, as her father was in behalf of the men. Through the exertions of herself and other benevolent women, an asylum for these poor outcasts, called THE HOME, was established and sustained. Friend Hopper took a deep interest in that institution, and frequently went there on Sunday evening, with his wife and daughters, to talk with the inmates in a manner most likely to soothe and encourage them. They were accustomed to call him "Father Hopper," and always came to him for advice when they were in trouble.

When the Prison Association petitioned to be incorporated, it encountered a great deal of opposition, on the ground that it would be likely to interfere with the authority of the State over prisons. During two winters, Friend Hopper went to Albany frequently to sustain the measure. He commanded respect and attention, by the good sense of his remarks, his dignified manner, and readiness of utter-

ance. The Legislature were more inclined to have
confidence in him, because he was known to be a
benevolent, conscientious Quaker, entirely uncon-
nected with party politics. In fact, the measure
was carried mainly by the exertion of his personal
influence. He sustained the petition of the Association in a speech before the Legislature, which excit
ed much attention, and made a deep impression on
those who heard it. Judge Edmonds, who was one
of the speakers on the same occasion, often alluded
to it as a remarkable address. He said, "It elicited
more applause, and did more to carry the end in
view, than anything that was said by more practised
public speakers. His eloquence was simple and direct, but most effective. If he was humorous, his
audience were full of laughter ; if solemn, a death-
like stillness reigned ; if pathetic, tears flowed all
around him. He seemed unconscious of his power
in this respect, but I have heard him many times before large assemblies at our Anniversaries, and in the
chapel of the State Prison, and I have been struck,
over and over again, with the remarkable sway he
had over the minds of those whom he addressed."

The business of the Association made it necessary
for Friend Hopper to visit that city many times afterward. He came to be so well known there, and
was held in such high respect, that whenever he
made his appearance in the halls of legislation, the

Speaker sent a messenger to invite him to take a seat near his own.

He often applied to the Governor to exert his pardoning power, where he thought there were mitigating circumstances attending the commission of a crime; or where the mind and health of a prisoner eemed breaking down; or where a long course of good conduct seemed deserving of reward. When Governor Young had become sufficiently acquainted with him to form a just estimate of his character, he said to him, "Friend Hopper, I will pardon any convict, whom you say you conscientiously believe I ought to pardon. If I err at all, I prefer that it should be on the side of mercy. But so many cases press upon my attention, and it is so difficult to examine them all thoroughly, that it is a great relief to find a man in whose judgment and. integrity I have such perfect confidence, as I have in yours." On the occasion of one of these applications for mercy, the following quaint correspondence passed between him and the Governor:

"Esteemed Friend,
John Young:
.   Thou mayst think this mode of address rather too familiar; but as it is the spontaneous effusion of my heart, and entirely congenial with my feelings, I hope thou wilt hold me excused.

Permit me to embrace this opportunity to con-

gratulate thee upon thy accession to the office of
Chief Magistrate of the State. I have confidence its
duties will be faithfully performed. I rejoice that
thou hast had independence enough to restore to
liberty, and to their families, those infatuated men
called Anti-Renters. Some, who live under the old
dispensation, that demanded 'an eye for an eye, and
a tooth for a tooth,' will doubtless censure this act
of justice and mercy. But another class will be
glad; those who have embraced the Christian faith,
and live under the benign influence of its spirit,
which enjoins forgiveness of injuries. The approbation of such, accompanied with an approving conscience, will, I trust, more than counterbalance any
censure that may arise on the occasion.

The object I particularly have in view in addressing thee now, is, to call thy attention to the case of
Allen Lee, who was sentenced to twelve years' imprisonment for horse-stealing, in Westchester County. He has served for eleven years and two months
of that time. It is his first offence, and he has conducted well during his confinement. His health is
much impaired, and he has several times had a slight
hæmorrhage of the lungs. Allen's father was a regular teamster in the army during all the revolutionary
war. Though poor, he has always sustained a fair
reputation. He is now ninety years old, and he is
extremely anxious to behold the face of his son.

Permit me, most respectfully, but earnestly, to ask thy early attention to this case. The old man is confined to his bed, and so low, that he cannot continue many weeks. Unless Allen is very soon released, there is no probability that he will ever see him. I have no self-interested motives in this matter, but am influenced solely by considerations of humanity. With sincere desires for thy health and happiness, I am very respectfully thy friend,

"ISAAC T. HOPPER."

Governor Young promptly replied as follows.

"My worthy friend, Isaac T. Hopper,

"I have often thought of thee since we last met. I have received thy letter; and because thou hast written to me, and because I know that what thou writest is always truth, and that the old man, before he lays him down to die, may behold the face of his son, I will restore Allen to his kindred. When thou comest to Albany, I pray thee to come and see me. Very respectfully thy friend, JOHN YOUNG."

The monitor within frequently impelled Friend Hopper to address the assembled convicts at Sing Sing, on Sunday. The officers of the establishment were very willing to open the way for him; for according to the testimony of Mr. Harman Eldridge, the warden, "With all his kindness, and the encouragement he was always ready to give, he was guarded and cautious in the extreme, that nothing should be said to conflict with the discipline of the prison." His exhortations rendered the prisoners more docile, and stimulated them to exertion by keeping hope alive in their hearts. On such occasions, I have been told that a large portion of his unhappy audience were frequently moved to tears; and the warmth of their grateful feelings was often manifested by eagerly pressing forward to shake hands with him, whenever they received permission to do so. The friendly counsel he gave on such occasions sometimes produced a permanent effect on their characters. In a letter to his daughter Susan, he says: "One of these poor fellows attacked the life of the keeper, and I soon after had a private interview with him. He received what I said kindly, but declared that he could not govern his temper. He said he had no ill-will toward the keeper; that what he did was done in a gust of passion, and he could not help it. I tried to convince him that he had power to control his temper, if he would only exercise it. A year and a half afterward, on First Day, after meeting, he asked permission to speak to me. He then told me he was convinced that what I had said to him was true; for he had not given way to anger since I talked to him on the subject. He showed me many certificates from the keepers, all testifying to his good conduct. I hardly ever saw a man more changed than he is."

I often heard my good old friend describe these scenes in the Prison Chapel, with much emotion. He used to say, the feeling of confidence and safety which prevailed, was sometimes presented to his mind in forcible contrast with the state of things in Philadelphia, in 1787, as related by his worthy friend, Dr. William Rogers, who was on the committee of the first Society formed in this country "for relieving the miseries of public prisons." That kind-hearted and conscientious clergyman proposed to address some religious exhortation to the prisoners, on Sunday. But the keeper was so unfriendly to the exertion of such influence, that he assured him his life would be in peril, and the prisoners would doubtless escape, to rob and murder the citizens. When an order was granted by the sheriff for the performance of religious services, he obeyed it very reluctantly; and he actually had a loaded cannon mounted near the clergyman, and a man standing ready with a lighted match all the time he was preaching. His audience were arranged in a solid column, directly in front of the cannon's mouth. This is supposed to have been the first sermon addressed to the assembled inmates of a State Prison in this country.

Notwithstanding Friend Hopper's extreme benevolence, he was rarely imposed upon. He made it a rule to give very little money to discharged convicts.

He paid their board till employment could be obtained, and when they wished to go to their families, in
distant places, he procured free passage for them in
steamboats or cars; which his influence with cap-
tains and conductors enabled him to do very easily.
If they wanted to work at a trade, he purchased
tools, and hired a shop, when circumstances seemed
to warrant such expenditure. After they became
well established in business, they were expected to
repay these loans, for the benefit of others in the
same unfortunate condition they had been. Of
course, some who expected to receive money whenever they told a pitiful story, were disappointed and
vexed by these prudential regulations. Among the
old gentleman's letters, I find one containing these
expressions: "When I heard you talk in the Prison
Chapel, I thought there was something for the man
that had once left the path of honesty to hope for
from his fellow-men; but I find that I was greatly
mistaken. You are men of words. You can do the
wind-work first rate. But when a man wants a little assistance to get work, and get an honest living,
you are not there. Now I wish to know where
your philanthropy is."

But such instances were exceptions. As a general
rule, gratitude was manifested for the assistance rendered in time of need; though it was always limited
to the urgent necessities of the case. One day,

the following letter, enclosing a dollar bill for the Association, was addressed to Isaac T. Hopper: "Should the humble mite here enclosed be the means of doing one-sixteenth part the good to any poor convict that the sixteenth of a dollar has done for me, which I received through your hands more than once, when I was destitute of money or friends, then I shall have my heart's desire. With the blessing of God, I remain your most humble debtor."

From the numerous cases under Friend Hopper's care, while Agent of the Prison Association, I will select a few; but I shall disguise the names, because the individuals are living, and I should be sorry to wound their feelings by any unnecessary exposure of past delinquences.

C. R. about twenty-nine years old, called at the office, and said he had been lately released from Moyamensing prison; having been sentenced for two years, on account of selling stolen goods. When Friend Hopper inquired whether it was his first offence, he frankly answered, "No. I have been in Sing Sing prison twice for grand larceny. I served five years each time."

"Thou art still very young," rejoined Friend Hopper; "and it seems a large portion of thy life has been spent in prison. I am afraid thou art a bad man. But I hope thou seest the error of thy ways, and art now determined to do better. Hast thou any friends ?"

He replied, "I have a mother ; a poor hard-working woman, who sells fruit and candies in the streets. If you will give me a start, I will try to lead an honest life henceforth ; for I want to be a comfort and support to her. I have no other friend in the world, and nobody to help me. When I left prison, I was advised to come to you. I am a shoemaker ; and if I had money to buy a set of tools, I would work at my trade, and take care of my mother."

Necessary tools were procured for him, and he seemed very grateful ; saying it was the first time in his life that he had found any one willing to help him to be honest, when he came out of prison. Great doubts were entertained of the success of this case ; because the man had been so many times convicted. But he occasionally called at the office, and always appeared sober and respectable. A few months after his first introduction, he sent Friend Hopper a letter from Oswego, enclosing seven dollars for his mother. He immediately delivered it, and returned with a cheerful heart to enter it on his Record ; adding, "The poor old woman was much pleased that her son remembered her, and said she believed he was now going to do well."

After that, C. R. frequently sent five or ten dollars to his mother, through the same channel, and

paid her rent punctually. He refunded all the mo
ney the Association had lent him, and made some
small donations, in token of gratitude. Having behaved in a very exemplary manner during four years
and a half, Friend Hopper, at his earnest request,
applied to the Governor to have all the rights of citi-
zenship restored to him. This was readily obtained
by a full and candid statement of the case. It is
entered on the Record, with this remark: "C. R.
has experienced a wonderful change for the better
since he first called upon us. He said he should always remember the kindness that had been extended
to him, and hoped he should never do anything to
make us regret it."

He afterward opened a store, with a partner, and
up to this present time, is doing well, both in a moral
and worldly point of view. Five years and a half
after he began to reform, Dr. Russ, of New-York,
sent a discharged prisoner to him, in search of work.
He wrote in reply, as follows: "I have obtained
good employment for the bearer of your note; and
it gives me much pleasure at my heart to do something for him that wishes to do well. So leave him
to me; and I trust you will be gratified to know the
end of charity from a discharged convict." A week
elapsed before the man could enter on his new employment; and C. R paid his board during that
time.

A person, whom I will call Michael Stanley, was sentenced to Sing Sing for two years; being convicted of grand larceny when he was about twenty-two years old. When his term expired, he called upon the Prison Association, and obtained assistance in procuring employment. He endeavored to establish a good character, and was so fortunate as to gain the affections of a very orderly, industrious young woman, whom he soon after married. In his Register, Friend Hopper thus describes a visit to them, little more than a year after he was discharged from prison: "I called yesterday to visit M. S. He lives in the upper part of a brick house, nearly new. His wife is a neat, likely-looking woman, and appears to be a nice housekeeper. Everything about the premises indicates frugality, industry, and comfort. They have plain, substantial furniture, and a good carpet on the floor. Before their door is a grass-plot, and the margin of the fence is lined with a variety of plants in bloom. He and his wife, and her mother, manifested much gratification at my visit."

In little more than two years after he began to retrieve the early mistakes of his life, M. S. established a provision shop on his own account, in the city of New-York, and was successful. He and his tidy little wife called on Friend Hopper, from time to time, and always cheered his heart by their respecta-

ble appearance, and the sincere gratitude they manifested. The following record stands in the Register: "M. S. called at my house, and spent an hour
with me. He is a member of the Society of Methodists, and I really believe he is a reformed man. It
is now more than four years and a half since he was
released from Sing Sing; and his conduct has ever
since been unexceptionable."

Another young man, whom I will call Hans Over-
ton, was the son of very respectable parents, but unfortunately he formed acquaintance with unprincipled men when he was too young and inexperienced
to be a judge of character. Being corrupted by
their influence, he forged a check on a bank in Albany. He was detected, and sentenced to the State
Prison for two years. When he was released, at
twenty-two years of age, he did the best he could to
efface the blot on his reputation. But after having
obtained respectable employment, he was discharged
because his employer was told he had been in prison.
He procured another situation, and the same thing
again occurred. He began to think there was no
use in trying to redeem his lost character. In this
discouraged state of mind, he applied to the Prison
Association for assistance. Inquiries were made o1
the two gentlemen in whose employ he had been
more than a year. They said they had found him
capable, industrious, and faithful; and their distrust

of him was founded solely on the fact of his being a discharged convict. For some time, he obtained only temporary employment, now and then ; and the Association lent him small sums of money whenever his necessities required. At one time, he was charged with being an accomplice in a larceny ; but upon investigation, it was ascertained that he had become mixed up with an affair, which made him appear to disadvantage, though he had no dishonest intentions in relation to it. Finally, through the influence of the Association he obtained a situation, in a drug store. His employer was fully informed concerning his previous history, but was willing to take him on trial. He remained there five years, and conducted in the most exemplary manner. Having married meanwhile, he was desirous to avail himself of an opportunity to obtain a higher salary ; and the druggist very willingly testified that his conduct had been entirely satisfactory during the time he had been with him. But in about eight months, his new employer discovered that he had been in prison, and he immediately told him he had better procure some other situation ; though he acknowledged that he had no fault to find with him. Friend Hopper sought an interview with this gentleman and represented the youthfulness of H. O. at the time he committed the misdemeanor, which had so much injured the prospects of his life. He urged his subsequent

good conduct, and the apparent sincerity of his efforts to build up a reputation for honesty. He finally put the case home to him, by asking how he
would like to have others conduct toward a son of
his own, under similar circumstances. It was a
point of view from which the gentleman had never
before considered the question, and his mind was
somewhat impressed by it; but his prejudices were
not easily overcome. Meanwhile, the druggist was
very willing to receive the young man back again;
and he returned. It seems as if it would have been
almost impossible for him to have avoided sinking into the depths of discouragement and desperation, if
he had not received timely assistance from the Prison
Association. How highly he appreciated their aid
may be inferred from the following letter to Isaac T.
Hopper:

"My dear friend, as business prevents me from seeing you in the day-time, I take this method to express
my thanks for the noble and generous mention made
of me in your remarks before the Association; which
remarks were as pleasant and exciting to me, as they
were unexpected. I need scarcely assure you, my
kind and generous friend, (generous not only to so
humble an individual as myself, but to all your fellow creatures,) that it is out of my power to find
words to thank you adequately, or to express my
feelings on that occasion. I was the more gratified

because my dear wife was present with me, and also my brother-in-law. Oh, what a noble work the Society is engaged in. My most fervent prayer is that your name may remain on its list for many years to come. Then indeed should I have no fears for those poor unfortunates, whose first unthinking error places them unconditionally within the miasma of vice and crime. That you may enjoy a very merry Christmas, and many happy New-Years, is the sincere desire of my wife and myself."

T. B., who has been for several years in the employ of the Association, was raised by their aid from the lowest depths of intemperance, and has become a highly respectable and useful citizen.

J. M., who was in Sing Sing Prison four years, for grand larceny, was aided by the Association at various times, and always repaid the money precisely at the appointed day. His industry and skilful management excited envy and jealousy in some, who had less faculty for business. They taunted him with having been a convict, and threw all manner of obstacles in the way of his making an honest living. Among other persecutions, a suit at law was instituted against him, which cost him seventy-five dollars. The charge was entirely without foundation, and when brought before the court, was promptly dismissed. It is now about six years since. J. M. re solved to retrieve his character, and he still perseveres in the right course.

Ann W. was an illegitimate child, and early left an orphan. She went to live with an aunt, who kept a boarding-house in Albany. According to her own account, she was harshly treated, and frequently taunted with the circumstances of her birth. At the early age of fourteen, one of the boarders offered to marry her, and induced her to leave the house with him. She lived with him some time, always urging the fulfilment of his promise; and at last he pacified her by going to a person, who performed the marriage-ceremony. She was strongly attached to him, and being a capable, industrious girl, she kept everything nice and bright about their lodgings. He pretended to have a great deal of business in New-York; but in fact his frequent visits to that city were for purposes of gambling. On one of those occasions, when he had been absent much longer than usual, she followed him, and found him living with another woman. He very coolly informed her that the marriage-ceremony between them was a mere sham; the person who performed it not having been invested with any legal authority. Thus betrayed, deserted, and friendless, the poor young creature became almost frantic. In that desperate state of mind, she was decoyed by a woman, who kept a disreputable house. A short career of reck-

less frivolity and vice ended, as usual, in the hospital
on Blackwell's Island. When she was discharged,
she tried to drown her sorrow and remorse in intemperance, and went on ever from bad to worse, till
she became a denizen of Five Points. In her brief
intervals of sobriety, she was thoroughly disgusted
with herself, and earnestly desired to lead a better
life. Being turned into the street one night, in a
state of intoxication, she went to the prison called
The Tombs, because its architecture is in imitation
of the ancient sepulchral halls of Egypt. She humbly asked permission to enter this gloomy abode, in
hopes that some of the ladies connected with the
Prison Association would visit her, and find some
decent employment for her. Her case being represented to Friend Hopper, he induced his wife to
take her into the family, as a domestic. As soon as
she entered the house, she said, "I don't want to
deceive you. I will tell you everything." And she
told all the particulars of her history, without attempting to veil any of its deformity. She was very
industrious, and remarkably tidy in her habits. She
kept the kitchen extremely neat, and loved to deco-
rate it with little ornaments, especially with flowers.
Poor shattered soul! Who can tell into what blossom of poetry that little germ might have expanded,
if it had been kindly nurtured under gentle and re
fining influences? She behaved very well for several

months, and often expressed gratitude that she could now feel as if she had a home. Friend Hopper took great interest in her, and had strong hopes that she would become a respectable woman. Before a year expired, she relapsed into intemperate habits for a time; but he overlooked it, and encouraged her to forget it. As she often expressed a great desire to see her cousins in Albany, he called upon them, and told the story of her reformation. They sent some little presents, accompanied with friendly messages, and after a while invited her to visit them. For a time, it seemed as if the excursion had done her good, both physically and mentally; but the sight of respectable relatives, with husbands and children, made her realize more fully the utter loneliness of her own position. She used opium in large quantities, and had dreadful fits in consequence. Sometimes, she stole out of the house in the evening, and was taken up by the police in a state of intoxication. When she recovered her senses, she would be very humble, and during an interval of weeks, or months, would make an effort to behave extremely well. I forget how often Friend Hopper received her back, after she had spent the night in the Station House; but it was many, many times. His patience held out long after everybody else was completely weary. She finally became so violent and ungovernable, and endangered the household so much in her frantic fits,

that even he felt the necessity of placing her under
the restraining influences of some public institution.
The Magdalen Asylum at Philadelphia consented to
receive her, and after much exhortation, she was
persuaded to go. While she was there, his daughters
in that city called on her occasionally, at his request,
and he and his wife made her a visit. He wrote to
her frequently, in the kindest and most encouraging
manner. In one of these epistles, he says: "I make
frequent inquiries concerning thee, and am generally
told thou art getting along *pretty* well. Now I want
to hear a different tale from that. I want thy
friends at the Asylum to be able to say, 'She is
doing *exceedingly* well. Her health is good, she is
satisfied with her condition, and we are all much
gratified to find that she submits to the advice of her
friends.' When they can speak thus of thee, I shall
begin to think about changing thy situation. The
woman who fills thy place in my family does very
well. Every day, she puts on the table the mug
thou gavest me, and she keeps it as bright as silver.
Our little garden looks beautiful. The Morning
Glories, thou used to take so much pleasure in,
have grown finely. All the family desire kind re-
membrances. Farewell. May peace and comfort
be with thee."

In another letter, he says: "Thy Heavenly Father
has been kind, and waited long for thee; and He has

now provided a way for thy redemption from the
bondage under which thou hast suffered so much. I
hope thou wilt not think of leaving the Asylum for
some time to come. Thou canst not be so firmly
established yet, as not to be under great temptation
elsewhere. What a sorrowful circumstance it would
be, if thou shouldst again return to the filthy and
wicked habit of stupifying thyself with that pernicious drug! I am glad thou hast determined to
take my advice. If thou wilt do so, I will never
forsake thee. I will do all I can for thee; and thou
shalt never be without a home."

Again he writes: "Thy letter occasioned joy and
sorrow. Sorrow to find thou hast not always treated
the matron as thou oughtest to have done. I am
sure that excellent person is every way worthy of
thy regard; and I hope my ears will never again be
pained by hearing that thou hast treated her un-
kindly or disrespectfully. I did hope that after a
year's discipline, thou hadst learned to control thy
temper. Until thou canst do so, thou must be
aware that thou art not qualified to render thyself
useful or agreeable in any family. But after all, I
am glad to find that thou art sensible of thy error,
and hast a disposition to improve. When thou
liest down at night, I want thee to examine the
deeds of the past day. If thou hast made a hasty
reply, or spoken impertinently, or done wrong in any

other way, be careful to acknowledge thy fault.
Ask thy Heavenly Father to forgive thee, and be
careful to do so no more. I feel a great regard for
thee ; and I trust thou wilt never give me cause to
regret thy relapse into vice. I hope better things
for thee, and I always shall."

But his hopefulness and patience proved of no
avail in this instance. The wreck was too complete
to admit of repair. The poor creature occasionally
struggled hard to do better ; but her constitution
was destroyed by vice and hardship ; her feelings
were blunted by suffering, and her naturally bright
faculties were stupified by opium. After she left the
Asylum, she lived with a family in the country for
awhile ; but the old habits returned, and destroyed
what little strength she had left. The last I knew
of her she was on Blackwell's Island ; and she will
probably never leave it, till she goes where the weary
are at rest.

An uncommon degree of interest was excited in
Friend Hopper's mind by the sufferings of another
individual, whom I will call Julia Peters. She was
born of respectable parents, and was carefully tended
in her early years. Her mother was a prudent, re-
ligious-minded woman ; but she died when Julia was
twelve years old. The father soon after took to
drinking and gambling, and spent all the property he
possessed. His daughter was thus brought into the

midst of profligate associates, at an age when impulses are strong, and the principles unformed. She led a vicious life for several years, and during a fit of intoxication married a worthless, dissipated fellow. When she was eighteen years old, she was imprisoned for perjury. The case appeared doubtful at the time, and from circumstances, which afterward came to light, it is supposed that she was not guilty of the alleged crime. The jury could not agree on the first trial, and she remained in jail two years, awaiting a decision of her case. She was at last pronounced guilty; and feeling that injustice was done her, she made use of violent and disrespectful language to the court. This probably increased the prejudice against her; for she was sentenced to Sing Sing prison for the long term of fourteen years. She was naturally intelligent, active and energetic; and the limitations of a prison had a worse effect upon her, than they would have had on a more stolid temperament. In the course of a year or two, her mind began to sink under the pressure, and finally exhibited signs of melancholy insanity. Friend Hopper had an interview with her soon after she was conveyed to Sing Sing, and found her in a tate of deep dejection. She afterward became completely deranged, and was removed to the Lunatic Asylum at Bloomingdale. He and his wife visited her there, and found her in a state of temporary

rationality. Her manners were quiet and pleasing,
and she appeared exceedingly gratified to see them.
The superintendent granted permission to take her with
them in a walk through the grounds, and she enjoyed
this little excursion very highly. But when one of
the company remarked that it was a very pleasant
place, she sighed deeply, and replied, "Yes, it is a
pleasant place to those who can leave it. But chains
are chains, though they are made of gold; and mine
grow heavier every day."

Her temperament peculiarly required freedom, and
chafed and fretted under restraint. Insanity returned
upon her with redoubled force, soon after. She used
blasphemous and indecent language, and cut up her
blankets to make pantaloons. She picked the lock
of her room, and tried various plans of escape.
When Friend Hopper went to see her again, some
weeks later, he found her in the masculine attire,
which she had manufactured. She tried to hide
herself, but when he called her back in a gentle, but
firm tone, she came immediately. He took her
kindly by the hand, and said, "Julia, what does all
this mean?"

"It is military costume," she replied. "I am an
officer of state."

"I am sorry thou art not more decently clad,"
said he. "I intended to have thee take a walk with
me; but I should be ashamed to go with thee in

that condition." She earnestly entreated to go, and promised to change her dress immediately. He accordingly waited till she was ready, and then spent more than an hour walking round the grounds with her. She told him the history of her life, and wept bitterly over the retrospect of her erroneous course. It seemed a great relief to have some one to whom she could open her over-burdened heart. She was occasionally incoherent, but the fresh air invigorated her, and the quiet talk soothed her perturbed feelings. At parting, she said, "I thank you. I thought I had n't a friend in the world. I was afraid everybody had forgotten me."

"I am thy sincere friend," he replied; "and I promise that I will never forget thee."

I make the following extract from a letter, which he wrote to her soon after: "Now, Julia, listen to me, and mind what I say; for thou knowest I am thy friend. I want thee, at all times, and upon all occasions, to be very careful of thy conduct. Never suffer thyself to use vulgar or profane language. It would grieve me, and I am sure thou dost not wish to do that. Besides, it is very degrading, and very wicked. Be discreet, sober, and modest. Be kind, courteous, and obliging to all. Thou wilt make many friends by so doing, and wilt feel more cheerful and happy thyself. Do be a lady. I know thou canst, if thou wilt. More than all, I want thee to be a Christian. I sympathize with thee, and intend to come and see thee soon."

Dr. Earle, physician of the Asylum, said the letter had a salutary effect upon her. Friend Hopper went out to see her frequently, and was often accompanied by his wife, or daughters. Her bodily and mental health continued to improve; and in the course of five or six months, the doctor allowed her to accompany her kind old friend to the city, and spend a day and night at his house. This change of scene was found so beneficial, that the visit was repeated a few weeks after. Before winter set in, she was so far restored that she spent several days in his family, and conducted with the greatest propriety. He soon after applied to the Governor for a pardon, which was promptly granted. His next step was to procure a suitable home for her; and a worthy Quaker family in Pennsylvania, who were acquainted with all the circumstances, agreed to employ her as chambermaid and seamstress. When it was all arranged, Friend Hopper went out to the Asylum to carry the news. But fearful of exciting her too much, he talked upon indifferent subjects for a few minutes, and then asked if she would like to go into the city again to spend a fortnight with his family. She replied, "Indeed I would." He promised to take her with him, and added, "Perhaps thou wilt stay longer than two weeks." At last, he said, "It may be that thou wilt not have to return here again. She sprang up instantly, and looking in his face with intense anxiety, exclaimed, "Am I pardoned? *Am* I pardoned?"

"Yes, thou art pardoned," he replied; "and I have come to take thee home." She fell back into her seat, covered her face with her hands, and wept aloud. Friend Hopper, describing this interview in a letter to a friend, says: "It was the most affecting scene I ever witnessed. Nothing could exceed the joy I felt at seeing this child of sorrow relieved from her sufferings, and restored to liberty. I had seen this young and comely looking woman, who was endowed with more than common good sense, driven to the depths of despair by the intensity of her sufferings. I had seen her a raving maniac. Now, I saw her 'sitting and clothed in her right mind.' I was a thousand times more than compensated for all the pains I had taken. I had sympathized deeply with her sufferings, and I now partook largely of her joy."

As her nerves were in a very excitable state, it was thought best that she should remain a few weeks under the superintendence of his daughter, Mrs. Gibbons, before she went to the home provided for her. She was slightly unsettled at times, but was disposed to be industrious and cheerful. Having earned a little money by her needle, the first use she made of it, was to buy a pair of vases for Friend Hopper; and proud and pleased she was, when she brought them home and presented them! He always kept them on the parlor mantel-piece, and often told their history to people who called upon him.

When she had become perfectly calm and settled, he and his wife accompanied her to Pennsylvania, and saw her established among her new friends, who received her in the kindest manner. A week after his return, he wrote to assure her that his interest in her had not abated. In the course of the letter, he says: "I need not tell thee how anxious I am that thou shouldst conduct so as to be a credit to thyself, and to those who have interested themselves in thy behalf. I felt keenly at parting with thee, but I was comforted by the reflection that I had left thee with kind friends. Confide in them upon all occasions, and do nothing without their advice. Thy future happiness will depend very much upon thyself. Never suffer thy mind to become excited. Remember that kind friends were raised up for thee in the midst of all thy sorrows, and that they will always continue to be thy friends, if thou wilt be guided by their counsels. Thou wert with us so long, that we feel toward thee like one of the family. All join me in love to thee."

In her reply, she says: "Your letter was to me what a glass of cold water would be when fainting.

I have pored over it so much, that I have got it by
heart. Friend Hopper, you first saw me in prison
and visited me. You followed me to the Asylum.
You did not forsake me. You have changed a bed
of straw to a bed of down. May Heaven bless and
reward you for it. No tongue can express the gratitude I feel. Many are the hearts you have made
glad. Suppose all you have dragged out of one
place and another were to stand before you at once!
I think you would have more than you could shake
hands with in a month ; and I know you would shake
hands with them all."

For a few months, she behaved in a very satisfactory manner, though occasionally unsettled and depressed. She wrote that the worthy woman with
whom she lived was 'both mother and friend to her.'
But the country was gloomy in the winter, and the
spirit of unrest took possession of her. She went to
Philadelphia and plunged into scenes of vice for a
week or two; but she quickly repented, and was
rescued by her friends. I have seldom seen Friend
Hopper so deeply pained as he was by this retrograde
step in one whom he had rejoiced over, "as a brand
plucked from the burning." After awhile, he addressed a letter to her, in which he says: "I should
have written to thee before, but I have been at a loss
what to say. I have cared for thee, as if thou hadst
been my own child. Little did I think thou wouldst

ever disgrace thyself, and distress me, by associating
with the most vile. Thou wert wonderfully snatched
from a sink of pollution. I hoped thou wouldst appreciate the favor, and take a fresh start in life, determined to do well. Better, far better, for thee to
have lingered out a wretched existence in Blooming
dale Asylum, than to continue in such a course a
that thou entered upon in Philadelphia. My heart is
pained while I write. Indeed, thou art seldom out
of my mind. Most earnestly, and affectionately, I
beseech thee to change thy course. Restrain evil
thoughts and banish them from thee. Try to keep
thy mind quiet, and stayed upon thy Heavenly Father. He has done much for thee. He has followed thee in all thy wanderings. Ask him to forgive thy iniquity, and he will have mercy on thee.
Thou mayest yet be happy thyself, and make those
happy who have taken a deep interest in thy welfare.
But if thou art determined to pursue evil courses, after all that has been done for thee, let me tell thee
thy days will be brief and full of trouble; and I
doubt not thou wilt end them within the walls of a
prison. I hope better things of thee. If thou doest
well, it will afford encouragement to assist others;
but if thy conduct is bad, it may be the means or
prolonging the sufferings of many others. I am still
thy friend, and disposed to do all I can for thee."

In her answer, she says: "Oh, frail woman! No

steps can be recalled.   It is all in the future to make
amends for the past.   After all the good counsel
some receive, they return to habits of vice.   They
repent when it is too late.   How true it is that virtue
has its reward, and vice its punishment.   I know
that the way of transgressors is hard.   If I only had
a few years of my life to live over again, how different would I live!   For the many blessings Providence has bestowed on me, may I be grateful.   In
all my troubles, He has raised me up a friend.   I believe He never forsakes me ; so there is hope for me.
Don't be discouraged that you befriended me ; for,
with God's blessing, you shall have no reason to re
pent of it."

He wrote thus to her, a short time after : "I very
often think of thee, and I yet hope that I shall one
day see thee a happy and respectable woman.   I
have lately had a good deal of conversation with the
Governor concerning 'my friends,' as he calls those
whom he has pardoned at my request.   I did not tell
him thou hadst behaved incorrectly.   I hope I shall
never be obliged to do so.   I have had pleasant accounts concerning thee lately, and I do not wish to
remember that thou hast ever grieved me.   As I
passed down the river yesterday, from Albany, I saw
Bloomingdale Asylum.   I remembered how I used
to walk with thee about the grounds ; and my mind
was for a time depressed with melancholy reflections.

I had deeply sympathized in thy sufferings; and I had rarely, if ever, experienced greater pleasure than when I was the happy messenger of thy redemption from the grievous thraldom, under which thou wert suffering. Thou art blessed with more than common good sense, and thou knowest how to make thyself agreeable. I earnestly advise thee to guard well thy thoughts. Never allow thyself to use an immodest word, or to be guilty of an unbecoming action. On all occasions, show thyself worthy of the regard of those who feel an interest in thy welfare. 'There is joy in heaven over one sinner that repenteth, more than over ninety and nine just persons that need no repentance.' With ardent solicitude for thy welfare, I remain thy sincere friend."

About two years afterward, Friend Hopper made the following record in his Register: "J. P. continues to conduct very satisfactorily. She makes a very respectable appearance, is modest and discreet in her deportment, and industrious in her habits. As a mark of gratitude for the attentions, which at different times I have extended to her, she has sent me a pair of handsome gloves, and a bandana handkerchief. Taking into consideration all the circumstances attending this case, this small present affords me much more gratification than ten times the value from any other person." Six months later, he made this record : "The Friend, with whom J. P. lives, called upon me to say that she sent a world of love to Isaac T. Hopper, whose kindness she holds in grateful remembrance." The same Friend afterward wrote, "She is all that I could wish her to be."

Many more instances might be quoted ; but enough has been told to illustrate his patience and forbearance, and his judicious mode of dealing with such characters. Dr. Russ, one of the most active and benevolent members of the Prison Association, thinks it is a fair statement to say that at least three-fourths of those for whom he interested himself eventually turned out well ; though in several cases, it was after a few backslidings. The fullness of his sympathy was probably one great reason why he obtained such influence over them, and made them so willing to open their hearts to him. He naturally, and without effort, put *his* soul in *their* soul's stead. This rendered it easy for him to disregard his own interests, and set aside his own opinions, for the benefit of others. In several instances, he procured another place for a healthy, good-looking domestic, with whose services he was well satisfied, merely because some poor creature applied for work, who was too lame, or ill-favored, to obtain employment elsewhere. When an insane girl, from Sing Sing, was brought to his house to wait for an opportunity to return to her parents in Canada, he sent for the Catholic Bishop to come and minister to her spiritual wants, because he found she was very unhappy without religious consolation in the form to which she had been accustomed in childhood.

The peculiar adaptation of his character to this mission of humanity was not only felt by his fellow laborers in the New-York Association, but was acknowledged wherever he was known. Dr. Walter Channing, brother of the late Dr. William Ellery Channing wrote to him as follows, when the Boston Prison Association was about being formed ; "I was rejoiced to learn that you would stay to help at our meetings in behalf of criminals. The demand which this class of brothers has upon us is felt by every man, who examines his own heart, and his own life. How great is every man's need of the kindness and love of his brethren! Here is the deep-laid cause of sympathy. Here is the secret spring of that wide effort, which the whole world is now making for the happiness and good of the race. I thank you for what you have done in this noble work. I had heard with the sincerest pleasure, of your labors for the down trodden and the poor. God bless you for these labors of love! Truly shall I thank you for the light you can so abundantly give, and which will make the path of duty plain before me."

Incessant demands were made upon his time and attention. A great many people, if they happened to have their feelings touched by some scene of distress, seemed to think they had fulfilled their whole duty by sending the sufferer to Isaac T. Hopper. Few can imagine what an arduous task it is to be such a thorough philanthropist as he was. Whoever wishes for a crown like his, must earn it by carrying the martyr's cross through life. They must make up their minds to relinquish their whole time to such pursuits ; they must be prepared to encounter envy and dislike ; to be misrepresented and blamed, where their intentions have been most praiseworthy ; to be often disheartened by the delinquences, or ingratitude, of those they have expended their time and strength to serve ; above all, they must be willing to live and die poor.

Though attention to prisoners was the mission to which Friend Hopper peculiarly devoted the last years of his life, his sympathy for the slaves never abated. And though his own early efforts had been made in co-operation with the gradual Emancipation Society, established by Franklin, Rush, and others, he rejoiced in the bolder movement, known as modern anti-slavery. Of course, he did not endorse everything that was said and done by all sorts of temperaments engaged in that cause, or in any other cause. But no man understood better than he did the fallacy of the argument that modern abolitionists had put back the cause of emancipation in the South. He

often used to speak of the spirit manifested toward
William Savery, when he went to the South to
preach, as early as 1791. Writing from Augusta,
Georgia, that tender-hearted minister of Christ says :
"They can scarcely tolerate us, on account of our
abhorrence of slavery. This was truly a trying place
to lodge in another night." At Savannah the landlord
of a tavern where they lodged, ordered a cruel flogging to be administered to one of his slaves, who had
fallen asleep through weariness, before his daily task
was accomplished. William Savery says : "When
we went to supper, this unfeeling wretch craved a
blessing ; which I considered equally abhorrent to the
Divine Being, as his curses." In the morning, when
the humane preacher heard sounds of the lash, accompanied by piteous cries for mercy, he had the
boldness to step in between the driver and the slave ;
and he stopped any further infliction of punishment,
for that time. He says : "This landlord was the
most abominably wicked man that I ever met with ;
full of horrid execrations, and threatenings of all
Northern people. But I did not spare him ; which
occasioned a bystander to express, with an oath, that
I should be 'popped over.' We left them distressed
in mind ; and having a lonesome wood of twelve
miles to pass through, we were in full expectation of
their waylaying, or coming after us, to put their
wicked threats in execution.'

As early as 1806, James Lindley, of Pennsylvania, had a large piece of iron hurled at him, as he was passing through the streets, at Havre de Grace, Maryland. Three of his ribs were broken, and several teeth knocked out, and he was beaten till he was supposed to be dead. All this was done merely because they mistook him for Jacob Lindley, the Quaker preacher, who was well known as a friend to fugitives from slavery.

In view of these, and other similar facts, Friend Hopper was never disposed to blame abolitionists for excitements at the South, as many of the Quakers were inclined to do. He had a sincere respect for the integrity and conscientious boldness of William Lloyd Garrison; as all have, who know him well enough to appreciate his character. For many years, he was always an invited and welcome guest on the occasion of the annual meeting of the Anti-Slavery Society in New-York. Mr. Garrison's feelings toward him are manifested in the following answer to one of his letters: "As there is no one in the world for whom I entertain more veneration and esteem than for yourself, and as there is no place in New-York, that is so much like home to me, as your own hospitable dwelling, be assured it will give me the utmost pleasure to accept your friendly invitation to remain under your roof during the approach-

ing anniversary week." It was on one of these
occasions, that Garrison addressed to him the following sonnet :

"Thou kind and venerable friend of man,
    In heart and spirit young, though old in years!
The tyrant trembles when thy name he hears,
And the slave joys thy honest face to scan.
A friend more true and brave, since time began,
    Humanity has never found : her fears
    By thee have been dispelled, and wiped the tears
Adown her sorrow-stricken cheeks that ran.
If like Napoleon's appears thy face,
    Thy soul to his bears no similitude.
He came to curse, but thou to bless our race.
    Thy hands are pure ; in blood were his imbrued.
His memory shall be covered with disgrace,
    But thine embalmed among the truly great and good."

Until the last few years of his life, Friend Hopper
usually walked to and from his office twice a day,
making about five miles in the whole ; to which he
sometimes added a walk in the evening, to visit
children or friends, or transact some necessary business. When the weather was very unpleasant, he
availed himself of the Harlem cars. Upon one of
these occasions, it chanced that the long, ponderous
vehicle was nearly empty. They had not proceeded
far, when a very respectable-looking young woman
beckoned for the car to stop. It did so ; but when
she set her foot on the step, the conductor, some-

what rudely pushed her back; and she turned away, evidently much mortified. Friend Hopper started up and inquired, "Why didst thou push that woman away?"

"She's colored," was the laconic reply.

"Art thou instructed by the managers of the rail-road to proceed in this manner on such occasions?' inquired Friend Hopper.

The man answered, "Yes."

"Then let me get out," rejoined the genuine republican. "It disturbs my conscience to ride in a public conveyance, where any decently behaved person is refused admittance." And though it was raining very fast, and his home was a mile off, the old veteran of seventy-five years marched through mud and wet, at a pace somewhat brisker than his usual energetic step; for indignation warmed his honest and kindly heart, and set the blood in motion. The next day, he called at the rail-road office, and very civilly inquired of one of the managers whether conductors were instructed to exclude passengers merely on account of complexion.

"Certainly not," was the prompt reply. "They have discretionary power to reject any person who is drunk, or offensively unclean, or indecent, or quarrelsome."

Friend Hopper then related how a young woman of modest appearance, and respectable dress, was

pushed from the step, though the car was nearly
empty, and she was seeking shelter from a violent
rain.

"That was wrong," replied the manager. "We
have no reason to complain of colored people as passengers. They obtrude upon no one, and always
have sixpences in readiness to pay; whereas fash-
ionably dressed white people frequently offer a ten
dollar bill, which they know we cannot change, and
thus cheat us out of our rightful dues. Who was
the conductor, that behaved in the manner you have
described? We will turn him away, if he does n't
know better how to use the discretionary power with
which he is entrusted."

Friend Hopper replied, "I had rather thou wouldst
not turn him out of thy employ, unless he repeats
the offence, after being properly instructed. I have
no wish to injure the man. He has become infected
with the unjust prejudices of the community without
duly reflecting upon the subject. Friendly conversation with him may suggest wiser thoughts. All I
ask of thee is to instruct him that the rights of the
meanest citizen are to be respected. I thank thee
for having listened to my complaint in such a candid
and courteous manner."

"And I thank you for having come to inform us
of the circumstance," replied the manager. They
parted mutually well pleased; and a few days after,

the same conductor admitted a colored woman into
the cars without making any objection. This improved state of things continued several weeks. But
the old tyrannical system was restored, owing to
counteracting influence from some unknown quarter.
I often met colored people coming from the country
in the Harlem cars; but I never afterward knew one
to enter from the streets of the city.

Many colored people die every year, and vast
numbers have their health permanently impaired, on
account of inclement weather, to which they are exposed by exclusion from public conveyances. And
this merely on account of complexion! What a tor-
nado of popular eloquence would come from our
public halls, if Austria or Russia were guilty of any
despotism half as mean! Yet the great heart of the
people is moved by kind and sincere feelings in its
outbursts against foreign tyranny. But in addition
to this honorable sympathy for the oppressed in other
countries, it would be well for them to look at home,
and consider whether it is just that any well-behaved
people should be excluded from the common privileges of public conveyances. If a hundred citizens
in New-York would act as Friend Hopper did, the
evil would soon be remedied. It is the almost universal failure in individual duty, which so accumu-
lates errors and iniquities in society, that the ultra-
theories, and extra efforts of reformers become abso-

lutely necessary to prevent the balance of things from being destroyed; as thunder and lightning are required to purify a polluted atmosphere. Godwin, in some of his writings, asks, "What is it that enables a thousand errors to keep their station in the world? It is cowardice. It is because the majority of men, who see that things are not altogether right, yet see in so frigid a way, and have so little courage to express their views. If every man to-day would tell all the truth he knows, three years hence, there would scarcely be a falsehood of any magnitude remaining in the civilized world."

In the summer of 1844, Friend Hopper met with a Methodist preacher from Mississippi, who came with his family to New-York, to attend a General Conference. Being introduced as a zealous abolitionist, the conversation immediately turned upon slavery. One of the preacher's daughters said, "I could'nt possibly get along without slaves, Mr. Hopper. Why I never dressed or undressed myself, till I came to the North. I wanted very much to bring a slave with me."

"I wish thou hadst," rejoined Friend Hopper.

"And what would you have done, if you had seen her?" she inquired.

He replied, "I would have told her that she was a free woman while she remained here; but if she went back to the South, she would be liable to be sold, like a pig or a sheep."

They laughed at this frank avowal, and when he invited them to come to his house with their father, to take tea, they gladly accepted the invitation. Again the conversation turned toward that subject, which is never forgotten when North and South meet. In answer to some remark from Friend Hopper, the preacher said, "Do you think I am not a Christian?"

"I certainly do not regard thee as one," he replied.

"And I suppose you think I cannot get to heaven?" rejoined the slaveholder.

"I will not say that," replied the Friend. "To thy own Master thou must stand or fall. But slavery is a great abomination, and no one who is guilty of it can be a Christian, or Christ-like. I would not exclude thee from the kingdom of heaven; but if thou dost enter there, it must be because thou art ignorant of the fact that thou art living in sin."

After a prolonged conversation, mostly on the same topic, the guests rose to depart. The Methodist said, "Well, Mr. Hopper, I have never been treated better by any man, than I have been by you. I should be very glad to have you visit us."

"Ah! and thou wouldst lynch me; or at least, thy friends would," he replied, smiling.

"Oh no, we would treat you very well," rejoined

the Southerner. " But how would you talk about
slavery if you were there ?"

"Just as I do here, to be sure," answered the
Quaker. "I would advise the slaves to be honest,
industrious, and obedient, and never try to run away
from a good master, unless they were pretty sure of
escaping; because if they were caught, they would'
fare worse than before. But if they had a safe opportunity, I should advise them to be off as soon as
possible." In a more serious tone, he added, "And
to thee, who claimest to be a minister of Christ, I
would say that thy Master requires thee to give deliverance to the captive, and let the oppressed go
free. My friend, hast thou a conscience void of offence? When thou liest down at night, is thy mind
always at ease on this subject? After pouring out
thy soul in prayer to thy Heavenly Father, dost thou
not feel the outraged sense of right, like a perpetual
motion, restless within thy breast? Dost thou not
hear a voice telling thee it is wrong to hold thy fellow men in slavery, with their wives and their little
ones?"

The preacher manifested some emotion at this earnest appeal, and confessed that he sometimes had
doubts on the subject; though, on the whole, he had
concluded that it was right to hold slaves. One of
his daughters, who was a widow, seemed to be more
deeply touched. She took Friend Hopper's hand, at

parting, and said, "I am thankful for the privilege
of having seen you. I never talked with an abolitionist before. You have convinced me that slave-
holding is sinful in the sight of God. My husband
left me several slaves, and I have held them for five
years; but when I return, I am resolved to hold a
slave no longer."

Friend Hopper cherished some hope that this
preaching and praying slaveholder would eventually
manumit his bondmen; but I had listened to his
conversation, and I thought otherwise. His conscience seemed to me to be asleep under a seven-fold
shield of self-satisfied piety; and I have observed
that such consciences rarely waken.

At the time of the Christiana riots, in 1851, when
the slave-power seemed to overshadow everything,
and none but the boldest ventured to speak against
it, Friend Hopper wrote an article for the Tribune,
and signed it with his name, in which he maintained
that the colored people, "who defended themselves
and their firesides against the lawless assaults of an
armed party of negro-hunters from Maryland," ought
not to be regarded as traitors or murderers "by men
who set a just value on liberty, and who had no conscientious scruples with regard to war."

The first runaway, who was endangered by the
passage of the Fugitive Slave Law in 1850, happened to be placed under his protection. A very good-

looking colored man, who escaped from bondage, resided some years in Worcester, Massachusetts, and
acquired several thousand dollars by hair-dressing.
He went to New-York to be married, and it chanced
that his master arrived in Worcester in search of
him, the very day that he started for that city.
Some person friendly to the colored man sent information to New-York by telegraph; but the gentleman to whom it was addressed was out of the city.
One of the operators at the telegraph office said,
"Isaac T. Hopper ought to know of this message;"
and he carried it himself. Friend Hopper was then
eighty years old, but he sprang out of bed at midnight, and went off with all speed to hunt up the fugitive. He found him, warned him of his danger,
and offered to secrete him. The colored man hesitated. He feared it might be a trick to decoy him
into his master's power. But the young wife gazed
very earnestly at Friend Hopper, and said, "I would
trust the countenance of that Quaker gentleman
anywhere. Let us go with him." They spent the
remainder of the night at his house, and after being
concealed elsewhere for a few days, they went to
Canada. This slave was the son of his master, who
estimated his market-value at two thousand five hundred dollars. Six months imprisonment, and a fine
of one thousand dollars was the legal penalty for
aiding him. But Friend Hopper always said, "I

have never sought to make any slave discontented
with his situation, because I do not consider it either
wise or kind to do so; but so long as my life is
spared, I will always assist any one, who is trying to
escape from slavery, be the laws what they may."

A black man, who had fled from bondage, married
a mulatto woman in Philadelphia, and became the
father of six children. He owned a small house in
the neighborhood of that city, and had lived there
comfortably several years, when that abominable law
was passed, by which the Northern States rendered
their free soil a great hunting-ground for the rich
and powerful to run down the poor and weak. In
rushed the slaveholders from all quarters, to seize
their helpless prey! At dead of night, the black
man, sleeping quietly in the humble home he had
earned by unremitting industry, was roused up to receive information that his master was in pursuit of
him. His eldest daughter was out at service in the
neighborhood, and there was no time to give her notice. They hastily packed such articles as they
could take, caught the little ones from their beds,
and escaped before the morning dawned. A gentleman, who saw them next day on board a steamboat,
bserved their uneasiness, and suspected they were
"fugitives from injustice." When he remarked this
to a companion, he replied, "They have too much
luggage to be slaves." Nevertheless, he thought it

could do no harm to inform them that Isaac T. Hopper of New-York was the best adviser of fugitives Accordingly, a few hours afterward, the whole co lored colony was established in his house; where the genteel-looking mother, and her bright, pretty little children excited a very lively interest in all hearts They made their way to Canada as soon as possible, and the daughter who was left in Philadelphia, was soon after sent to them.

Friend Hopper's resolute resistance to oppression, in every form, never produced any harshness in his manners, or diminished his love of quiet domestic life. He habitually surrendered himself to pleasant influences, even from events that troubled him at the time, he generally extracted some agreeable incident and soon forgot those of opposite character. It was quite observable how little he thought of the instances of ingratitude he had met with. He seldom, if ever, alluded to them, unless reminded by some direct question; but the unfortunate beings who had persevered in reformation, and manifested gratitude, were always uppermost in his thoughts.

Though always pleased to hear that his children were free from pecuniary anxiety, he never desired wealth for them. The idea of money never seemed to occur to him in connection with their marriages. It was a cherished wish of his heart to have them united to members of the Society of Friends; yet he

easily yielded, even on that point, as soon as he saw
their happiness was at stake. When one of his sons
married into a family educated under influences totally foreign to Quaker principles, he was somewhat
disturbed. But he at once adopted the bride as a
beloved daughter of his heart; and she ever after
proved a lovely and thornless Rose in the pathway
of his life. Great was his satisfaction when he discovered that she was grandchild of Dr. William
Rogers, Professor of English and Oratory in the
University of Pennsylvania, who, sixty years before,
had preached the first sermon to inmates of the State
Prison, in Philadelphia. That good and gifted clergyman was associated with his earliest recollections;
for when he was on one of his pleasant visits to his
uncle Tatem, at six years old, he went to meeting
with him for the first time, and was seated on a stool
between his knees. The proceedings were a great
novelty to him; for Dr. Rogers was the first minister he ever saw in a pulpit. He never forgot the
text of that sermon. I often heard him repeat it,
during the last years of his life. The remembrance
of these incidents, and the great respect he had for
the character of the prison missionary, at once established in his mind a claim of old relationship between him and the new inmate of his household.

He had the custom of sitting with his wife on the
front-door-step during the summer twilight, to catch

the breeze, that always refreshes the city of New-
York, after a sultry day. On such occasions, the
children of the neighborhood soon began to gather
round him. One of the most intelligent and interesting pupils of the Deaf and Dumb Institution had
married Mr. Gallaudet, Professor in that Institution,
and resided in the next house. She had a bright
lively little daughter, who very early learned to imitate her rapid and graceful way of conversing by
signs. This child was greatly attracted toward
Friend Hopper. The moment she saw him, she
would clap her tiny hands with delight, and toddle
toward him, exclaiming, "Opper! Opper!" When
he talked to her, she would make her little fingers
fly, in the prettiest fashion, interpreting by signs to
her mute mother all that "Opper" had been saying.
Her quick intelligence and animated gestures were a
perpetual source of amusement to him. When he
went down to his office in the morning, all the nurses
in the neighborhood were accustomed to stop in his
path, that he might have some playful conversation
with the little ones in their charge. He had a pleasant nick-name for them all; such as "Blue-bird,"
or "Yellow-bird," according to their dress. They
would run up to him as he approached home, calling
out, "Here's your little Blue-bird!"

His garden was another source of great satisfaction to him. It was not bigger than a very small

bed-room, and only half of it received the sunshine. But he called the minnikin grass-plot his meadow, and talked very largely about mowing his hay. He covered the walls and fences with flowering vines, and suspended them between the pillars of his little piazza. Even in this employment he revealed the tendencies of his character. One day, when I was helping him train a woodbine, he said, "Fasten it in that direction, Maria; for I want it to go over into our neighbor's yard, that it may make their wall look pleasant."

In the summer of 1848, when I was staying in the country, not far from New-York, I received the following letter from him: "Dear Friend, the days have not yet come, in which I can say I have no pleasure in them. Notwithstanding the stubs against which I hit my toes, the briars and thorns that sometimes annoy me, and the muddy sloughs I am sometimes obliged to wade through, yet, after all, the days have *not* come in which I have no enjoyment. In the course of my journey, I find here and there a green spot, by which I can sit down and rest, and pleasant streams, where I sometimes drink, mostly in secret, and am refreshed. I often remember the saying of a beloved friend, long since translated from this scene of mutation to a state of eternal beatitude: 'I wear my sackcloth on my loins; I don't wish to afflict others by carrying a sorrowful coun-

tenance.' A wise conclusion. I love to diffuse happiness over all with whom I come in contact. But
all this is a kind of accident. I took up my pen to
tell thee about our garden. I never saw it half so
handsome as it is now. Morning Glories are on
both sides of the yard, extending nearly to the
second story windows; and they exhibit their glories
every morning, in beautiful style. There are Cy-
press vines, twelve feet high, running up on the pil-
lar before the kitchen window, and spreading out
each way. They blossom most profusely. The
wooden wall is entirely covered with Madeira vines,
and the stone wall with Woodbine. The grass-plot
is very thrifty, and our borders are beautified with a
variety of flowers. How thou wouldst like to look
at them !"

I replied as follows: "My dear and honored
friend : Your kind, cheerful epistle came into my
room as pleasantly as would the vines and flowers
you describe. I am very glad the spirit moved you
to write; for, to use the words of the apostle, 'I
thank my God for every remembrance of you.' I do
not make many professions of friendship, because
neither you nor I are much given to professions; but
there is no one in the world for whom I have a higher
respect than yourself, and very few for whom I cherish a more cordial affection. You say the time has
not *yet* come when you have no pleasure. I think,

my friend, that it will *never* come. To an ever-
green heart, like yours, so full of kindly sympathies,
the little children will always prattle, the birds will
always sing, and the flowers will always offer in-
cense. *This* reward of the honest and kindly heart
is one of those, which 'the world can neither give
nor take away.'

"I should love to see your garden now. There is
a peculiar satisfaction in having a very *little* patch
all blooming into beauty. I had such an one in my
humble home in Boston, some years ago. It used to
make me think of Mary Howitt's very pleasant poetry :

> "Yes, in the poor man's garden grow
>   Far more than herbs and flowers ;
> Kind thoughts, contentment, peace of mind,
>   And joy for weary hours."

I have one enjoyment this summer, which you cannot have in your city premises. The birds ! not only
their sweet songs, but all their little cunning manœu-
vres in courting, building their nests, and rearing
their young. I watched for hours a little Phœbe-
bird, who brought out her brood to teach them to
fly. They used to stop to rest themselves on the
naked branch of a dead pear-tree. There they sat
so quietly, all in a row, in their sober russet suit of
feathers, just as if they were Quakers at meeting.
The birds are very tame here ; thanks to Friend Joseph's tender heart. The Bob-o-links pick seed from

the dandelions, at my very feet. May you sleep like a child when his friends are with him, as the Orientals say. And so farewell."

Interesting strangers occasionally called to see Friend Hopper, attracted by his reputation. Frederika Bremer was peculiarly delighted by her interviews with him, and made a fine sketch of him in her collection of American likenesses. William Page, the well-known artist, made for me an admirable drawing of him, when he was a little past seventy years old. Eight years after, Salathiel Ellis, of New-York, at the suggestion of some friends, executed an uncommonly fine medallion likeness. A reduced copy of this was made in bronze at the request of some members of the Prison Association. The reverse side represents him raising a prisoner from the ground, and bears the appropriate inscription, "To seek and to save that which was lost."

Young people often sent him pretty little testimonials of the interest he had excited in their minds. Intelligent Irish girls, with whom he had formed acquaintance in their native land, never during his life ceased to write to him, and occasionally sent some tasteful souvenir of their friendship. The fashionable custom of New-Year's and Christmas offerings was not in his line. But though he always dined on humble fare at Christmas, as a testimony against the

observance of holy days, he secretly sent turkeys to
poor families, who viewed the subject in a different
light; and it was only by accidental circumstances
that they at last discovered to whom they owed the
annual gift.

Members of the Society of Friends often came to
see him; and for many of them he cherished high
respect, and a very warm friendship. But his character grew larger, and his views more liberal, after
the bonds which bound him to a sect were cut asunder. Friends occasionally said to him, "We miss
thy services in the Society, Isaac. Hadst thou not
better ask to be re-admitted? The way is open for
thee, whenever thou hast an inclination to return."
He replied, "I thank thee. But in the present state
of the Society, I don't think I could be of any service to them, or they to me." But he could never
relinquish the hope that the primitive character of
Quakerism would be restored, and that the Society
would again hold up the standard of righteousness
to the nations, as it had in days gone by. Nearly
every man, who forms strong religious attachments
in early life, cherishes similar anticipations for his
sect, whose glory declines, in the natural order of
things. But such hopes are never realized. The
spirit has a resurrection, but not the form. "Soul
never dies. Matter dies off it, and it lives elsewhere." Thus it is with truth. The noble princi-

ples maintained by Quakers, through suffering and
peril, have taken root in other sects, and been an in-
calculable help to individual seekers after light,
throughout the Christian world. Like winged seed
scattered in far-off soils, they will produce a forest-
growth in the future, long after the original stock is
dead, and its dust dispersed to the winds.

In Friend Hopper's last years, memory, as usual
with the old, was busily employed in reproducing the
the past; and in his mind the pictures she presented
were uncommonly vivid. In a letter to his daughter,
Sarah Palmer, he writes: "I was deeply affected on
being informed of the death of Joseph Whitall. We
loved one another when we were children; and I
never lost my love for him. I think it will not be
extravagant if I say that my soul was knit with his
soul, as Jonathan's was to David's. I have a letter,
which I received from him in 1795. I have not
language to express my feelings. Oh, that separation! that cruel separation! How it divided very
friends!"

In a letter to his daughter Susan, we again find
him looking fondly backward. He says: "I often,
very often remember the example of thy dear mother,
with feelings that no language can portray. She
was neat and tasteful in her appearance. Her dress
was elegant, but plain, as became her Christian profession. She loved sincere Friends, faithfully main-

tained all their testimonies, and was a diligent at-
tender of meetings. She was kind and affectionate
to all. In short, she was a bright example in her
family, and to all about her, and finally laid down
her head in peace. May her children imitate her
virtues."

Writing to his daughter Sarah in 1845, he thus
returns to the same beloved theme : "I lately happened to open the Memoirs of Sarah Harrison. It
seemed to place me among my old friends, with
whom I walked in sweet unity and Christian fellowship, in days that are gone forever. I there saw the
names, and read the letters, of William Savery,
Thomas Scattergood, and a host of others, who have
long since gone to their everlasting rest. I hope,
however unworthy, to join them at some day, not
very distant."

"Next day after to-morrow, it will be fifty years
since I was married to thy dear mother. How fresh
many of the scenes of that day are brought before
me ! It almost seems as if they transpired yesterday. These reminiscences afford me a melancholy
pleasure, and I love to indulge in them. No man
has experienced more exquisite pleasure, or deeper
sorrows than I have."

Perhaps the reader will say that I have spoken
little of his sorrows ; and it is true. But who does
not know that all the sternest conflicts of life can

never be recorded! Every human soul must walk
alone through the darkest and most dangerous paths
of its spiritual pilgrimage; absolutely alone with
God! Much, from which we suffer most acutely,
could never be revealed to others; still more could
never be understood, if it were revealed; and still
more ought never to be repeated, if it could be understood. Therefore, the frankest and fullest biography must necessarily be superficial.

The old gentleman was not prone to talk of his
troubles. They never made him irritable, but rather
increased his tenderness and thoughtfulness toward
others. His naturally violent temper was brought
under almost complete subjection. During the nine
years that I lived with him, I never saw him lose his
balance but twice; and then it was only for a
moment, and under very provoking circumstances.

The much-quoted line, "None knew him but to
love him, none named him but to praise," was probably never true of any man; certainly not of any one
with a strong character. Many were hostile to
Friend Hopper, and some were bitter in their enmity.
Of course, it could not be otherwise with a man who
battled with oppression, selfishness, and bigotry,
wherever he encountered them, and whose rebukes
were too direct and explicit to be evaded. Moreover, no person in this world is allowed to be peculiar and independent with impunity. There are

always men who wish to compel such characters
to submit, by the pressure of circumstances. This
kind of spiritual thumb-screw was often, and in various ways, tried upon Friend Hopper; but though
it sometimes occasioned temporary inconvenience,
it never induced him to change his course.

Though few old men enjoyed life so much as he
did, he always thought and spoke of death with
cheerful serenity. On the third of December, 1851,
he wrote thus to his youngest daughter, Mary:
"This day completes my eightieth year. 'My eye
is not dim, nor my natural force abated.' My head
is well covered with hair, which still retains its usual
glossy dark color, with but few gray hairs sprinkled
about, hardly noticed by a casual observer. My life
has been prolonged beyond most, and has been truly
'a chequered scene.' I often take a retrospect of it,
and it fills me with awe. It is marvellous how many
dangers and hair-breadth escapes I have experienced.
If I may say it without presumption, I desire not to
live until I am unable to take care of myself, and
become a burden to those about me. If I had my
life to live over again, the experience I have had
might caution me to avoid many mistakes, and perhaps I might make a more useful citizen; but I
don't know that I should greatly improve it. Mercy
and kindness have followed me thus far, and I have
faith that they will continue with me to the end."

But the bravest and strongest pilgrim, when he is travelling toward the sunset, cannot but perceive that the shadows are lengthening around him. He did not, like most old people, watch the gathering gloom; but during the last two or three years of his life, he seemed to have an increasing feeling of spiritual loneliness. He had survived all his co-temporaries; he had outlived the Society of Friends, as it was when it took possession of his youthful soul; and though he sympathized with the present generation remarkably for so old a man, still he was *among* them, and not *of* them. He quieted this feeling by the best of all methods. He worked continually, and he worked for others. In this way, he brought upon himself his last illness. A shop had been built very far up in the city, for a discharged convict, and the Association had incurred considerable expense on his account. He was remarkably skilful at his trade, but after awhile he manifested slight symptoms of derangement. Friend Hopper became extremely anxious about him, and frequently travelled back and forth to examine into the state of his affairs. This was in the severe winter of 1852, and he was past eighty years old. He took heavy colds, which produced inflammation of the lungs, and the inflammation subsequently extended to his stomach. In February of that year, declining health made it necessary to resign his office in the Prison Association. His letter to that effect was answered by the following Resolutions, unanimously passed at a meeting of the Executive Committee :

"This Association has received, with undissembled sorrow, the resignation of Isaac T. Hopper, as their agent for the relief of discharged convicts.

"He was actively engaged in the organization of the Society, and has ever since been its most active member.

"His kindness of heart, and his active zeal in behalf of the fallen and erring, whom he has so often befriended, have given to this Society a lofty character for goodness, which, being a reflection of his own, will endure with the remembrance of him.

"His forbearance and patience, combined with his great energy of mind, have given to its action an impetus and a direction, which, it is to be earnestly hoped, will continue long after it shall have ceased to enjoy his participation in its active business.

"His gentleness and propriety of deportment toward us, his associates, have given him a hold upon our affections, which adds poignancy to our grief at parting with him.

"And while we mourn his loss to us, our recollection of the cause of it awakens within us the belief that the good he has done will smooth his departure from among us, and gives strength to the cheering hope that the recollection of a life well spent may add even to the happiness that is in store for him hereafter."

He sent the following reply, which I believe was the last letter he ever wrote:

"Dear Friends :—I received through your committee, accompanied by Dr. Russ, your resolutions of the 13th of February, 1852, commendatory of my course while agent for Discharged Convicts. My bodily indisposition has prevented an earlier acknowledgment.

The kind, friendly, and affectionate manner in which you have been pleased to express yourselves on this occasion, excited emotions which I found it difficult to repress. The approbation of those with whom I have long labored in a deeply interesting and arduous concern, I value next to the testimony of a good conscience. Multiplied years and debility of body admonish me to retire from active life as much as may be, but my interest in the work has not abated. Much has been done, and much remains to be done.

In taking a retrospect of my intercourse with you, I am rejoiced to see that the great principles of humanity and Christian benevolence have risen above and overspread sectarian prejudice, that bane of Christianity, and while each has been allowed to enjoy his own religious opinions without interference from his fellows, we have labored harmoniously together for the promotion of the great object of our Association.

May He who clothes the lilies, feeds the ravens, and

provides for the sparrows, and without whose Providential regard, all our endeavors must be vain, bless your labors, and stimulate and encourage you to persevere, so that having, through His aid, fulfilled all your relative and social duties, you may in the end receive the welcome, "Come, ye blessed of my Father, inherit the kingdom prepared for you from the foundation of the world: for I was an hungered, and ye gave me meat; I was thirsty, and ye gave me drink; I was a stranger, and ye took me in; naked, and ye clothed me; I was sick, and ye visited me; I was in prison, and ye came unto me."

That this may be our happy experience, is the fervent desire of your sincere and affectionate friend,

ISAAC T. HOPPER.

NEW-YORK, 4th mo. 15, 1852."

Early in the Spring, he was conveyed to the house of his daughter, Mrs. Gibbons, in the upper part of the city; it being supposed that change of air and scene might prove beneficial. It was afterward deemed imprudent to remove him. His illness was attended with a good deal of physical suffering; but he was uniformly patient and cheerful. He often observed, "There is no cloud. There is nothing in my way. Nothing troubles me." His daughters left all other duties, and devoted themselves exclusively to him. Never were the declining hours of an old man watched over with more devoted affection. Writing to his daughter Mary, he

says : "I have the best nurses in New-York, thy
mother and sisters. I have every comfort that industry and ingenuity can supply."

Among the Quakers who manifested kindness and
sympathy, several belonged to the branch called
Orthodox; for a sincere respect and friendship had
grown up between him and individuals of that
Society, in New-York, after the dust of controversy
had subsided. He was always glad to see them;
for his heart warmed toward the plain dress and the
plain language. But I think nothing during his
illness gave him more unalloyed satisfaction than a
visit from William and Deborah Wharton, Friends
from Philadelphia. He loved this worthy couple
for their truly Christian character; and they were,
moreover, endeared to him by many tender and
pleasant associations. They stood by him generously during his severe pecuniary struggles; they
had been devoted to his beloved Sarah, whose long
illness was cheered by their unremitting attentions;
and she, for many years, had received from Hannah
Fisher, Deborah's mother, the most uniform kindness. William's father, a wealthy merchant, had
been to him an early and constant friend; and his
uncle, the excellent mayor of Philadelphia, had sustained him by his influence and hearty co-operation,
in many a fugitive slave case, that occurred in years
long past. It was, therefore, altogether pleasant to

clasp hands with these tried and trusty friends, before life and all its reminiscences faded away.

His physician, Dr. John C. Beales, was very assiduous in his attentions, and his visits were always interesting to the invalid, who generally made them an occasion for pleasant and animated conversation; often leading the doctor off the professional track, by some playful account of his symptoms, however painful they might be. He had been his medical adviser for many years, and as a mark of respect for his disinterested services to his fellow-men, he uniformly declined to receive any compensation.

Neighbors and acquaintances of recent date, likewise manifested their respect for the invalid by all manner of attentions. Gentlemen sent choice wines, and ladies offered fruit and flowers. Market people, who knew him in the way of business, brought delicacies of various kinds for his acceptance. He was gratified by such tokens of regard, and manifested it in many pleasant little ways. One of his sons had presented him a silver goblet, with the word "Father" inscribed upon it; and whenever he was about to take nourishment, he would say, "Give it to me in John's cup." When his little grand-daughter brought flowers from the garden, he was careful to have them placed by the bedside, where he could see them continually. After he was unable to rise to take his meals, he asked to have two cups and plates brought to him, if it were not too much trouble ; for he said it would seem pleasant, and like old times, to have Hannah's company. So his wife ate with him, as long as he was able to partake of food. A china bird, which a ransomed slave had given to his daughter, when she was a little girl, was placed on the mantel-piece, because he liked to look at it. A visitor, to whom he made this remark one day, replied, "It must be very pleasant to you now to remember how many unfortunate beings you have helped." He looked up, and answered with frank simplicity, "Yes, it *is* pleasant."

He made continual efforts to conceal that he was in pain. When they asked why he was so often singing to himself, he replied, "If I didn't sing, I should groan." Even as late as the day before he died, he indulged in some little "Cheeryble" pleasantries, evidently intended to enliven those who were nearly exhausted by their long attendance on him. At this period, his son-in-law, James S. Gibbons, wrote to me thus : "Considering his long bodily weakness, now ten weeks, he is in an extraordinary state of mental strength and clearness. Reminiscences are continually falling from his lips, like leaves in autumn from an old forest tree ; not indeed green, but rich in the colors that are of the tree, and characteristic. Thou hast known him in the extraordinary vigor and freshness of his old age; cheat-

ing time even out of turning his hair gray. But
thou shouldst see him now; when, to use his own
words, he feels that 'the messenger has come.' All
his thoughts have tended to, and reached this point.
The only question with him now is of a few more
days. Though prostrate in body, his mind is like a
sturdy old oak, that don't care which way the wind
blows. As I sat by his bedside, last evening, I
thought I never had seen so beautiful a close to a
good man's life."

He had no need to make a will; for he died, as he
had lived, without property. But he disposed of his
little keepsakes with as much cheerfulness as if he
had been making New-Year's presents. He seemed
to remember everybody in the distribution. His
Quaker library was left in the care of his children,
with directions that it should be kept where members of the Society of Friends or others interested
could have ready access to it. To his daughter Sarah he entrusted the paper written by her mother, at
fourteen years of age; still fastened by the pin she
had placed in it, which her dear hand had invested
with more value than a diamond, in his eyes. He
earnestly recommended his wife to the affectionate
care of his children; reminding them that she had
been a kind and faithful companion to him during
many years. He also gave general directions concerning his funeral. "Don't take the trouble to

make a shroud," said he. "One of my night-shirts will do as well. I should prefer to be buried in a white pine coffin; but that might be painful to my family; and I should not like to afflict them in *any* way. It may, therefore, be of dark wood; but be sure to have it entirely plain, without varnish or inscription. Have it made by some poor neighbor, and pay him the usual price of a handsome one; for I merely wish to leave a testimony against vain show on such occasions." He appeared to be rather indifferent where he was buried; but when he was informed that his son and daughter had purchased a lot at Greenwood Cemetery, it seemed pleasant to him to think of having them and their families gathered round him, and he consented to be laid there.

I was summoned to his death-bed, and arrived two days before his departure. I found his mind perfectly bright and clear. He told over again some of his old reminiscences, and indulged in a few of his customary pleasantries. He spoke of rejoining his beloved Sarah, and his ancient friends William Savery, Nicholas Waln, Thomas Scattergood, and others, with as much certainty and pleasure as if he had been anticipating a visit to Pennsylvania. Sometimes, when he was much exhausted with physical pain, he would sigh forth, "Oh, for rest in the kingdom of heaven!" But nothing that approached nearer to complaint or impatience escaped his lips.

On the last day, he repeated to me, what he had previously said to others, that he sometimes seemed to
hear voices singing, "We have come to take thee
home." Once, when no one else happened to be
near him, he said to me in a low, confidential tone,
"Maria, is there anything peculiar in this room?" I
replied, "No. Why do you ask that question?"
"Because," said he, "you all look so beautiful; and
the covering on the bed has such glorious colors, as
I never saw. But perhaps I had better not have said
anything about it." The natural world was transfigur-
ed to his dying senses; perhaps by an influx of light
from the spiritual; and I suppose he thought I should
understand it as a sign that the time of his departure
drew nigh. It was a scene to remind one of Jeremy
Taylor's eloquent words : "When a good man dies,
one that hath lived innocently, then the joys break
forth through the clouds of sickness, and the conscience stands upright, and confesses the glories of
God : and owns so much integrity, that it can hope
for pardon, and obtain it too. Then the sorrows of
sickness do but untie the soul from its chain, and let
it go forth, first into liberty, and then into glory."

A few hours before he breathed his last, he rallied
from a state of drowsiness, and asked for a box containing his private papers. He wished to find one,
which he thought ought to be destroyed, lest it should
do some injury. He put on his spectacles, and looked

at the papers which were handed him; but the old man's eyes were dimmed with death, and he could not see the writing. After two or three feeble and ineffectual attempts, he took off his spectacles, with a trembling hand, and gave them to his beloved daughter, Sarah, saying, "Take them, my child, and keep them. They were thy dear mother's. I can never use them more." The scene was inexpressibly affecting; and we all wept to see this untiring friend of mankind compelled at last to acknowledge that he could work no longer.

Of his sixteen children, ten were living; and all but two of them were able to be with him in these last days. He addressed affectionate exhortations to them at various times; and a few hours before he died, he called them, one by one, to his bedside, to receive his farewell benediction. At last, he whispered my name; and as I knelt to kiss his hand, he said in broken accents, and at long intervals, "Maria, tell them I loved them——though I felt called to resist——some who claimed to be rulers in Israel ——I never meant——." His strength was nearly exhausted; but after a pause, he pressed my hand, and added, "Tell them I love them *all*." I had previously asked and obtained permission to write his biography; and from these broken sentences, I understood that he wished me to convey in it a message to the Society of Friends; including the "Or-

thodox" branch, with whom he had been brought into
painful collision, in years gone by.

After several hours of restlessness and suffering,
he fell into a tranquil slumber, which lasted a long
time. The serene expression of his countenance remained unchanged, and there was no motion of limb
or muscle, when the spirit passed away. This was
between eight and nine o'clock in the evening, on the
seventh of May, 1852. After a long interval of silent weeping, his widow laid her head on the shoulder of one of his sons, and said, "Forty-seven years
ago this very day, my good father died; and from
that day to this, he has been the best friend I ever
had."

No public buildings were hung with crape, when
news went forth that the Good Samaritan had gone.
But prisoners, and poor creatures in dark and desolate corners, wept when they heard the tidings. Ann
W. with whose waywardness he had borne so patiently, escaped from confinement, several miles distant, and with sobs implored "to see that good old
man once more." Michael Stanley sent the following
letter to the Committee of the Prison Association:
"When I read the account of the venerable Friend
Hopper's death, I could not help weeping. It touched a tender chord in my heart, when I came to the
account of his being the prisoner's friend. My soul
responded to that; for I had realized it. About six

years ago, I was one of those who got good advice
from 'the old man.' I carried it out, and met with
great success. I was fatherless, motherless, and
friendless, with no home, nobody to take me by the
hand. I felt, as the poet has it,

> 'A pilgrim stranger here I roam,
> From place to place I'm driven;
> My friends are gone, and I'm in gloom;
> This earth is all a lonely tomb;
> I have no home but heaven.'

Go on in the work of humanity and love, till the
Good Master shall say, 'It is enough. Come up
higher.'"

Nearly all the domestics in Friend Hopper's neighborhood attended the funeral solemnities. One of
these said with tears, "I am an orphan; but while
he lived, I always felt as if I had a father. He always had something pleasant to say to me, but now
everything seems gone." A very poor man, who
had been an object of his charity, and whom he had
employed in many little services, could not rest till
he had earned enough to buy a small Arbor-vitæ,
(Tree of Life,) to plant upon his grave.

The Executive Committee of the Prison Association met, and passed the following Resolutions:

"*Resolved:*—That the combination of virtues which
distinguished and adorned the character of our lamented
friend, eminently qualified him for the accomplishment of

those benevolent and philanthropic objects to which he unremittingly devoted *a life* far more extended than ordinarily falls to man's inheritance.

"That in our intimate associations with him for many years, he has uniformly displayed a character remarkable for its disinterestedness, energy, fearlessness, and Christian principle, in every good word and work.

"That we tender to the family and friends of the deceased our sincere condolence and sympathy in their sore bereavement, but whilst sensible that words, however truly uttered, cannot compensate for the loss of such a husband, father, and guide, we do find both for ourselves and for them, consolation in the belief that his peaceful end was but the prelude to the bliss of Heaven.

"That in the death of Isaac T. Hopper, the community is called to part with a citizen of transcendent worth and excellence; the prisoner, with an unwearied and welltried friend; the poor and the homeless, with a father and a protector; the church of Christ, with a brother whose works ever bore unfailing testimony to his faith; and the world at large, with a philanthropist of the purest and most uncompromising integrity, whose good deeds were circumscribed by no sect, party, condition or clime."

The American Anti-Slavery Society received the tidings while they were in session at Rochester. Mr. Garrison, after a brief but eloquent tribute to the memory of the deceased, offered the following Resolution:

"*Resolved :*—That it is with emotions too profound for utterance, that this Society receives the intelligence of the decease of the venerable Isaac T. Hopper, on Tuesday evening last, in the city of New-York; the friend of the friendless—boundless in his compassion—exhaustless in his benevolence—untiring in his labors—the most intrepid of philanthropists, who never feared the face of man, nor omitted to bear a faithful testimony against injustice and oppression—the early, steadfast, heroic advocate and protector of the hunted fugitive slave, to whose sleepless vigilance and timely aid multitudes have been indebted for their deliverance from the Southern House of Bondage ;—in whom were equally blended the gentleness of the lamb with the strength of the lion—the wisdom of the serpent with the harmlessness of the dove ; and who, when the ear heard him, then it blessed him, when the eye saw him, it gave witness to him, because he delivered the poor that cried, and the fatherless, and him that had none to help him. The blessing of him that was ready to perish came upon him, and he caused the widow's heart to sing for joy. He put on righteousness, and it clothed him; his judgment was as a robe and a diadem. He was eyes to the blind, and feet was he to the lame. The cause which he knew not he searched out, and he broke the jaws of the wicked, and plucked the spoil out of its teeth.

He moved that a copy of this resolution be forwarded in an official form to the estimable partner of his life, and the children of his love, accompanied by an assurance of our deepest sympathy, in view of their great bereavement.

Several spoke in support of the Resolution, which was unanimously and cordially adopted.

The Committee of the Prison Association desired to have public funeral solemnities, and the family complied with their wishes. Churches of various denominations were immediately offered for the purpose, including the meeting-houses of both branches of the Society of Friends. The Tabernacle was accepted. Judge Edmonds, who had been an efficient co-laborer, and for whom Friend Hopper had a strong personal affection, offered a feeling tribute to the virtues and abilities of his departed friend. He was followed by Lucretia Mott, a widely known and highly respected minister among Friends. In her appropriate and interesting communication, she dwelt principally upon his efforts in behalf of the colored people; for whose sake she also had encountered obloquy.

The Society of Friends in Hester-street, to which he had formerly belonged, offered the use of their burying-ground. It was kindly meant; but his children deeply felt the injustice of their father's expulsion from that Society, for no other offence than following the dictates of his own conscience. As his soul had been too much alive for them, when it was in the body, their unity with the lifeless form was felt to avail but little.

The body was conveyed to Greenwood Cemetery, followed only by the family, and a very few intimate friends. Thomas McClintock, a minister in the Society of Friends, addressed some words of consolation to the bereaved family, as they stood around the open grave. Lucretia Mott affectionately commended the widow to the care of the children. In the course of her remarks, she said, " I have no unity with these costly monuments around me, by which the pride and vanity of man strive to extend themselves beyond the grave. But I like the idea of burial grounds where people of all creeds repose together. It is pleasant to leave the body of our friend here, amid the verdant beauty of nature, and the sweet singing of birds. As he was a fruitful bough, that overhung the wall, it is fitting that he should not be buried within the walls of any sectarian enclosure."

Three poor little motherless German boys stood hand in hand beside the grave. Before the earth was thrown in, the eldest stepped forward and dropped a small bouquet on the coffin of his benefactor. He had gathered a few early spring flowers from the little garden plot, which his kind old friend used to cultivate with so much care, and with childish love and reverence he dropped them in his grave.

Soon after the funeral Lucretia Mott called a meeting of the colored people in Philadelphia, and delivered an address upon the life and services of their friend and protector. There was a very large audience; and among them were several old people, who well remembered him during his residence in that city. At the Yearly Meeting also she paid a tribute to his virtues; it being the custom of Friends, on such occasions, to make tender allusion to the worthies who have passed from among them in the course of the year.

The family received many letters of sympathy and condolence, from which I will make a few brief extracts. Mrs. Marianne C. D. Silsbee, of Salem, Massachusetts, thus speaks of him, in a letter to his son John: "I have thought much of you all, since your great loss. How you must miss his grand, constant example of cheerful trust, untiring energy, and love to all! What a joy to have had such a father! To be the son of such a man is ground for honest pride. The pleasure of having known him, the honor of having been in social relations with him, will always give a charm to my life. I cherish among my most precious recollections the pleasant words he has so often spoken to me. I can see him while I write, as vividly as though he were with me now; and never can his benign and beautiful countenance lose its brightness in my memory. Dear old friend!

We cannot emulate your ceaseless good works ; but we can follow, and we can love and remember."

Mrs. Mary E. Stearns, of Medford, Massachusetts, wrote as follows to Rosalie Hopper : "The Telegraph has announced that the precious life you were all so anxiously watching has 'passed on,' and that mysterious change we call death has taken it from your midst forever. It is such a beautiful day ! The air is so soft, the grass so green, and the birds singing so joyously ! The day and the event have become so interwoven with each other, that I cannot separate them. I think of his placid face, sleeping its last still sleep ; and through the open window, I see the springing grass and the bursting buds. My ears are filled with bird-music, and all other sounds are hushed in this Sabbath stillness. All I see and hear seems to be hallowed by his departed spirit. Ah, it is good to think of his death in the Spring time ! It is good that his soul, so fresh, so young and hopeful, should burst into a higher and more glorious life, as if in sympathy with the ever beautiful, ever wonderful resurrection of nature. Dear, blessed old man ! I shall never see his face again ; but his memory will be as green as this springing grass, and we shall always think and talk of our little experience with him, as one of the golden things that can never pass away."

Dr. Russ, his beloved co-laborer in the Prison Association, wrote thus in a note to Mrs. Gibbons : "I have found it for my comfort to change the furniture of the office, that it might not appear so lonely without your dear, venerable father. I felt for him the warmest and most enduring friendship. I esteemed him for his thousand virtues, and delighted in his social intercourse. I am sure no one out of his own immediate family, felt his loss more keenly than myself."

James H. Titus, of New-York, thus expresses himself in a letter to James S. Gibbons : "I have ever considered it one of the happiest and most fortunate events of my life, to have had the privilege of an acquaintance with Friend Hopper. I shall always recur to his memory with pleasure, and I trust with that moral advantage, which the recollection of his Christian virtues is so eminently calculated to pro duce. How insignificant the reputation of riches, how unsatisfactory the renown of victory in war, how transient political fame, when compared with the history of a long life spent in services rendered to the afflicted and the unfortunate !"

Ellis Gray Loring, of Boston, in a letter to John Hopper, says : "We heard of your father's death while we were in Rome. I could not restrain a few tears, and yet God knows there is no room for tears about the life or death of such a man. In both, he was a blessing and encouragement to all of us. He really lived out all the life that was given him; filling it up to such an age with the beauty of goodness, and consecrating to the divinest purposes that wonderful energy of intellect and character. In a society full of selfishness and pretension, it is a great thing to have practical proof that a life and character like his are possible."

Edmund L. Benzon, of Boston, writing to the same, says; "You will imagine, better than I can write, with what deep sympathy I learned the death of your good father, whom I have always esteemed one of the best of men. I cannot say I am sorry for his death. My only regret is that more of us cannot live and die as he has done. I feel with regard to all good men departed, whom I have personally known, that there is now another witness in the spirit, before whose searching eyes my inmost soul lies open. I shall never forget him; not even if such a green old age as his should be my own portion. If in the future life I can only be as near him as I was on this earth, I shall deem myself blest."

From the numerous notices in papers of all parties and sects, I will merely quote the following: The New-York Observer thus announces his death:

"The venerable Isaac T. Hopper, whose placid benevolent face has so long irradiated almost every public meeting for doing good, and whose name, influence, and labors have been devoted with an apostolic simplicity and constancy to humanity, died on Friday last, at an advanced age. He was a Quaker of that early sort illustrated by such philanthropists as Anthony Benezet, Thomas Clarkson, Mrs. Fry, and the like.

He was a most self-denying, patient, loving friend of the poor, and the suffering of every kind; and his life was an unbroken history of beneficence. Thousands of hearts will feel a touch of grief at the news of his death, for few men have so large a wealth in the blessings of the poor, and the grateful remembrance of kindness and benevolence, as he."

The New-York Sunday Times contained the following:

"Most of our readers will call to mind in connection with the name of Isaac T. Hopper, the compact, well-knit figure of a Quaker gentleman, apparently about sixty years of age, dressed in drab or brown clothes of the plainest cut, and bearing on his handsome, manly face the impress of that benevolence with which his whole heart was filled.

He was twenty years older than he seemed. The fountain of benevolence within, freshened his old age with its continuous flow. The step of the octogenarian, was elastic as that of a boy, his form erect as the mountain pine.

His whole *physique* was a splendid sample of nature's handiwork. We see him now with our "mind's eye"— but with the eye of flesh we shall see him no more.

Void of intentional offence to God or man, his spirit has joined its happy kindred in a world where there is neither sorrow nor perplexity."

I sent the following communication to the New-York Tribune:

"In this world of shadows, few things strengthen the soul like seeing the calm and cheerful exit of a truly good man; and this has been my privilege by the bedside of ISAAC T. HOPPER.

He was a man of remarkable endowments, both of head and heart. His clear discrimination, his unconquerable will, his total unconsciousness of fear, his extraordinary tact in circumventing plans he wished to frustrate, would have made him illustrious as the general of an army; and these qualities might have become faults, if they had not been balanced by an unusual degree of conscientiousness and benevolence. He battled courageously, not from ambition, but from an inborn love of truth. He circumvented as adroitly as the most practised politician; but it was always to defeat the plans of those who oppressed God's poor; never to advance his own self-interest.

Few men have been more strongly attached to any religious society than he was to the Society of Friends, which he joined in the days of its purity, impelled by his own religious convictions. But when the time came that he must either be faithless to duty in the cause of his enslaved brethren, or part company with the Society to which he was bound by the strong and sacred ties of early religious feeling, this sacrifice he also calmly laid on the altar of humanity.

During nine years that I lived in his household, my respect and affection for him continually increased. Never have I seen a man who so completely fulfilled the Scripture injunction, to forgive an erring brother "not only seven times, but seventy times seven." I have witnessed relapse after relapse into vice, under circumstances which seemed like the most heartless ingratitude to him; but he joyfully hailed the first symptom of repentance, and was always ready to grant a new probation.

Farewell, thou brave and kind old Friend! The prayers of ransomed ones ascended to Heaven for thee, and a glorious company have welcomed thee to the Eternal City."

On a plain block of granite at Greenwood Cemetery, is inscribed:

ISAAC T. HOPPER,
BORN, DECEMBER 3D, 1771,
ENDED HIS PILGRIMAGE, MAY 7TH, 1852.

"Thou henceforth shalt have a good man's calm,
A great man's happiness; thy zeal shall find
Repose at length, firm Friend of human kind."